Speaking Philosophically

Also Available from Bloomsbury

A New Philosophy of Discourse: Language Unbound, Joshua Kates
The Linguistic Condition: Kant's Critique of Judgment and the Poetics of Action, Claudia Brodsky
Husserl's Phenomenology of Natural Language: Intersubjectivity and Communality in the Nachlass, Horst Ruthrof

Speaking Philosophically

*Communication at the Limits
of Discursive Reason*

Thomas Sutherland

BLOOMSBURY ACADEMIC
LONDON • NEW YORK • OXFORD • NEW DELHI • SYDNEY

BLOOMSBURY ACADEMIC
Bloomsbury Publishing Plc
50 Bedford Square, London, WC1B 3DP, UK
1385 Broadway, New York, NY 10018, USA
29 Earlsfort Terrace, Dublin 2, Ireland

BLOOMSBURY, BLOOMSBURY ACADEMIC and the Diana logo are trademarks of
Bloomsbury Publishing Plc

First published in Great Britain 2023
This paperback edition published in 2024

Copyright © Thomas Sutherland, 2023

Thomas Sutherland has asserted his right under the Copyright, Designs and
Patents Act, 1988, to be identified as Author of this work.

For legal purposes the Acknowledgements on p. viii constitute an extension
of this copyright page.

Cover image: Fichte, Johann Gottlieb, 19.5.1762- 29.1.1814, German philosopher, lecturing
his 'Reden an die deutsche Nation' (Addresses to the German Nation), winter 1807 / 1808,
later made wood engraving, 19th century (© INTERFOTO / Alamy Stock Photo)
Series design by Charlotte Daniels

All rights reserved. No part of this publication may be reproduced or transmitted
in any form or by any means, electronic or mechanical, including photocopying,
recording, or any information storage or retrieval system, without prior
permission in writing from the publishers.

Bloomsbury Publishing Plc does not have any control over, or responsibility for, any
third-party websites referred to or in this book. All internet addresses given in this
book were correct at the time of going to press. The author and publisher regret any
inconvenience caused if addresses have changed or sites have ceased to exist,
but can accept no responsibility for any such changes.

A catalogue record for this book is available from the British Library.

A catalog record for this book is available from the Library of Congress.

ISBN: HB: 978-1-3501-6082-8
PB: 978-1-3503-7396-9
ePDF: 978-1-3501-6083-5
eBook: 978-1-3501-6084-2

Typeset by Deanta Global Publishing Services, Chennai, India

To find out more about our authors and books visit www.bloomsbury.com and
sign up for our newsletters.

The most important remark which I can suggest as a caution to those who approach a great system of philosophy as if it were a series of riddles and their answers, is this: no complex or very important truth was ever yet transferred in full development from one mind to another: truth of that character is not a piece of furniture to be shifted.

Thomas De Quincey, 'Letters to a Young Man whose Education has been Neglected, No. V: On the English Notices of Kant' (1823)

Contents

Acknowledgements   viii

Introduction: A philosophical manner of speaking   1

1   Escaping the noise of the city: Heraclitus' *logos*   17
2   In the presence of truth: Plato and dialectic   29
3   A question of tone: Mysticism and propriety in Immanuel Kant   45
4   Speaking from the heart: J. G. Fichte on the role of the scholar   63
5   A new breed of philosophers: Friedrich Nietzsche's tyrannical impulse   85
6   The mark of a true Christian: Søren Kierkegaard on solitude   107
7   Aspiring to a higher good: Speaking of affliction with Simone Weil   123
8   Writing at the limits of history: Michel Foucault and unreason   135
9   Talking with borrowed words: Strategic mimesis in Luce Irigaray   153

Notes   173
Bibliography   213
Index   228

Acknowledgements

The central ideas of this book have germinated over a rather long stretch of time, almost a decade, and are the result of countless interactions and discussions throughout this period. Most of the writing also occurred during successive Covid-19 lockdowns – an oddly solitary context for producing a book on communication. Many thanks to Scott Wark, Marie Thompson, Gábor Gergely, Thao Phan, Chris O'Neill and Ben Nicoll, among so many other people, for helpful and stimulating discussions during this strange time. Thanks also to my cat Morris, for his unflagging support – a friend whose communication has no need of discursive reason. Above all, my sincerest gratitude to Elliot Patsoura for his generous feedback, suggestions and encouragement regarding almost every aspect of the book.

Introduction

A philosophical manner of speaking

Near the end of *The Laws*, his final, unfinished dialogue, Plato argues, via the character of the Athenian Stranger, that mastery of knowledge requires 'previous instruction and plenty of intimate discussion'.[1] This simple statement sums up the distinctive theory of communication extending across the Platonic dialogues. As he makes clear in the *Meno*, a love of wisdom does not involve absorbing facts one has obtained from others; on the contrary, it demands the recollecting of knowledge that has always existed within one's soul.[2] And one must foster this recollection (*anamnēsis*) through a particular mode of dialogue and disputation: the dialectical method of *elenchus*. Through this method, we can enquire into the truth of things, allowing others to help guide us towards ideas we must ultimately locate within ourselves. Plato's emphasis on the need to train in and continue to refine one's approach to dialectic does not stem from the hope he might be able to communicate propositions adequate to the ideal truths towards which he points; in fact, it reflects his desire to *not* reduce philosophizing to a mere transmission of propositions.

Invoking a distinction occasionally employed by Samuel Taylor Coleridge, we might say Plato, like many philosophers, is less concerned with *verbal* accuracy, 'the correspondence of a given fact to given words', than he is with *veracity*, which entails speaking 'to convey truth, not merely to say it'.[3] This is plainly discernible in his style of writing. His philosophy, and the question of which claims made in his dialogues can be ascribed to his own beliefs, is complicated by his use of the dialogic genre and the various *dramatis personae* via whom these claims are put forward. Identifiable propositions, in the form we typically encounter them in philosophical writing, are scarce. He does not want his audience to accept passively what he states as true; he wants to cultivate an audience capable of engaging in a discourse – a philosophical *manner of speaking* – by which the limits of any such statements are tested.

Plato seeks an audience who can exchange and debate views in accordance with the ideal truths he identifies, rather than talking about these ideas as if they were mundane platitudes. The public, he worries, have not been 'adequately exposed to discussions which aren't dishonourable and mean, but are designed for a thorough and intense quest for the truth, for the sake of knowledge'.[4] In this respect, he draws inspiration from his Presocratic forebears Heraclitus and Parmenides, both of whom suggest, in quite distinct fashions, that learning *how* to communicate is as important, if not more important, to the philosopher as the question of *what* is communicated. In all three of these thinkers, overcoming *doxa* – a non- or extra-philosophical manner of speaking – is posited as the fundamental goal of philosophizing, allowing for a truth to be apprehended *in the very act of speech itself* that remains impossible to represent as a discursive concept. Veracity is privileged over verbal accuracy.

If Plato is chiefly responsible for the proliferation of written philosophy (despite his unease about the effects of this medium), it is Aristotle who should be credited with (or blamed for) supplying the field with its most familiar style. For although later philosophers replicated the dialogic genre (Aristotle himself wrote many dialogues, although none have survived in more than the most meagre fragments), it has never come close to being the predominant style of Western philosophical writing. Instead, the dense, prosaic, often tedious quality of Aristotle's acroamatic writings (probably records of or accompaniments to his lectures), devoid of literary embellishment – exhibiting what Arthur Schopenhauer once generously described as a 'brilliant dryness' – has had the greatest influence on the philosophical mode of expression (implemented, above all, through the pedantic systematism of the mediaeval scholastics), even while the Platonic dialogue is still often lauded as somehow exemplary of a certain philosophical spirit.[5]

Compared to his Greek predecessors, Aristotle displays scant interest in aspects of philosophical discourse that might exceed propositional knowledge. Foregrounding the role of syllogisms and definitions as the basis of knowledge acquisition, he regards the boundaries of this knowledge as coextensive with those of expressibility. This is made apparent in the first chapter of the *Posterior Analytics*, wherein he explains that both deductive and inductive arguments 'effect their teaching through what we already know, the former assuming items which we are presumed to grasp, the latter proving something universal by way of the fact that the particular cases are plain' – which is to say, both forms of argumentation depend upon preexistent knowledge: definitions on the one hand and manifest evidence on the other hand.[6] Aristotle conceives of knowledge as a straightforward accumulation of facts, which in turn provide the basis for subsequent reasoning. Although he also alludes to rhetoric in the same passage, he clarifies that rhetorical arguments, while structurally homologous, are distinct from 'teaching and learning of an intellectual [*dianoētikē*] kind', inasmuch as the former are concerned with persuasion rather than determination of knowledge.[7] Rhetoric might help in imparting knowledge and fostering learning, but it is not itself a necessary precondition *for* knowledge.

'One of philosophy's self-images', argues Max Deutscher, 'is of producing evident premises and valid reasoning all within an impersonal voice that would speak the same truth, with the same reason, to any reader.'[8] Aristotle is exemplary in this respect: all knowledge, as he conceives of it, can be expressed in propositional form – that is, in 'a sentence that affirms or denies something of something'.[9] He subordinates his philosophy's communicative function to the position of a means, rather than an end: content is privileged over form; the message over the medium. He takes his own discourse's universal communicability for granted. To speak philosophically, in Aristotelian terms, is nothing more than to transmit philosophical knowledge to those listening or reading in an accurate and persuasive manner. The question of veracity in philosophical speech has, however, refused to disappear.[10]

Though the specifics may vary, we witness the same basic mentality I have just attributed to Plato in various philosophers throughout the history of Western thought, up to the present day. This notion of veracity – speaking (or writing) in a properly or peculiarly philosophical manner, in accordance with the truth, but without claiming to articulate that truth – turns out to be an intriguing heuristic for cutting across philosophical history, identifying parallels and homologies between distinct thinkers separated by thousands of years' distance. Furthermore, it indicates one of the many ways in which philosophers have sought, whether consciously or otherwise, to define not just the characteristics of the philosophical enterprise, but its limits. Not the limits of its ambit or the applicability of its concepts, but the limits of what and who has the right to reside within the domain of philosophical discursivity. As Michèle Le Dœuff observes,

> philosophical discourse is a discipline, which means that it is a discourse obeying (or claiming to obey) a finite number of procedural rules or operations, and as such it represents a closure, a delimitation which denies the (actually or potentially) indefinite character of modes of thought, a form of containment restricting the number of possible (admissible) statements.[11]

The gap posited between genuine discourse and mere gossip or opinion – *dialektos* or *logos* (speaking usually in the name of *alētheia* or *epistēmē*) on the one hand, *doxa* on the other hand – is one mechanism by which this delimitation takes place. And while this gap is often defined on straightforward methodological grounds (speaking philosophically often means little more than conducting enquiries in a rigorous and systematic fashion), in the works of certain philosophers it takes on a much more profound significance, to the extent that speaking (and comprehending others' speech) in the correct manner comes to be deemed a necessary condition for acquisition of knowledge or wisdom.

When Plato, in a conspicuously odd analogy, compares his idealized guardians of the city-state to well-bred dogs, he does so on the basis that the latter 'get fierce with strangers even before the slightest harm has been done them, and they welcome familiar people even if they've never been benefited by them'.[12] This trait 'shows how naturally smart they are and how genuinely they love knowledge [*philosophon*]'.[13] The sole criterion on which such a dog judges whether a person is friendly or hostile is whether they know them. 'Now,' he goes on to argue, 'anything that relies on familiarity and unfamiliarity to define what is congenial and what is alien must prize learning [*philomathes*]', and loving learning is 'the same thing as loving knowledge'.[14] And 'the same,' he suggests, 'goes for a human being too – that if he's going to be gentle with his friends and acquaintances, he must be an innate lover of knowledge and learning'.[15] The proper *comportment* of the philosopher (i.e. a love of knowledge or wisdom), Plato insinuates, has nothing to do with gaining new knowledge, but is about orienting oneself towards everything with which one is already familiar (as his account of *anamnēsis* makes apparent), and distancing oneself from everything that is unknown or alien. It is, as Sara Ahmed puts it, 'the same thing as telling the difference between what you know and don't know, which is the same thing as smelling the difference between the friend and the foe', an expulsion of all strangeness or alterity from 'a community of those whose epistemic privilege is a form of loving'.[16] Discourse, for Plato, is the terrain upon which this community is formed and those who belong to it identified.[17] And this struggle over discourse constitutes the chief concern of this book.

This is not a book about right and wrong ways of speaking, or the distinction between technical and everyday forms of language – these debates crop up in all fields of knowledge and study. Nor is it a book about philosophical style or rhetoric, and the role this might play in the amassing of cultural capital and the alienation of potential audiences. The contention I wish to put forward in this book is very specific, bearing upon certain tendencies that have cropped up sporadically across thousands of years of philosophy. I focus upon a specific presupposition expressed, with varying degrees of equivocality, by a number of philosophers: namely, that in order to philosophize authentically, one must adopt a certain mode of address or method of instruction – that is, take on a certain type of comportment – and that to comport oneself in this manner capacitates a truthfulness or veracity for which speaking directly, in a propositional form, will never allow. This prioritization of form over content, valorizing a privileged idiom or syntax of philosophy, I argue, furnishes a mechanism (albeit just one of many) via which the boundaries of philosophical discourse can be circumscribed, positioning this discipline in opposition to everyday thought, eluding the doxastic misrepresentations of common speech, and, above all else, giving the philosopher the power to decide *who should be deemed capable of speaking philosophically*.

To reiterate, when I refer to direct speech, this is in no way a stylistic judgement – I am not concerned with distinctions between, say, ordinary language philosophy on the one side and the difficult prose of much continental philosophy on the other.[18] Speaking directly, in this context, has nothing to do with speaking clearly or transparently. One could reflect at length upon the manifold styles and approaches taken in the dissemination of philosophy (from Lucretius' didactic poetry to Frege's concept writing, Saint Thomas' scholastic disputation to Spinoza's geometrical method, etc.), but in most cases these enquiries would bear upon nothing more than the question of the most effective style for transmitting ideas. Instead, I refer to the implicit assumption, underpinning most philosophical doctrines (and indeed, most accounts of language), that concepts can be transmitted integrally from one mind to another in a discursive or propositional form.

The 'transmission model' is a well-known motif and object of derision within contemporary philosophies of communication, usually associated with the Shannon-Weaver mathematical theory of communication, which was originally formulated in the context of electrical engineering (telephony) but soon universalized as a means for representing any communications system. The Shannon-Weaver schema is based upon a hylomorphic conception of the message as a pre-existent entity that can, at least hypothetically, be transported with complete accuracy (assuming one had access to a noiseless channel) in a linear fashion from a sender to a receiver.[19] In recent decades, this model has faced sustained critique – as Régis Debray notes, scholars now widely recognize that:

> the 'thing to communicate' does not exist prior to and independently of the one who communicates it and the one to whom it is communicated. Sender and

receiver are modified from the inside by the message they exchange, and the message itself modified by its circulation.[20]

But similar, albeit less formally sophisticated transmission models have recurred for centuries or more. How else can we interpret Saint Augustine's claim that 'there is no reason for us to signify something (that is, to give a sign) except to express and transmit to another's mind what is in the mind of the person who gives the sign'?[21] The operative image in such a semiotics is one of transport or exchange: a sign moving from one mind to another.

Another example would be John Locke's account of the use and abuse of words in *An Essay Concerning Human Understanding* (1689), in which he distinguishes between two modalities of communication via words: civil and philosophical.[22] Where the former refers to 'a communication of thoughts and ideas by words, as may serve for the upholding common conversation and commerce, about the ordinary affairs and conveniences of civil life, in the societies of men, one amongst another', the latter by contrast designates 'a use of them as may serve to convey *the precise notions of things*, and to express in general propositions *certain and undoubted truths*, which the mind may rest upon and be satisfied with in its search after true knowledge'.[23] In both cases, the 'chief end of language in communication' is 'to be understood', and this can only occur, he states, when a word is able to excite in the hearer the same idea envisioned and conveyed by the speaker.[24] Locke seeks an optimal transparency of communication between a speaker and their audience in the face of an inherently imperfect language.[25] More specifically though, Locke frames the *philosophical use* of words as predicated upon a transmission of propositions expressing veridical ideas, enabling true knowledge to pass from one individual to another.

These linear, integral models of transmission, argues Debray, need to be grasped as reflecting a limited set of circumstances, and placed alongside much more profound, albeit profuse forms of promulgation that enable the creation and perpetuation of durable meanings. In doing so, Debray suggests, 'the communicational fiction of the lone individual producing and receiving meaning gives way to people establishing membership in a group (even if only one they seek to found) and to coded procedures signaling that group's distinction from others'.[26] The latter, rather than taking place between individuals, 'uses collegial methods and collective settings, frameworks, and management'.[27] And as opposed to merely involving transportation, it 'necessitates transformation if not conversion', bringing its audience into the fold.[28] It is exactly this kind of communication that interests me in this book: the use of discourse, and particular modes of address, as a way of identifying those who belong to a group defined by its shared values, aims and ethos. The extent to which the delineation of a philosophical manner of speaking can serve to construct and regulate an imagined philosophical community.[29]

Dissemination among an audience is a prerequisite for philosophizing (lest we conflate the latter with the mere act of thinking). This ongoing interchange, however, need not be reduced solely to the transmission of concepts from mind to mind. Many philosophers have sought to underscore the existence of modes of dialogic communication outside the confines of integral transmission, foregrounding deliberation, consensus and intersubjective rationality. But seldom do they reflect upon the communicative presuppositions underpinning the composition and dissemination of their own philosophy. A *knowledge by description*, which would aim at rendering the most adequate, intelligible propositional definition of an object even in the latter's absence, is assumed.[30] Hence my aim in this book to highlight philosophers who *have* tried to take into account the ways in which philosophy itself is and should be communicated, devising protreptic approaches that reject the possibility of an integral transmission of philosophical concepts. We might characterize these latter philosophers as privileging some form of *knowledge by acquaintance*, conceiving of the dissemination of knowledge as proceeding not from the mere transmission of an accurate definition, but from a certain accord or propinquity vis-à-vis its object – a veracious mode of speaking (and equally, of listening).

These philosophers of veracity are trying to square the circle, so to speak, of philosophical discursivity, furnishing a means to communicate something which cannot be straightforwardly expressed under discursive reason's strictures. 'Philosophy has no doubt *defined* itself from its inception as the desire or the will to signify,' remarks Jean-Luc Nancy, 'but it has also *determined* itself from its inception according to the demand of a meaning that is in excess of signification.'[31] Most times, this excess is rendered signifiable through recourse to apophatic theology, pointing towards the divine or infinite by speaking only in terms of what they are not. In contrast, I turn my attention towards philosophers who are adamant that one need not maintain a sedulous silence in the face of the inexpressible – that by inducting their audience into a specialized or even esoteric mode of discourse distinct from ordinary speech, one can speak of that which cannot be straightforwardly or integrally described within discursive reason's limits. Again, speaking in a way according with or proceeding from truth, rather than speaking *of* truth itself.

There is an obvious intersection between my investigation here and Pierre Hadot's influential postulation of ancient philosophy as comprising a series of spiritual exercises. For Hadot, the various schools of Graeco-Roman philosophy did not consider their discipline to be concerned merely with the accumulation and promulgation of knowledge; rather, they viewed it as a way of life, defined by 'an effort to live and think according to the norm of wisdom'.[32] We have been far too willing, he opines, to project our modern expectations regarding what philosophizing is and how one engages in it upon ancient doctrines that place little emphasis on precision, methodological rigour and systematicity, but strive instead to effect a profound transformation in their disciples' vision of the world.

Although Hadot himself concentrates almost exclusively on philosophies of antiquity, a number of scholars have fruitfully taken up this notion of spiritual exercises in other settings.[33] Most notable among them is Ian Hunter, who argues that by treating philosophies (in particular, what he describes as the European tradition of 'university metaphysics') as *paideiā* rather than *theōríā* – formative intellectual regimens requiring adherents to undergo self-transformative work in line with a given ethos before they can gain access to promised knowledge – we can 'open the door to a fundamentally non-Kantian approach to the self, treating this not in terms of a subjectivity transcendentally presupposed by experience, but in terms of one historically cultivated to meet the purposes of a particular way of life'.[34] Rather than judging university metaphysicians' systems on their success in acquiring the knowledge to which they aspire, Hunter instead chooses to view their desire for metaphysical knowledge, and their denigration of empirical reality in the name of a higher spiritual truth attainable only through metaphysical abstraction, as part of an ascetic inner labour by which neophytes are inducted into the rites of academic philosophy. He suspends these systems' claims to epistemic authority by highlighting their anthropological function as spiritual exercises.

My aims are not dissimilar, insofar as I wish to comprehend several distinct philosophical positions on the basis of the communicative techniques they demand from their audience in exchange for the ability to philosophize authentically. At the same time, my focus is narrower than either those of Hadot or Hunter. Even though we could interpret the various philosophers discussed in this book as advocating a particular way of life or means for transforming the self, my interest lies instead in identifying how they account for the question of communicability with respect to their own philosophy, and how they mobilize this question as a way of both demarcating the boundaries of philosophical discourse and inducting their audience into this discourse. It may well be the case that, as Hadot complains, 'philosophical discourse now tends to have as its object nothing but more philosophical discourse', churning out the kinds of commentary once more associated with mediaeval Scholasticism.[35] But the exegetic trend Hadot is describing (and to which this book is no exception) still concentrates in the main upon the *content* of philosophical discourse, offering expositions of and extrapolations from canonical texts, treating these texts as storehouses of concepts and propositions receptive to interminable analysis, critique and logomachy. Less common, particularly in the wake of Aristotelian logic, are those who take philosophical discourse *as such* as their object of enquiry, bringing it to bear upon itself.

Now, one might protest that I am conflating two different practices here: on the one hand, a self-reflexive attunement to the communicative functions of philosophy; and, on the other, an attempt to communicate at and beyond the extreme boundaries of discursion, speaking in accordance with truth rather than of truth itself. But we should hardly be surprised that this attunement tends to crop up in those accounts where the capabilities of integral transmission, discursive reason and propositional knowledge are challenged. The perceived need to reflect upon one's own communicative practices tends to arise on occasions where such a model of transmission no longer seems self-evident.[36]

When Gilles Deleuze and Félix Guattari declare, for example, that 'philosophy does not contemplate, reflect, or communicate', they are referring to communication in the sense of consensus building, attempting to formulate shared understandings, values and norms.[37] To conceive of philosophy as a mode of communication, they suggest, is to diminish the former's productive capacities, limiting it to a 'perpetual discussion' between participants who will always talk past one another.[38] Likewise, when they argue that 'philosophy is not a discursive formation, because it does not link propositions together', they are drawing a distinction between propositions and concepts, the former defined and justified by their relation to a particular state of affairs, and the latter consisting in the act of creation, surveying and reshaping every state of affairs.[39] In this dismissal of communication and discursivity as properly philosophical attributes, however, Deleuze and Guattari are not actually rejecting communication or discourse in the broad senses of these terms; rather, they are rejecting communication *qua* transmission and discourse *qua* propositional knowledge, respectively. They are advocating for what they regard as a peculiarly philosophical kind of concept, the point of departure for a heterogenetic constructivism which forecloses the possibility of any transcendent truth claims diminishing the nature of the real (and the thought coterminous with it) in advance.

Dissatisfaction with integral transmission and propositional knowledge does not always result in a fully fledged repudiation of communication and discursivity. Some philosophers attempt to set out other modes of address that do not fall back into unwanted tendencies. Uniting these otherwise disparate approaches is an interest in circumscribing the boundaries of the philosophical. And it is for exactly this reason that this book underlines the antinomies and ambivalences characterizing the previously mentioned attunement towards the communicative properties of philosophy, not only highlighting its efficacy in engendering critical viewpoints towards the world as given but also acknowledging its propensity to give rise to exclusions and discriminations. My concern relates to the coupling of this self-reflexive standpoint vis-à-vis philosophical discursivity with a desire to gesture towards the incommunicable via a self-professedly veracious mode of address. For in this coupling, I contend, we can locate the adoption of a very particular method for deciding who belongs to the sphere of philosophical discourse – and thus, who is deemed able to speak in a properly philosophical manner.

In order to advance this argument, I must first bracket out the question of whether or not certain aspects of the real (e.g. the physical world, lived experience, affective states, unconscious drives, etc.) remain inexpressible or unrepresentable within the strictures of discursive reason. In place of this question, I want to regard all gestures at or beyond the limits of discursive reason as being nothing more than further discursive significations. From this standpoint, we must understand any such gesture not as a truth claim offering access to some otherwise inaccessible or occulted knowledge, but as a performative utterance: by identifying something (whatever it might be) as incommunicable, it delegitimizes any subsequent attempts to speak directly of that thing, and instead authorizes a particular discursive framework by which the philosopher can allude to this thing without making the same error. Or to put this another way, it is the delimitation of an 'other' discourse – characterized as a naive or dogmatic propositional discourse – in order to exclude it from the realm of veracity.

In understanding all claims to incommunicability as performative rather than constative in this fashion, I have two aims. First, to foreclose from the outset any implication that I am judging these philosophies on their comparative efficacy in transmitting knowledge, expressible or otherwise. For my concern lies with the effect these claims have, rather than the truth they may or may not reveal. Secondly and concomitantly, to engage in a reading of the history of philosophical communication that does not take transmission, as a straightforward transferral of concepts and ideas, for granted. As Jacques Derrida maintains:

> the performative is a 'communication' which does not essentially limit itself to transporting semantic content that is already constituted and guarded by its own orientation toward truth (truth as an *unveiling* of that which is in its Being, or as an *adequation* between a judicative statement and the thing itself).[40]

I wish to investigate the manifold forms of exclusion that come part and parcel with the circumscription of philosophical discourse – exclusion of the masses, exclusion of the uninitiated, exclusion of specific groups of people, exclusion of particular ways of speaking or thinking and so on – and the ways in which the struggle over discourse has offered philosophers the opportunity to posit *a priori* decisions by which this exclusion is justified.

The type of communication that interests me is that which actively seeks to exclude, and does so through the delineation and gatekeeping of a specific sort of speech, identifying who is and who is not a philosopher. The type of communication that, in Debray's words, 'stakes out territory [. . .] consolidates a whole, draws borderlines, defends itself, and exiles others'.[41] My intention in doing so is not to supply a transcendental rubric for interpreting the history of philosophy but to demonstrate the diverse ways in which appeals to the transcendental surety of a properly philosophical discourse are embroiled in mundane, empirical concerns relating to the audience of this discourse. An investigation of the variable conditions under which and protocols according to which philosophizing has taken place.

In an age dominated by the 'compulsion to communicate and to secure the communicability of anything at all', as Jean-François Lyotard once described it (as accurate a description now as it was then), there is a real potency in affirming that which stubbornly eludes all representation.[42] This book makes no appeal for greater transparency in philosophy, but it also refuses to take it as self-evident that gestures towards the unpresentable or ineffable possess inherent value, let alone that they are necessarily emancipatory. I admire the philosophers examined in the ensuing chapters to the extent they provide a rationale for their own communicative practices – that is, inasmuch as they use their demarcation of discursive limits as an opportunity to reflect upon the other ways and means by which one might point towards truth and help one's followers acquire knowledge in the absence of a viable prospect for integral transmission. Yet they do not, in my estimation, go far enough. They do not recognize the performative rationale guiding their approach, and thus fail to reflect upon the circumscriptive function it performs. Hence my own intervention, however tentative it might be.

This book can be roughly divided into four sections, each of which deals with a set of complementary philosophers. It begins in ancient Greece, with Heraclitus and Plato, and their respective conceptualizations of the *logos*: in the former, the *logos* is a divine law and discourse governing the cosmos and all who live within it, even though most remain deaf to its enigmatic signs; in the latter, the term refers to a reasoned account of things, delivered in a manner conforming to their ideal nature. In both philosophers' writings, there is a palpable scepticism or even fear of the citizenry of the Greek *polis*, and it is in juxtaposition to the confused, doxastic speech circulated by the *polloi* that they put forward their own, distinctive forms of philosophical discourse – modes of address identifying one as a true lover of wisdom. For Heraclitus, the divine truth the *logos* speaks will never be adequately captured within the words of mortals, and thus, the philosopher must act as a mediator between these two realms, gesturing towards a unity of opposites through their presentation of enigmatic, seemingly paradoxical statements. The mark of the philosopher, in this case, is that they do not speak in the direct, uncomplicated manner of the masses. For Plato, who contrastively favours a kind of supersensible reasoning that transcends the vicissitudes of sensible reality, the philosopher is defined by their ability to speak of the ideal nature of things, unalloyed by empirical residua – to communicate pure identity. But to speak in such a manner requires more than just the mindless repetition of memorized facts; the philosopher must adopt a particular bearing, engaging in dialectical enquiry with others, debating and testing their claims, while either orienting themselves towards the superlative idea of the Good (in *The Republic*) or grounding their speech in a certain type of presence (in the *Phaedrus*). In this way, Plato draws a sharp line between his own philosophical discourse and the sophistry he despises.

For all we know, reflections upon the discursive character of philosophy may well have played a prominent role in the day-to-day affairs of the Graeco-Roman schools, but little evidence of this remains in the writings available to us. And although we can discern traces of them in the neo-Platonic framing of early Christian theology (especially Pseudo-Dionysius, though he is not alone on this count), the disproportionate sway Aristotelian doctrines held over mediaeval philosophy (whether Jewish, Christian or Islamic), combined with the universalist, encyclopaedic optimism of Renaissance and Enlightenment thought, left little room to contemplate the limits of philosophical communicability. I thus pick up my argument again in the late eighteenth century, at the birth of German Idealism, looking at the kindred philosophies of Immanuel Kant and J. G. Fichte. In relation to this topic, Kant is almost certainly best known for his arguments regarding aesthetic judgement and its subjective universal communicability. I, however, focus instead upon a more obscure aspect of his critical project: namely, the labour demanded by genuine philosophizing, and the need to produce rational cognitions through input of one's own reason, rather than adopting objectified (i.e. historical) cognitions borrowed from others. Emphasizing the need for students to be inducted into philosophy from a young age, he reckons those who have honed their cognition in such a fashion will not only be able to gain knowledge of the world around them (within the bounds of possible experience) but will adopt a fitting tone when speaking about metaphysical ideas about which no cognition will ever be reached. As for Fichte, who views the scholar as having a unique ethical duty to educate humankind by virtue of their capacity to access a speculative standpoint removed from ordinary experience, he contends discursive reason can never represent freedom itself, the first principle of his philosophical system. All the scholar can do is help their audience locate this freedom within themselves, requiring them to address this audience in a certain manner. In both Kant and Fichte though, I argue, the distinction between mere transmission of propositions on the one hand and properly philosophical intellection on the other hand, acts as a mechanism by which they can justify the arbitrary exclusion of certain groups (on the basis of gender, race or metaphysical inclination) from the philosophical enterprise.

With an epistemological confidence characteristic of the era in which they lived, Kant and Fichte both circumscribe the realm of the transmissible in order to shore up cognition (in Kant's case, ensuring claims to knowledge are not subject to reason's enthusiastic flights of fancy; in Fichte's, securing his system's coherence by grounding all demonstration in an indemonstrable first principle). In doing so, however, they both appeal, albeit in quite divergent ways, to a subjective interiority, one's own reason, in which all genuine cognition must find its foundation. This leads me to the third section of the book, on Friedrich Nietzsche and Søren Kierkegaard, both of whom (despite their glaring differences) extol the solitary life of the thinker, spurning customary values and ways of speaking, and despise those intransigent institutions, authorities and traditions acting as impediments to the individual's flourishing. For Nietzsche, who is almost entirely dismissive of philosophical conventions, this manifests in a rejection of communication (i.e. the establishment of fixed, shared designations), which he believes can only obscure the vigour of singular experience and the infinite perspectives or interpretations constituting the real. But needing a justification for the continued dissemination of philosophy in the absence of communication, Nietzsche gravitates towards a tyrannical, expressly inegalitarian mode of address, whereby the philosopher elevates themselves above the rabble by seeking to impose concepts upon them. For Kierkegaard, who is dismissive of philosophy as a whole, setting his sights instead upon a Christian theology shorn of philosophical trappings (albeit still heavily influenced by certain philosophers, mainly Plato and Hegel), it manifests in a repudiation of objective, dispassionate knowledge and organized religion, demanding that individuals instead turn inward, exercising a passionate, subjective interest in their own eternal happiness. He thus adopts a strategy of indirect communication, trying to guide his audience towards a truth they must discover for themselves, within themselves. Consequently, while faith is meant to be wholly singular and personal, the manner in which individuals communicate becomes a means by which one can distinguish between true Christians and those merely concerned with social propriety.

If Nietzsche and Kierkegaard are both interested in how a manner of speaking can distinguish the authentic, self-possessed individual from the compliant rabble, beholden to inherited traditions, in the final section of the book, which is situated in the mid-twentieth century, I conversely investigate three iconoclastic philosophers – Simone Weil, Michel Foucault and Luce Irigaray – who discern the possibility of using language differently, giving voice to those who remain inaudible within the confines of philosophical discourse proper. Which is to say, they all seek to circumscribe this discourse's reach in order to gesture towards aspects of reality it has suppressed. They hope to undermine rather than undergird philosophy's totalizing pretensions. Weil's thought, both philosophical and theological in character, shares many attributes with that of Kierkegaard: most notably, a distrust of the collective, an antipathy towards organized religion, and an emphasis upon the personal nature of faith and salvation. But the component of her work I concentrate upon is her reflections upon the power of language. Weil believes certain words can be used to orient readers or listeners towards higher ideals (viz. truth, beauty and justice), and in doing so, might make it possible to articulate the pained cries of the afflicted, whose voices are usually stifled by the discourse of rights and its attendant juridical procedures. Likewise, Foucault seeks to write a history of madness that, in some odd sense, will allow the experience of madness itself to speak. Not the subjective experience of those who have been pronounced mad or diagnosed with what would now be labelled mental illness but the objective yet historically variable experience of division, segregation and exclusion. A history of limits, as he describes it – a history of those who have been pushed to the margins, separated from reason. In tracing this separation, though, Foucault also sees a chance to position his history at these limits, seizing upon an indistinct figure – which he designates Unreason – lying outside all conceptual mastery, all sense and signification, outside the continuity of history, and yet in some way constitutive of these 'rational' discourses, insofar as they are classified as such via reason's separation from itself. Lastly, Irigaray aims to both identify the latent metaphysical logic underwriting the psychoanalytic account of psychosexual development and to provide a psychoanalytic reading of philosophical discourse itself, bringing the conditions of possibility for its coherence and systematicity into relief. Such a reading, she maintains, provides the starting point for a different mode of address, a playful, strategic mimesis making no pretensions to speaking *of* the concept or identity of woman, but instead proposing to speak *as* a woman, in accordance with sexual difference as such. Speaking in such a manner, she believes, allows us to gesture towards everything the dominant, phallogocentric discourse reduces to silence.

One can probably already appreciate the substantial diversity in perspectives and procedures with which we will grapple in this book. There are, however, several themes and motifs that carry throughout most, if not all the chapters: a distinction between authentic and inauthentic speech; a privileging of subjectivity, interiority and presence, from which a truly living discourse might spring forth; an emphasis upon the peculiar pedagogical prerequisites for philosophizing; and a disdain for ordinary, trite or received ways of conveying the truth of things. Above all else, what all the thinkers scrutinized in this book share is a belief that communication has more to offer than simply describing or explaining things such that everyone might immediately grasp them – and that, in fact, philosophy itself must be located beyond the limits of discursive reason and propositional knowledge. One can also perceive an implicit narrative working its way through these various case studies: namely, a growing awareness among the thinkers mentioned (who may or may not label themselves philosophers) of philosophy's shortcomings, and a desire to delimit discursion not in order to bolster this discipline's totalizing proclivities but to empower other voices traditionally excluded from the sphere of the properly philosophical. We already see this awareness in Kant and Fichte, both of whom abhor the dogmatic conviction that all aspects of the real are straightforwardly transmissible in the form of propositions, convinced this will erode rational beings' capacity to grasp their own freedom (and that, in the case of Kant, it will also eliminate any room for faith). But it is most discernible in the book's two concluding sections, in the course of which all three thinkers seek, in some way, to mitigate the stifling, oppressive or delusive tendencies of philosophical discourse. What should also be discernible, though, by the end of the book, is that this increasing self-reflexivity does not alter the overall manoeuvre under examination: discursive reason's limits come to be circumscribed so the thinker in question can posit another, superior manner of speaking not subject to these limits, allowing for the identification of those who are or are not capable of speaking in accordance with or proximity to the truth of things. Even thinkers who effect this manoeuvre under the aegis of another discipline (e.g. theology or psychoanalysis) still adhere to the same long-standing philosophical division between *logos* and *doxa*, the former established as a master discourse against which all other discourses can be judged and in which one must be instructed.

The 'presentation of philosophy as a discourse that announces, teaches, advises, indeed, even leads by example, is not only dependent on the thought of signification', argues Nancy, but 'itself constitutes a signification conferred upon philosophy'.[43] I wish to investigate why this signification, as a distinctly performative claim, may not be as innocent as it might initially seem. After all, communication is never innocent. There is no neutral manner of speaking.

1

Escaping the noise of the city
Heraclitus' *logos*

The history of philosophy is a corpus always only constituted in retrospect, as tempting as it might be to project upon it the appearance of necessity or presume its boundaries to be self-evident. Like any canon, the sheer arbitrariness of the valuation defining philosophy's inclusions and exclusions (at a basic level, the question of what we should and should not consider philosophical) puts rest to any assertion of a natural or linear progression of ideas. Any identification of a philosophical lineage, even one striving to decentre the traditional canon, must be regarded, in the words of Chiara Bottici, as yet another example of 'a long-lasting strategy of self-definition through a reappropriation of the past'.[1] Like any history, the history of philosophy is an abstraction derived from remaining accessible materials, however meagre. When we speak of a Western philosophical tradition, spanning the past 2,500 years, as some manner of continuum, this is a continuum constructed unavoidably *ex post facto*, based on whatever information remains available to us, either through extant texts or allusions and paraphrases presumed to be drawn from now-lost texts (or even vague recollections and oral transmissions).

Analysis of the Presocratics is hindered by the material fact that their writings have only been preserved in the form of fragmentary quotations and glosses, stripped of their context and structure. As Friedrich Nietzsche once put it:

> it is a veritable misfortune that we have so little extant of the works of the ancient masters and that not a single one of their works was handed down to us complete. We are involuntarily influenced by this loss, measuring therefore with false standards, and letting ourselves be disposed more favorably toward Plato and Aristotle by the sheer accident that they never lacked connoisseurs and copyists.[2]

In particular, the doxography has too often been taken in by Aristotle's reconstruction of philosophical history in terms of his own fourfold model of causality, portraying his forebears as *physiologoi* – natural philosophers – who 'thought that the starting-points of all things were of the material kind only'.[3] Thus, Heraclitus of Ephesus is depicted by Aristotle as a monist pronouncing the cosmos to be made of fire (just as Thales asserted it was made of water and Anaximenes air).[4]

Yet when one reads Heraclitus' statements on this matter alongside his other available writings, a more nuanced picture starts to emerge. In his description of the cosmos as 'an ever-living fire, kindled in measures and extinguished in measures', Heraclitus seems less interested in fire as a material cause (*hylē*) in the Aristotelian sense, and more in the harmonious play between contrary terms this image implies: ignited and doused, stoked or exhausted, time and time again, fire provides an apt metaphor for a cosmos united in its perpetual change – a perfect balance between generation and decay, coming to be and passing away.[5] Cutting across most of Heraclitus' fragments is not the image of a fiery cosmos, but the principle of a *unity of opposites*, pairing harmony and conflict, necessity and contingency.[6] This principle is what Heraclitus terms the *logos*, a divine law and discourse collecting within itself a deeper unity of superficially opposed terms, embracing such difference rather than pursuing its elimination. One does not locate the *logos* by escaping the vicissitudes of nature, for it is always contained with nature's protean flux, albeit hidden and usually misprized. One must instead learn to listen out for the *logos*, attuning oneself to its elucidative voice resonating throughout the world's chaotic becoming.

The crucial feature of Heraclitus' philosophy is, pace Aristotle, his account of the *logos*. Within this account we find the clearest and most decisive statements, however rudimentary they might be, regarding the communicative role of this nascent discipline. Heraclitus distances himself, as a philosopher, from the slumbering masses, who sleepwalk through life, deaf to the law guiding them. This distancing, the probable source of his reputation as a trenchant misanthrope, results in a quite idiosyncratic construction of the relationship between *doxa* and *sophia*. The desire for identity, he believes, mars ordinary speech, breaking down the ligature between contrary terms in order to privilege one over the other. And yet, even the philosopher is incapable of relinquishing this desire, for all human discourses are inadequate in relation to the *logos*. Some, however, can at least point towards its truth. To speak wisely, then, is not to form propositions *identifying* a specific truth regarding nature (which loves to conceal itself from such signification), but to use paradox and antinomy in order to evoke a greater unity, the unity of opposites. The philosopher acts as the mediator between the mortal and divine realms.

Heraclitus calls upon a divine *logos* which maintains its inexpressibility in the face of everyday language. A law and discourse that gathers and unifies difference, sensible in nature (since one must 'hear' it) and yet still divorced from ordinary, subjective experience and speech, preceding (conditioning) and exceeding (transcending) human laws and discourses.[7] Hence why Heraclitus does not claim to speak in the words of the *logos* but merely in a manner that might point us towards its unity. He implores us to listen to the *logos*, rather than to him personally.[8] In doing so, he marks a dividing line between proper and improper ways of speaking philosophically, the former consisting not in an integral transmission of knowledge but in a series of allusions indicating a unity that can never be adequately expressed in words.

Law and discourse: *Logos* and the unity of opposites

It is 'necessary to follow what is common', declares Heraclitus, but 'although the *logos* is common, most people live as if they had their own private understanding.'[9] This distinction between public and private, that which is held in common and that which is confined to individuals, runs throughout many of Heraclitus' fragments, underscoring the significance of *commun*ication – thinking the latter term in its strictest etymological acceptation – to his philosophy. Communication is, after all, at the most basic level, a sharing of and participating in the common. The *logos* for Heraclitus represents a divine law and discourse within which all people partake, whether or not they realize it. What distinguishes those with understanding from those who lack it then, in his estimation, is that the former adhere to what is common to all in the same way (and to a greater extent) that a city-state adheres to its own laws. 'For all human laws', Heraclitus declares, are 'nourished by one law, the divine law.'[10]

Heraclitus often depicts the *logos* as an impersonal discourse, speaking the law with absolute authority and jurisdiction: an eternal, unchanging divinity stripped of the anthropomorphic trappings that characterized the traditional Greek pantheon. This is not to say he identifies the *logos* with any given utterance, nor that he views it as commensurate with ordinary human speech; rather, the Heraclitean *logos* is best construed as the universal speech structuring all particular speech acts and the universal law conditioning all human laws. It is speech itself, communication in its ideal form: absolute truth and absolute law.[11] It forms the basis for the misguided, impoverished conversations in which the masses engage and the inferior, corrupted laws of the city-state from which Heraclitus would, according to doxography, one day extricate himself. Everyday speech is inimical to the *logos*, for 'although all things come to be in accordance with this *logos*, humans are like the inexperienced when they experience such words and deeds' – they always 'prove unable to understand it both before hearing it and when they have first heard it'.[12] Most of the population fail to recognize how this divine force drives their own destiny: in not hearing the discourse of the *logos*, they do not recognize its corresponding law either.

'Human nature has no insight', Heraclitus argues, 'but divine nature has it'.[13] The philosopher becomes the mediator between these two natures, showing a path by which his audience can escape worldly ignorance. As is the case also for his Presocratic contemporaries Parmenides of Elea and Xenophanes of Colophon, Heraclitus points towards the means by which one might traverse an otherwise unbreachable chasm between the divine and the mortal (again, in stark contradistinction to the anthropomorphic gods of prior mythology). And this in turn corresponds to the difference he posits between the philosopher (who is not himself divine but acts as an intermediary for the divine *logos*) and the general populace.[14] 'The philosopher', writes Conche, 'is not simply a divine being, nor is he simply a human being. He rises from the human to the divine; he is the mediator and the *daimōn*'.[15] This mediation is achieved by the philosopher by speaking in accordance with the *logos*.

Whether or not the testimonies regarding Heraclitus' life are at all accurate, it is clear from the surviving fragments of his work that Heraclitus holds most of his fellow citizens in contempt, frustrated by their willingness to remain ignorant and speak of little other than falsehoods. 'Eyes and ears are bad witnesses to people if they have barbarian souls', he complains, conceiving of understanding as analogous to comprehending a language (the descriptor *barbaros* referring in his time to all non-Greek speakers, contrasted against *hellēnikos*): sensible data is not on its own sufficient for apprehending the truth of nature; one must learn to speak the language of the law governing this nature.[16] Heraclitus treats the love of wisdom as synonymous with a *comprehension* of the truth of things, not in the sense of a mere knowledge of facts but a more foundational capacity to make sense of the enduring medium through which such contingent facts might be transmitted. 'Just as the meaning of what is said is actually "given" in the sounds which the foreigner hears, but cannot understand', explains Charles Kahn, 'so the direct experience of the nature of things will be like the babbling of an unknown tongue for the soul that does not know how to listen'.[17] A failure to speak in accordance with the *logos* indicates an inability to grasp its truth.[18]

The *logos*, in Conche's words, 'is pure light, a light that leaves no shadow': a law which holds true for everything that is and a discourse which reveals everything as it is.[19] To comprehend the *logos* is to hear it as a medium without a message, to grasp its form instead of its content; its total effect.[20] Most people, therefore, *do* have barbarian souls in Heraclitus' conception, for even though they hear the language of the *logos*, they do not understand it. They remain as foreigners, even as they live under its ambit. Truth is communicated by and through the *logos* (or more precisely, truth lies in the mere fact of its communication), but few are willing or able to listen to that which surrounds them: 'uncomprehending when having heard, they are like the deaf'.[21]

Whereas Heraclitus is alert to this divine law guiding his own thought and actions, 'other people fail to notice what they do when awake, just as they forget what they do while asleep'.[22] Even when ordinary citizens are ostensibly awake, spiritually they are still sleeping, for they remain clueless when it comes to recognizing the force that guides them. They abide in a state of perpetual somnambulism: walking, talking, working, but never listening to (and comprehending) their environs. 'Thinking is common to all', but it is exactly in this common thought that most people *do not* partake, for they remain mere sleepwalkers, trapped inside their private worlds, not realizing the extent to which their actions are guided and governed by the *logos*, and thus unable to participate in the universality of the wisdom afforded by the latter.[23] Yet even though the somnolent masses do not consciously participate in the *logos*, they are still not exempt from its dominion. Just like the laws of a city-state, whether directed by the citizenry or instituted by a tyrant, one is held to this divine law even if one does not voluntarily assent to it.[24] The *logos* rules over all.

Heraclitus draws a sharp line between himself, as someone who listens to the *logos*, and the masses, who are mostly deaf to this law directing their lives. At the same time though, for all his apparent pessimism, he still implores his fellow citizens to listen to the *logos*. He does not just store its message away for himself.[25] In fact, he does not even claim to possess the truth of the *logos*, but merely regards himself as capable of hearing it. If one listened to the speech of Heraclitus alone, notes Conche, this would still be 'the language of opinion and desire, the usual human language, one particular language amongst others', a language that does not speak in accordance with the real, but of an invented world, subject to the whims of the individual.[26] Heraclitus derives his authority to speak on philosophical matters from the *logos*, but this simply means he claims to speak in accordance with it, pointing towards that which escapes the fetters of subjective judgement. To be wise is to recognize the necessary distance between the words of mortals and the objects to which these words refer. The masses, he argues, 'put their trust in popular bards and take the mob for their teacher', swayed by rhapsodes and demagogues.[27] Heraclitus does not abandon the rhapsodic mode of communication, but he transposes its authority from the whims of the public and the revered poetry of Homer and Hesiod to an abstract, divine discourse impervious to any such human concerns – a truth that literally communicates itself, and in doing so, imputes an inherent *meaningfulness* upon all things, providing the justification and impetus for philosophy as a project.

The enigmatic expression of nature

The *logos* determines the nature (*physis*) of all things, and as Heraclitus declares, 'nature loves to hide'.[28] Nature in this context refers neither to identifiable physical phenomena (as we typically use this term today) nor to a fixed, innate essence of things; instead, it would seem to designate a productive or generative power synonymous with the world as such. It is a perpetual becoming, an equilibrial movement of creation and destruction, an eternal propagation of differences, all kept in balance by the law of the *logos*. This is not a law that applies to people alone but a fundamental law governing the *cosmos* in its totality: a law holding these differences together in a *unity of opposites*.[29] Nature, then, loves to hide insofar as it obscures its own protean dynamism and differentiality behind the immediate appearance of the beings it produces: in their apparently constitutive stability and identity, their seemingly unassailable distinctness, the endless becoming underpinning these beings effaces itself.

The *logos* is not just the law governing nature though; it is also the medium via which this nature – and the carefully balanced equipoise of its contrary forces – is brought to our attention. Such elucidation does not occur, however, in a transparent and clear-cut manner. Although Heraclitus depicts it as a discourse, the *logos* resists all straightforward transmission of meaning, all reduction of communication to mere expression or representation. 'The Lord whose oracle is at Delphi', claims Heraclitus, 'neither speaks nor conceals but gives a sign'.[30] Evoking an association between the Pythia (the high priestess of the Temple of Apollo at Delphi), who according to some accounts delivered frenzied, almost impenetrable utterances, and the discursive quality of the *logos*, we can infer that the latter, as a medium of pure elucidation, similarly exists outside the semantic criteria according to which one judges ordinary language. The *logos* neither reveals nor obfuscates, for it does not transmit messages at all, and therefore proffers nothing to be interpreted (or left uninterpreted, as the case may be). It only communicates to those whose ears are open, who can extend their capacity for listening beyond the ambit of individual utterances and attend to this discourse as such in its pure, elucidative truth.

Viewing himself as a mortal conduit of this divine discourse and wanting no truck with the straight-talking language of everyday *doxa*, Heraclitus correspondingly inaugurates a distinctive mode of philosophical communication, which makes little attempt to convey arguments in the way one would expect, but instead supplies concise, elegant riddles – centred upon the collocation of apparently contrary terms – designed to spur on philosophical enquiry. He inaugurates 'not only a new manner of speaking', writes Maurice Blanchot, 'but one that invents simplicity, discovering the richness of sparse words and the illuminating power of a speech that is brief, deprived of images, and, in a sense, ascetic'.[31] With 'a perceptive knowledge of its resources', Blanchot continues, 'Heraclitus' language comes to deploy the enigmatic power proper to it in order to seize, in the network of its duplicities, the disjointed simplicity to which the enigma of the variety of things corresponds'.[32] Although they might at first seem implacably contradictory, Heraclitus makes it clear that the reader should not take his aporetic statements at face value; instead, one must interrogate them in order to draw out a deeper harmony, which does not reconcile these aporias by elevating one term and subordinating another, but gathers them together in their mutual complementarity and concert, without dampening their antagonistic tension.[33] Such interrogation will lead one towards the law of the unity of opposites governing this harmony. 'It is wise', as Heraclitus proclaims, 'to agree that all things are one': unity and plurality, identity and difference, agreement and opposition are all held in harmonious tension by this law.[34]

For Heraclitus, argues Conche, 'one does not comprehend more or less: one either comprehends fully, or not at all' – just like the Delphic oracle and the *logos* itself, he gestures beyond the false dichotomy of clarity and obscurity, towards a chiaroscuro uniting these terms within an all-encompassing discourse.[35] Heraclitus' abstruse style of exposition, dealing in paradox, contradiction and antinomy, becomes a means of veraciously communicating this unity of opposites (to those capable of and willing to listen), but doing so without straightforwardly expressing it.[36] Speaking in accordance with the *logos* without making propositional claims on its behalf. To do anything else would risk travestying this discourse and leading his audience astray.

An interesting parallel can be observed between Heraclitus' attitude towards speech and that of Parmenides. There is a still-common conception, ancient in provenance, which maintains these two roughly contemporaneous philosophers (albeit from opposite sides of Magna Graecia) posited competing theories regarding the nature of being: the former viewing it as defined by stasis, the latter by flux.[37] A number of pertinent similarities, however, can be identified between these two crucial figures: not least that they both present their respective philosophies as challenging prevailing *doxa*, marking their own conception of philosophical discourse as qualitatively distinct from ordinary speech. In fact, we find in Parmenides' proem (which is, in both style and structure, still reminiscent of epic poetry, and as such, likely intended to bring to mind the conventions of the Greek curriculum) the only other notable Presocratic deployment of the specifically philosophical conceptualization of *logos*: 'do not let habit, rich in experience', he warns, 'compel you along this route to direct an aimless eye and an echoing [*ēchēessan*] ear and tongue, but judge by reasoning [*logō*] the much-contested examination spoken by me'.[38] For Parmenides, *logos* does not refer to a divine force, but to a method of pure reasoning through which one can attain true belief (*alētheia*). It designates, in other words, a logical method posited by Parmenides as a continual corrective to thought, ensuring his audience stays on the right path, not following the dead-ended digressions of *doxa*.[39]

Parmenides' desire is to put discourse in the service of more fruitful ends, using the conceptual clarity of the *logos* to cut through the disorder of *doxa*. Through such a discourse, effectively identical with itself, we might only speak of *what is*, and avoid lapsing back into the hearsay and conjecture of *what is not*. Parmenides does not wish to impose his views upon his audience but encourages them to follow his line of reasoning, making explicit appeal to the goddess who, following the narrative of the proem, reveals this truth to him. 'If Parmenides represented the Truth which he announced as *his* own', remarks Conche, it would be nothing other than 'the opinion of a mortal', and so he instead portrays himself as the mere mouthpiece of the goddess, facilitating her message's dissemination within the mortal realm.[40] Unlike Heraclitus, who endeavours to complicate speech through paradox and antinomy, Parmenides' logical method tries to eliminate all the differences that crop up in our habitual ways of speaking, and which can only signify the non-existent. More conspicuously than any subsequent philosopher, Parmenides is driven by a desire for purity – justified via his dogged adherence to the principle of non-contradiction – that would strip away all empirical vestiges within speech, and in turn within thought, revealing an eternal being devoid of all difference, divisibility and change.

This may well be why Parmenides emphasizes the need for his audience to not take his claims at face value but to evaluate them in accordance with the logical method of reasoning he supplies. He is aware that his dream of a thought uncompromised by discursive representation, with all its ambiguities and contradictions, remains a superlative but unattainable ideal. To keep his audience on the right path, away from the distractions of *doxa*, the philosopher must continue to speak, guiding and directing them. For both Parmenides and Heraclitus then, the role of the philosopher is to gesture towards a unity remaining outside the grasp of human expression. What is notable about Heraclitus' approach though is his peculiar (perhaps even unique) positing of a philosophical discourse, suited to his mortal audience, that maintains conformity with a divine, everlasting discourse. Heraclitus wishes to help guide his audience, imploring them to look beyond the mundane and quotidian – and in particular, to shake out the types of speech to which they have become accustomed. But his oracular mode of communication is intended not just to help induct his audience into a philosophical community (brought together by their concern for what is held in common) but to determine the limits of this community, excluding vast swathes of the population (possibly everyone other than himself), who are, in their incomprehension of the *logos*, mere barbarians.[41] It separates those who can truly hear the *logos*, who have fostered a certain faculty of listening within themselves, from those still trapped in the echo chamber of gossip and hearsay.

Commonality and separation

It may seem strange that someone who so frequently underscores the common nature of truth would also claim that 'what is wise is set apart from all', and yet, this is exactly Heraclitus' position: given that 'most people are bad, and few are good', the *logos* can in no way be related to mass opinion, and in fact, the latter is only likely to obscure and distort the former's message.[42] For the general populace 'do not understand how, though at variance with itself, [the *logos*] agrees with itself'.[43] In order to understand this paradox, we must distinguish the *common* from the *popular*. As Mario Perniola argues, Heraclitus 'formulated the possibility of a conflict between the logos and the opinion of the majority, between what founds the social connection and what individuals agree upon, between rational society and the society of consensus', the latter remaining benighted and somnambulistic.⁴⁴ The masses do not make up a rational society; rather, the *polis*, in its typical form, remains just an agglomeration of private individuals, all sleepwalking together. Heraclitus gestures towards a more abstract commonwealth that conceals itself in these everyday interactions, and yet remains their ultimate condition. An imagined philosophical community set apart from the masses (even while the philosopher still may well live among them). A philosophical polity constituted not so much in terms of a physical or geographic location but as an audience united in its quest for a truth common to all and yet overlooked by most.

Thinking and speaking in accordance with the truth of the *logos* means forsaking the viewpoint of the individual, for the latter can only distract us, luring us away from the law common to all beings. Knowing ourselves means knowing our position within the cosmos. As Conche puts it,

> whereas the *logos*, the true discourse, reveals to us the world as it is *in itself*, i.e. independent of all particular approaches and subjectivizing gazes, men have in front of them only a world that correlates to their particular, subjective, self-interested approach, i.e. a particular world; they are absent in the world as it is in itself.⁴⁵

To think and speak in accordance with the *logos* is not to denounce or escape the physical world and the protean flux of nature but to recognize how all the differences this *cosmos* comprises are gathered by a universal law and spoken by a discourse that together compose a reality extending beyond all particularizing boundaries, and in which all people take part (even if they do not themselves recognize it). The truth sought by the philosopher is not a truth unique to them as an individual, nor even a wisdom common to humanity, but of a cosmic order.

Pivotal to Heraclitus' approach is this caveat that while the *logos* (which governs the cosmos as a whole) guides everyone, ordinary men and women are almost incorrigibly deaf to its discourse. Focused upon themselves, they are oblivious to what is held in common. In contrast, Heraclitus has attuned his ears, so that they can hear the truth of the *logos*, but to do this, he first had to learn to tune out the noise of the *polis*; to learn when *not* to listen. After all, Conche remarks, ordinary speech or *doxa* is 'a language of separation, which disunites opposites', representing the givens of experience by subordinating their complementary oppositions to their individual identities.⁴⁶ It wishes to speak of good without evil, peace without war, youth without ageing, treating these contrary terms as irreducibly *other*. The *logos*, by contrast, signifies the unity of these terms *in* their opposition. Importantly, what is common to all is not the *logos* itself; rather, the *logos* is both the condition of this commonality (inasmuch as it is the law of the unity of opposites in which all things share) and its presencing (whereby it *speaks for* this law).[47] Heraclitus effects a separation between ordinary speech and philosophical speech, the latter of which is guided by the *logos*' divine law, maintaining a hierarchy of philosophical superiority and mundane or quotidian inferiority that separates the philosopher from the rabble.

Conche proposes then that Heraclitus, faced with this separating language, puts forward his own set of separations: first, between 'the truth and the whole' (for the *logos* is external to nature *qua* totality, while simultaneously being the means by which the nature of this totality is disclosed); and then second, between 'the philosopher, the connoisseur of truth, and other men, the unintelligent, the inexpert, who are said to live in incomprehension of the *logos*, of true discourse'.[48] Philosophy thus resides in the harmonic, paradoxical unity of separation and commonality.[49] The philosopher separates himself from the masses because the latter think of themselves as individuals, and thus are unable to situate themselves within the totality of nature and the universality of the *logos* by which this totality is ordered. 'Every community has that which is common to all its members: its myths, its customs, its religion, its morality', writes Conche, but for Heraclitus this is 'a false universality, a universality within the limits of a particularity'.[50] The masses are still caught up in these traditions – false universals, confined to the walls of the *polis* – that conceal a more fundamental universality. The truth proffered by the *logos*, then, 'is accessible only to the individual who takes up along, in their solitude, the vocation of the knowledge of thought': to think the common, we must think in isolation, outside the walls of the city-state.[51] Heraclitus wishes to save the masses from their isolation, revealing to them the commonality of the discourse of which they were previously unmindful, and yet he can only do this by isolating himself from them. He finds it too difficult to philosophize when surrounded by the noise of *doxa*.

Heraclitus, at this foundational moment in the Western philosophical tradition, makes apparent a principle that has remained mostly obscure since. He dismisses the masses as the possessors of mere barbarian souls: they are foreigners in the philosophical *polis*, moving within this *topos* without knowledge or comprehension. And yet, they remain bound to its law regardless: the *logos* governs their actions, even while they are incapable of hearing it. The *logos* interpellates all people as subjects (in the politico-juridical sense of the term) of philosophy, even though its actual audience might be quite limited. Likewise, the philosopher speaks for and to all, even though he may not regard them as competent enough to speak back to him. More peculiarly, for Heraclitus the real is in its essence discursive, in an ontological sense: although humans may be incapable of integrally transmitting the truth of the *logos*, by its very nature, the latter remains communicable, for the precise fact that it is in itself a form of discourse. One just needs to be pointed towards it – hence the necessary role of the philosopher.

Heraclitus' book, argues Harold Cherniss, which by legend he himself deposited at the Temple of Artemis, 'though itself the expression of the "logos", was meant to be not a conveyance of this "logos" into the minds of others but a means of shaking them awake to the discovery of it within themselves'.[52] The purpose of philosophy for Heraclitus, it would seem, is not to represent the *logos* (thus avoiding the folly of attempting to faithfully express its truth, which cannot be compressed into the form of a message) but to gesture towards this medium itself, and to impress upon his audience the *imperative* to listen. Heraclitus attempts to communicate the incommunicable – or more precisely, to communicate his own inability to communicate this presence that can never be adequately represented. Through his writings (or what little of them we have left), Heraclitus hails and summons us as an audience, exhorting us to engage in the philosophical project, to take part in a movement away from opinion and false belief towards truth. He does this through appeal to a divine authority for whom he acts as a mediator, bridging the gap between the mortal and immortal, human and cosmic. This is not to suggest that he speaks to all people, or that all who listen will agree with his claims, but that his communicative strategy – resting upon this difference between *doxa* and *sophia* – seeks to situate its readers and listeners within this hierarchy, dividing them between those capable of hearing the *logos*, and those who take no notice of it. Those who can truly attend to the *logos* will always speak of it indirectly, in the strict manner Heraclitus himself demonstrates. And by speaking of it in this fashion, they are ultimately speaking in accordance with it.

2

In the presence of truth
Plato and dialectic

'Some might say that philosophy is certain arguments in certain books', notes Iris Murdoch, 'but for Plato (as indeed for many present-day philosophers) philosophy is essentially talk'.[1] Although not the first philosopher to store and disseminate his ideas in the written form, Plato is most responsible for transforming philosophy into a principally written enterprise. And yet, his body of writings comprises an elaborate and comprehensive defence of spoken philosophy in the face of such trends. Valorization of *elenchus* – cooperative but also argumentative spoken dialogue, bringing clarity to latent or unquestioned ideas through vigorous disputation – is an invariant feature of Plato's work, and arguably remains the idealized image of the philosophical enterprise to this day. In reading his philosophy, we are forced to ask whether, as Philippe Lacoue-Labarthe puts it, 'the dream, the desire that philosophy has entertained since its "beginning" for a *pure saying* (a speech, a discourse purely transparent to what it should immediately signify: truth, being, the absolute, etc.), has not always been compromised by the necessity of going through a text, through a process of writing'.[2] Plato's dialogues confront us with a strange situation, whereby he advocates for a supposedly self-present speech via the ancillary medium upon which he claims this speech has no dependence.

Philosophy, according to the Platonic model, writes Hadot, 'is not the solitary elaboration of a system, but the awakening of consciousness, and accession to a level of being which can only be reached in a person-to-person relationship'.[3] Following this line of thought, in this chapter I wish to identify a Platonic mode of discourse premised upon the question of *presence*. Seeing the act of philosophizing as equally one of communicating, Plato grounds his project in a belief that truth *does* have a genuine, ontological existence (in the middle-period dialogues, this takes the form of supersensible *ideas*, whereas in his later dialogues, it comes under the various *kinds* by which beings can be divided via *diairesis* and *synagōgē*), but also that the wisdom to which philosophy aspires lies not in the mere knowledge of such truths, nor even in their transmission, but in a holistic mode of speech which takes place in the *presence* of these truths. Such speech draws from the eternal wellspring of the soul, remaining clear, distinct and able to render a reasoned account, even if it cannot in every case fully articulate the identity of what it points towards. As Plato puts it in the *Symposium*, wisdom is not 'the sort of thing that could flow from the fuller to the emptier of us when we touch each other, like water, which flows through a piece of wool from a fuller cup to an emptier one'.[4]

I will centre my examination in this chapter upon two pivotal dialogues: *The Republic* and the *Phaedrus*. In the former, the paradigmatic middle-period dialogue, Plato worries that words can come to be distanced not only from their true referent but from the Good which binds them to this referent, acting as the basis by which one might apprehend all other ideas. In the latter, he gives voice to the terror of the author whose words are no longer their own as soon as they are inscribed upon the page, calling attention to the need for philosophical speech to be grounded in the presence of a soul trained in dialectic, oriented towards the truth of things (even if this remains ultimately inarticulable), and likewise able to point its audience towards this truth in a manner suited to these particular listeners or readers. A soul trained in such a fashion can communicate and defend its ideas, with the hope of teaching others as well, regardless of whether they are making speeches or writing texts. In both dialogues, the question of *how* one speaks (i.e. the *form* of discourse) is thus of as great an importance to him as the specific content of one's speech.

The hindrance to discussing Plato's work, of course, as I have already shown, is that his employment of the dialogic genre and its various *dramatis personae*, along with his frequent deployment of *aporia* and antinomy, works knowingly and artfully to undermine any attempt to reduce his philosophy to a series of propositional truth claims.[5] In particular, the depiction of a fictionalized version of his mentor Socrates exchanging views with a plethora of interlocutors makes attribution of any specific argument to Plato rather problematic.[6] Sarah Kofman gives quite a succinct rundown of the difficulties we face in this regard:

> How can one choose among the various images of Socrates? How can anyone sort out what belongs to Socrates and what to Plato? How can anyone manage to pry apart that inseparable couple and capture a 'pure and authentic' Socrates, a Socrates who has not been contaminated by his discipline, who has not been transfigured by someone who, under the influence of a somewhat excessive and suspect filial piety, attributes *all* his own thought to the other, someone who

never speaks in his own name, someone who practices, more than anyone else does, the mimetic discourse that is condemned Books II, III, and X of *The Republic*?[7]

These dialogues deliberately interfere with the direct transmission of knowledge, pushing their readers instead towards a dialectical mode of enquiry founded upon disputation and interchange.[8] Hence, when I ascribe particular claims to Plato in this chapter, I do so with the express caveat that he may intend them to be ironic, or provisional, and that they may well have no relation to his actual beliefs whatsoever. Such is the risk, Plato himself would aver, accompanying the evaluation of texts in the absence of their author, outside the sphere of animate speech.

Plato was anything but hermetic – he founded the Academy, utilizes writing as a pedagogical tool in a manner unprecedented by prior philosophers and seems at least somewhat invested in ensuring both the accessibility of his argumentation and the capacity for it to be disseminated – and this is perhaps why he is the first Greek philosopher whose corpus has been transmitted comparatively intact through to the present day. That being said though, his dialogues exhibit a great deal of anxiety regarding what we would now call mass communication, denouncing the citizens of the *polis* as driven by passions, swayed by casuistry and demagoguery, and unable to distinguish truth from falsehood. His dialogues consistently invoke the image of what Léon Robin describes as 'an association between teacher and pupil in the common search for truth, in which the teacher is merely a guide'.[9] The question of how one speaks and how one conveys knowledge thus also becomes a means by which he attempts to limit his audience, pushing back against the democratizing affordances of both speechmaking and writing, and striving to protect his discipline from those he perceives as unwanted intruders and charlatans.

The co-presence of speech

Near the conclusion of the *Phaedrus*, Plato lays out a broad critique of pedagogical methods dependent upon writing, arguing that this still-nascent medium will cause forgetfulness in the souls of those who use it, encouraging them to rely upon external marks rather than seeking the knowledge already lying within them.[10] This dialogue, observes John Durham Peters, 'sketches both the dream of direct communication from soul to soul and the nightmare of its breakdown when transposed into new media forms', uniting 'the hope of soul-to-soul contact with worries about its distortion'.[11] Writing, Plato propounds, is a supplement, an exteriority, separated from the vitality of living speech, and thus only capable of providing 'an appearance of wisdom, not the reality of it'.[12] As Robin puts it:

> writing kills the living activity of memory within thought; it can only artificially stand in for memory's laziness or failings; it is an alien aid which gets us out of the habit of inner effort. Progress in instruction can only result from the long-term patience of a cultivation directed by the man who knows, a cultivation appropriate to he who must receive it, presupposing on the part of the latter a communion with the teacher who confers it; far from furthering this progress, writing engenders the arrogant illusion of an uncritical knowledge, acquired too easily to have a solid foundation.[13]

Plato admonishes those who believe 'anything clear or certain will come from what is written down', arguing instead that written words can only act as a reminder for topics with which one is already familiar. And he underscores the difference in pedagogical efficacy between writing and speech, observing that 'when once it is written, every composition trundles about everywhere in the same way, in the presence both of those who know about the subject and of those who have nothing at all to do with it'.[14] Writing is able to be transmitted in the absence of its creator, left orphaned and illegitimate without the possibility of clarification or alteration, and in such a state is capable neither of tailoring its message towards a particular audience nor of defending itself against the censure of this audience. No matter how many questions one may ask of it, no matter who addresses it and in what manner, it will always provide the same answer. One can only guarantee the semantic surety of philosophical arguments by maintaining their connection to the speaking subject from which they spring.

This is not to say Plato wants to eradicate the use of the written word (naturally, given his own propensity for writing). Whether composing speeches, verses or written treatises, if one 'has composed these things knowing how the truth is, able to help his composition when he is challenged on its subjects, and with the capacity, speaking in his own person, to show that what he has written is of little worth', then he is, in Plato's estimation, worthy of the title of *philosopher*.[15] Whereas 'the man who doesn't possess things of more value than the things he composed or wrote' is nothing more than a poet, speechwriter or author.[16] It does not matter all that much whether one is using speech or writing to transmit one's arguments, for the real question is whether these arguments are communicated by or in the presence of someone who understands them, is able to speak truthfully in relation them, can defend them if needed and can modify or abandon them in light of convincing refutations. A memorized speech, recited by someone who does not comprehend what they are saying (precisely the kind of people the sophists were paid to teach), is no more helpful than a written disquisition studied without the presence of its author.[17] Plato defines effective communication as that which is congruent with the knowledge inscribed within the soul, 'capable of defending itself, and knowing how to speak and keep silent in relation to the people it should'.[18] Writing can be a useful instrument for philosophical instruction as long as one keeps it in its place, as an aid to spoken disputation, and uses it to clarify this divine, internal writing within each of us.

Although Plato foregrounds the co-presence of speech (or, more precisely, the right kind of speech) with the soul, he does not claim – at least in this dialogue – that this permits the philosopher to speak straightforwardly of the knowledge inscribed upon the latter. For to *assert* or *enunciate* these truths, to claim to articulate them *as such*, in a definitive and unambiguous form, would be to fall back into sophism, producing 'conviction without questioning or teaching' – it would do no better than writing in engendering genuine knowledge among its audience.[19] Plato does not define philosophical speech here in terms of an integral transmission or expression of truthful content; he defines it instead as speaking *in the presence* of truth: the clarity and veracity of that which is spoken is determined by the soul from which it arises.

Plato demurs at the notion that someone capable of such speechmaking should be called 'wise', for such a descriptor is 'fitting only in the case of a god', instead suggesting that 'to call him either a philosopher or something like that would both fit him more and be in better taste'.[20] To philosophize is to *love* wisdom, to pursue wisdom, it is not about accumulating knowledge.[21] The philosopher does not assert truth; they bring it to light, invoking its presence through dialogue. After all, none of us *need* such knowledge – it is already there, within our souls, waiting to be revealed, explained and enlivened. In this way, Plato resolutely reinforces the coupling of *philosophiā* and *logos*, conceiving of the former not in terms of the transmission of specific propositions, but of a general attitude or comportment, a fidelity to the originary conditions of knowledge, and a sensitivity to the means by which knowledge might be brought to light and disseminated.[22]

In *The Republic*, Plato describes painting as the creation of representations of representations; imitations of the already-corrupted copies given to us through sensible experience.[23] In the *Phaedrus*, Plato then in turn compares painting to writing, remarking that just as 'the offspring of painting stand there as if alive, but if you ask them something, they preserve a quite solemn silence', written words 'point to just one thing, the same every time'.[24] Both media at least *appear* to communicate, furnishing a semblance of truth (inasmuch as they re-present something), but this communication leaves them at the mercy of their audience. When someone attacks or misuses a written text, 'it always needs its father to help it; for it is incapable of either defending or helping itself'.[25] In writing, the father (usually) remains absent, resulting in an enervated, immobilized *logos*, disconnected from the soul of its author. In other words, the extended horizon of philosophical communicability enabled by writing becomes a problem for Plato, revealing how communication is grounded (and ungrounded) in its dissemination, its need for context – a problem he attempts to solve by suturing efficacious philosophical teaching to the presence or propinquity of the soul and the speaking subject.

This question of presence in Plato's philosophy is not at all straightforward: at the very minimum, it involves the presence of one's speech to one's own soul (the former being a direct exteriorization of the latter), the soul's presence to itself (its irreducible interiority, unsullied by any intrusion from without), and the face-to-face presence of speakers engaged in dialogue (an intercommunion of souls). So much of his philosophy can be understood as an attempt to tie together these three distinct types of presence, instituting a mode of dialogue that would not merely be an attempt to dazzle or fool its audience (as was, he asserts, the goal of the sophists' epideictic speeches), but to bring them into the fold of a properly philosophical community defined not only in terms of physical proximity but also in those of a particular *means* of communicating. Demonstrating, as he puts it in the *Protagoras*, that 'actually engaging with one another and talking things through [*dialogōn*]' is 'different from making long speeches [*dēmēgorein*]'.[26]

Furnishing a reasoned account

While this notion that wisdom must arise from adequately addressing and defending knowledge before one's audience is described most comprehensively in the *Phaedrus*, the accompanying claim that one's speech must be present to the soul from which it proceeds has a much broader status within the Platonic corpus. According to the *Phaedo*, Socrates began to develop his philosophical perspective at the moment he decided to spurn sensible knowledge and instead 'resort to *reasoned accounts* [*lógous*], and look into the truth of things in the world in them'.[27] Plato dedicates much of his writing to explaining how such an account (*logos*) might be furnished.[28] Although the specifics differ from dialogue to dialogue, what remains apparent is that philosophy is not just about transmission but *elenchus*, and its audience needs to be prepared for this, they need to be practiced in the rules of order (dialectic) under which this discussion is held.

Like Parmenides before him, Plato – within his middle-period dialogues, anyway – regards intra-empirical difference (e.g. change and becoming) as indicative of the sensible world's inherent difference from the supersensible world of the intellect. The 'true' difference is the *khorismos* between the pure identity of the ideas and their differential (and hence doxastic) representations: the job of the philosopher is thus to recognize this *khorismos*, of which the masses remain unaware, and to transcend the difference of the sensible world by giving an adequate account of it.[29] It is through *logos*, through the ability to give an account of a thing in its pure identity, unalloyed by any difference that we arrive at knowledge of this thing in itself. To know something, in Plato's conception, is to speak of it properly, to ensure one's words are adequate to its ideal nature, and this can only come through dialogue, and more specifically through dialectic.

In *The Republic*, Plato emphasizes the need to supply a rational and adequate account of the essence of a thing, 'to understand what it is to be any given thing'.[30] Anyone lacking in this ability will be incapable of grasping such a thing themselves, let alone explaining it to others. Such an account must begin by enquiring into the 'inherent difference and identity' of various things.[31] This connects to his observation of the need to argue for 'the separation and distinction of the character of goodness from everything else', presenting the idea of the Good as the superlative object towards which humans should direct their pursuit of knowledge, the similitude and difference from which we might derive all subsidiary ideas.[32] Secondly, though, he also stresses the need to be able to 'fight all the objections one by one and refute them (responding to them absolutely by referring to the reality of things, rather than to people's beliefs)', not asserting knowledge, but substantiating and defending it, avoiding recourse to empirical experience and instead appealing to a more pure intellection.[33] A reasoned account is therefore reached not through direct transmission, but by adopting a method of speaking that is borne of the Good and provides the means by which one may comport one's pursuit of knowledge with the Good.

The Good is more than just the superlative idea (which would position it as a mere object of knowledge); it is the 'source and provider of truth and knowledge'.[34] The Good 'gives the things we know their truth and makes it possible for people to have knowledge', and is thus more valuable than either.³⁵ It grants things their being – that is, their permanency, allowing them to remain unperturbed by the vicissitudes of empirical experience – so they can be grasped by the intellect and not the senses. Plato compares the Good to the sun, presenting them as intelligible and sensible counterparts, respectively. In the same way that the sun allows us to see things, but does not itself contain the faculty of sight, the Good furnishes the circumstances whereby we can possess knowledge, but it is not itself knowledge or understanding. One does not introduce sight to the eyes but turns them towards the light; likewise, one does not introduce knowledge to the soul but ensures it is heading in the right direction (i.e. towards goodness).³⁶

The consequence of all this is that the Good is not only an object the philosopher seeks via dialectical enquiry; rather, it is by trying to speak in conformity with the Good, spurning the world of sensibility (and becoming) in favour of that of intellection (and being), that the philosopher takes part in the dialectical method. Again, the Good is not just an object of knowledge, it is the ground of all knowledge. And dialectics is not just a means of reaching this object but a set of procedures for continually training the soul, hoping to make it capable of grasping the essence of all things, orienting it towards the Good as the basis of all such knowledge. So on the one hand, a person who persevered in dialectics could, eventually, grasp 'with his intellect the reality of goodness itself', even though Plato often seems very sceptical regarding the capacity of human beings, flawed as they are, to truly achieve this.³⁷ On the other hand, though, the very act of speaking dialectically must in itself demonstrate a certain orientation vis-à-vis the Good, for only through this orientation can one direct their enquiry towards the intelligible reality of things. A philosopher desires 'the whole of knowledge, not only some aspects of it'.³⁸

Dialectic for Plato, is not just 'the only field of enquiry which sets out methodically to grasp the reality of any and every thing', it is also the only one 'whose quest for certainty causes it to uproot the things it takes for granted in the course of its journey', helping to remove obstacles (*aporiai*) by questioning all given assumptions and received wisdom, so one might gradually approach the ideas one seeks.³⁹ It both facilitates and is facilitated by one's turning in the direction of the Ideas, away from the delusive distractions of quotidian experience. If the acquisition of knowledge, truth and wisdom (rather than their mere appearance) is the *telos* of the philosopher, Plato understands this goal not only in terms of giving an account of the ideas, although this is part of it, but also in terms of maintaining oneself within the presence of the Good, using dialectic as an instrument to keep oneself on the right path. The ability to challenge all of one's accreted preconceptions, to put all topics up for debate, and to supply an account of things that will allow others to also orient themselves in such a fashion, secures the status of the philosopher, much more than the specific answers they give.[40] For otherwise, even if a person 'does somehow manage to make contact with a reflection of goodness', their audience are liable to claim 'the contact is due to belief, not knowledge'.[41]

Of course, this is most obvious in Plato's early aporetic dialogues, wherein the interlocutors end up at a point of contradiction rather than confutation or clarity, finding themselves confronted with an impassable obstacle to further disputation.[42] And while these dialogues lack the weighty metaphysical armature characteristic of his later works, they are still significant, because they evidence not only a preoccupation regarding the incapacity of speech to consistently reach adequation with its object but a conviction that such inadequation does not in itself devalue the art of philosophical discussion.[43] Most times, notes Hadot, the 'task of dialogue' for Plato 'consists essentially in pointing out the limits of language, and its inability to communicate moral and existential experience' – these aporetic dialogues communicate the limits of the communicable (and thus, in some sense, attempt to communicate the incommunicability of the incommunicable).

It is readily apparent in many of his central, non-aporetic dialogues that Plato does not regard truth per se to be ineffable (or indeed, even uninscribable). But what is also apparent is his suspicion regarding the notion that mere description could ever be adequate as a means for pointing an audience towards the ideas, our experience of which comes not just by describing them, but *through* the process of reaching such a description (or reaching the limits of their description). The mystery of the ideas lies in their insinuation of a presence which exceeds all attempts to re-present it, hence the need for a speaking subject to articulate, innervate and defend all such representation (whether spoken or written). This subject supplies a veritable, inimitable presence any representation will lack.

Plato does not separate the act of philosophizing from that of transmission or communication. There is no meaningful distinction for him between knowing the essence of things and being able to convey this to one's audience, which together allows one to furnish a reasoned account and thus to philosophize. His dialogues offer no signs of philosophizing occurring anywhere other than in conversation with others (or as part of the inner conversation of the soul with itself).[44] As he warns in the *Sophist*, if we were deprived of speech, 'we'd be deprived of philosophy'.[45] *Logos*, and ultimately wisdom (as far as one can attain it), thus relates not just to the ability to think in accordance with the

Good but to invoke such thoughts within an audience as well, communicating in such a way that listeners or readers might themselves be able to reach the same conclusions.[46] And, we can surmise, even if we fail to ever adequately capture this essence through language (though we might get certain aspects of it across), there is still a utility in speaking about them veraciously, keeping our arguments in circulation – provided we take care not to treat this speech as an end in itself, but pursue it with another end in sight: the Good. Funnily enough, the famed principle of Socratic ignorance – that when one does not know things, one must not come to mistakenly believe that one knows them – bolsters the communicative impulse of the philosopher, obliging them to speak interminably of their failure to *know*.[47]

Lovers of wisdom

Situated in terms of Plato's broader corpus, the *Phaedrus* marks a midway point between his middle- and late-period dialogues (at least with respect to the question of dialectic). On the one hand, the emphasis in this dialogue upon the need for the presence of a knowing, speaking subject as a basis of all philosophical transmission is not at all an anomaly, fitting neatly into his broader conception of *logos* as the provision of a reasoned account, and even the foundational *khorismos* of the middle-period dialogues between an originary presentation and an ersatz re-presentation of the ideas. The *Phaedrus* still advocates a movement from sensible and embodied perceptions towards an ideal truth, sharing with the *Symposium* an emphasis upon Beauty, rather than the Good, as the superlative idea grounding knowledge. Plato treats the lover of beauty (*philokalos*) and lover of wisdom (*philosophos*) as one and the same, observing that although he who is enraptured with the beautiful people and things that surround him, and who for that reason sets his sights upward towards true Beauty, is often regarded as mad, he is in fact a lover in the truest sense, able to rise above mortal concerns and approach divinity – a journey that does not so much furnish him with new knowledge as it does remind him of those truths already inscribed upon his immortal soul.[48]

On the other hand, though, while the *Phaedrus* does not itself end up in aporia, it evinces much less confidence than many earlier dialogues in the notion that the instrument of language can do justice to the divine character of the ideas. Even those like the beauty-lover described earlier, who are able to use their experience of divinity in order to recollect knowledge of these ideas within themselves, are inevitably 'driven out of their wits with amazement' at such experience, incapable of fully comprehending that to which they have been witness.[49] To provide a reasoned account of the soul's immortality, Plato argues, would demand a divine power of exposition, whereas to merely speak of what it resembles is still within human capacities, providing a justification for the dialogue's subsequent use of extensive mythological metaphor.[50] Whereas in dialogues like *The Republic* or *Phaedo* there is a clear possibility of speech's adequation with the ideas, albeit one demanding the supplementation of description with disputation, ensuring that such speech arises from a subject oriented towards the Good, in the *Phaedrus*, the latter seems to take primacy, combined with a more pragmatic method of making speeches suited to their audience. The true orator, capable of constructing artful speeches, is a person who

> knows the truth about each of the things about which he speaks or writes, capable of defining the whole by itself, and having defined it, knows how to cut it up again according to its forms until it can no longer be cut; and until he has reached an understanding of the nature of soul along the same lines, discovering the form which fits each nature, and so arranges and orders his speech, offering a complex soul complex speeches containing all the modes, and simple speeches to a simple soul.[51]

Only this person can speak in a genuinely philosophical manner, avoiding all sophistic inferences.

The fact that Plato directs most of his animus in the *Phaedrus* towards written works reflects the extent to which this medium seems to him to give tangible form to the inadequacies of language. Semantic indeterminacy and malleability, after all, do not originate with the written word. Hence Plato's frequent comparisons of discourse to water or the ocean, alluding at one point to the need to 'try swimming to safety out of this sea of argument, hoping for some improbable rescue like a dolphin picking us up'.[52] The sea is unbounded, indefinite, *apeiron*, a space of apparent freedom, but also of fear and uncertainty; writing, likewise, is the visible manifestation of the unboundedness and indefinitude of language, a space in which one can so easily find oneself lost in aporia, unless one remains firmly moored to the surety of the Good. Not being bound to a particular place and time, writing foregrounds its own contextualized (and thus contingent) dissemination. The fixed nature of alphabetic letters, whether carved into stone, written on papyrus or scratched into wax, is antithetical to the eternal truth of the ideas, for one can only recall the latter, 'genuinely written in the soul', through the dynamic interchange and presence of spoken discussion.[53] Hence the importance of the Academy as a space in which Plato and his pupils affirmed and enacted this presence, with his written dialogues playing a merely hypomnematic role. A physical locus for philosophical disputation, cut off from the misological obstinacy of the broader *polis*. Writing for Plato, observes Robin,

> should only either be an accessory means of sustaining, for oneself as well as those with whom one associates, research and debates that have taken place within the School, or serve to offer insight for a wider public beyond these confines; an insight sufficient to pique curiosity, not to satisfy it.[54]

Whereas the sophists offer their rhetoric to anyone willing to pay, Plato is torn between wishing to disseminate his philosophy (convinced as he is of its universal applicability) and wishing to restrict its audience to prevent it from being misunderstood or distorted.

As Plato puts it in the *Parmenides*, it is not fitting for a philosopher to engage in debate 'in front of a crowd', for 'ordinary people don't know that without this comprehensive and circuitous treatment we cannot hit upon the truth and gain insight'.[55] The masses demand simple answers (the kind in which the sophists specialize), whereas dialectic requires sustained and oft-tortuous disputation. The sophists' epistemological scepticism, and their attendant conviction that speech is a medium not for the transmission of knowledge but for entertainment and persuasion, offers a discursive certitude quite distinct from Plato's method: there is no simpler answer to the problem of wisdom than to be told that it is nothing more than affect or rhetoric, that to be wise means simply to *appear* wise, that speech is cut loose from any grounding in reason. Their turgid oratory makes a mockery of the search for wisdom, and Plato wants to shield philosophy from any association with it. Dialectic is thus a serious endeavour for Plato, and he will not entrust it to just anyone, lest it be impugned by those who have no real ability to understand it. Dialectic is an instrument of *mastery*, a means of maintaining sway over one's propositions and not allowing them to fall into the wrong hands (as a written text so easily can, both literally and figuratively). After all, as he suggests in the *Theaetetus*, we as philosophers should not be in thrall to our arguments; rather, 'the arguments are *ours* – our slaves [*oiketai*], as it were, each waiting for our decision before it is completed', and unlike dramatists for instance, we do not have to suffer 'judge and audience set over us to criticize and control us'.[56]

By refusing to separate the question of philosophizing from that of speaking in a properly philosophical manner, a practice into which one must be inducted,

Plato does not merely pursue this circumscription of philosophy through the physical boundaries of the Academy. He also provides a philosophical means for differentiating between genuine lovers of wisdom and specious imposters. His philosophy contains within itself the rules for deciding who is or is not worthy of being privy to it, ensuring that those exposed to philosophical arguments are those deemed capable of philosophizing.

Graeco-Roman philosophy was an activity almost exclusively confined to the aristocratic class of male landowners. Along with the possibilities for transmission afforded by the *polis*, the written text and so forth, philosophizing found its material support in a strict social division that delegated the bulk of manual labour to chattel slaves.[57] Hence Plato's lengthy enumeration, in *The Republic*, of the inherent qualities needed for someone to be educated philosophically (which entails them becoming, in his imagined city-state, guardians of the community).[58] Since he believes it is 'an attribute of every child, woman, slave, free man, artisan, ruler, and subject that each individual does his own job without intruding elsewhere', and that these jobs should be assigned on the basis of an individual's specific nature, it is hardly surprising that he arrives at the conclusion that one's capacity for being trained in the art of philosophizing is determined on the basis of congenital traits.[59] His comparison between the unfitness to spurn sensible perception and recognize the truth of things, on the one hand, and physical blindness, on the other hand, marks the former as not merely a contingent inaptitude, capable of being mitigated, but as a connate characteristic.[60]

This is not to say that such enumeration does not sometimes lead to surprising results. Most notably, his suggestion that women are equally deserving of philosophical education, differing from men only in terms of physical strength, seems incongruous not only when compared to his Athenian peers (e.g. Aristotle's unequivocal misogyny) but also to philosophers millennia later.[61] Notwithstanding certain moments of apparent magnanimity though, Plato dedicates great swathes of his dialogues to circumscribing the boundaries of his philosophy and the community within which it is enacted in exclusionary terms dissonant with the purportedly universal applicability of its claims. To take just one germane example, in both the *Symposium* and the *Theaetetus*, the character of Socrates equates philosophy, peculiarly, with giving birth. In the latter dialogue, we find a succinct encapsulation of the role of the philosopher, with Socrates emphasizing that he himself is barren of wisdom, but acts instead as a midwife, helping those pregnant with concepts give birth, and then assessing these offspring to determine whether they are truthful or spurious.[62] Not communicating propositions directly, but encouraging their gestation within others' minds.

But this image of ratiocinative parturition is figured in strikingly gendered terms, with Socrates remarking that what differentiates his midwifery from the usual kind is that he 'practise[s] it on men instead of women, and supervise[s] the labour of their minds, not their bodies'.[63] Likewise, and even more pointedly, in the *Symposium*, Socrates extols the merits of the homosocial (and indeed, homoerotic) bond of male philosophers, which aims towards the mental reproduction of truths, counterposed against that of men and women, which conversely aims towards the physical reproduction of children. The former 'have a much closer partnership with each other and a stronger bond of friendship than parents have, because the children of their partnership are more beautiful and more immortal'.[64]

Thus, despite any inclusive gestures made elsewhere, what we find out in these two dialogues is: first, that the gestation of arguments (which, as we well know, is a necessary part of learning to philosophize) is a male activity, collocated against pregnancy in the usual sense, thus confining women to the inferior domain of the sensible and material world, denied access to the realm of ideal things; and second, that a philosophical community suited to this peculiar form of midwifery requires a kind of close coupling between speaker and listener that occurs between men and expressly excludes women – an ideal Love denuded of its unwanted feminine residua.[65] If Plato initiates, as Peters puts it, 'a long tradition that sees a reciprocal encounter with another person as a way to return to the homeland whence the soul has wandered', such reciprocity is already strictly circumscribed.[66]

Plato's emphasis in the *Phaedrus* on the significance of presence – which he views as providing the context (or perhaps more precisely, an eternal truth that avoids the facticity of any disseminative context) through which communication is enlivened and becomes truly meaningful, effecting knowledge rather than simulating its appearance through indemonstrable propositions – enables a redoubling, at the level of ideality, of the exclusionary conditions for philosophizing that Plato instituted through the Academy (and which were, in themselves, only supplements to the rigid hierarchization of Athenian society). Reacting against the perceived infinitude of the written form, Plato attempts to re-ground philosophy in the presence of spoken disputation, and in a specific manner of speaking. This must be regarded, then, as a reaction against the democratizing potential of writing as well: the attention that Plato pays to the audience of his philosophy is indicative of his desire to *limit* this audience, to insulate his philosophy from the masses, at the same time he presumes to assert its validity for and applicability to them.

When all is said and done, for Plato, merely enunciating a factually correct statement is no sign of wisdom, for anyone could – even by accident – stumble upon such a claim. The more important question is *how* they reached that conclusion (or how they failed to reach a definitive conclusion, as the case may be). A valuable principle, for sure, and one that on the face of it accords with most holistic accounts of pedagogy. But one that also, when coupled with Plato's emphasis upon a very particular philosophical manner of speaking, becomes a mechanism by which he safeguards philosophy's esotericism against the threat of popularizers, demagogues and those who are just not 'naturally suited for dialectic' – the latter category being determined, of course, on Plato's own idiosyncratic terms.[67]

3

A question of tone

Mysticism and propriety in Immanuel Kant

In the conclusion to one of his earliest noteworthy essays, 'Universal Natural History and Theory of the Heavens' (1755), Immanuel Kant observes that when one has reckoned with both humanity's place in the cosmos and its relationship with the highest being,

> the view of the starry sky on a clear night gives one a kind of pleasure that only noble souls feel. In the universal stillness of nature and the calmness of the senses the immortal spirit's hidden faculty of cognition speaks an ineffable language and provides undeveloped concepts that can certainly be felt but not described.[1]

Two implications of this passage stand out when considered in relation to Kant's later, 'critical' period: first, his appeal to an unspeakable language, furnishing concepts grounded in non-discursive cognition; and second, his intimation that these concepts offer an insight into the harmonious workings of nature not available (or at least not yet) to all rational beings. By the time he publishes the *Critique of Pure Reason* in 1781, little of this tacitly mystical viewpoint remains. Even though he still gestures towards indescribable aspects of reality (circumscription of the latter forming one of the central aspects of his critical approach), such gestures do not lead us to a mode of discourse that would allow us to get some purchase on them; they instead indicate the absolute impossibility of such a discourse being able to say *anything* with respect to these chimerical objects.[2] When he expresses his admiration, in the *Critique of Practical Reason*, for the starry heavens above and the moral law within himself, he makes clear that these are not 'veiled in obscurity', but accessible through his senses and intellect.[3]

This does not mean concerns relating to communicability disappear from Kant's work. In the wake of the underwhelming reception of the first edition of the *Critique of Pure Reason*, a certain pathos starts to pervade the critical project: namely, Kant's frustration at the incapacity of his peers to grasp the complexities of his new system, and his conviction that this is not the result of any fundamental error on his part with regard to his propositions or their grounds of proof, but merely a reflection of his ineffectual method of *presentation*. A pathos fuelled, in his own words, by 'the pain [felt] at being almost universally misunderstood'.[4] In the preface to the second edition of this *Critique*, published six years later, Kant bullishly asserts that the architectonic unity of his system remains unalterable, not only because of the scrutiny to which he has personally subjected it but because this system is inseparable from the unity of reason itself, such that 'the attempt to alter even the smallest part directly introduces contradictions not merely into the system, but into universal human reason'.[5] He does not fear refutation, only misunderstanding, and thus, aware of his advanced age, bequeaths his project to those 'deserving men, who combine well-groundedness of insight so fortunately with the talent for a lucid presentation', in the hope they might at last supply an elegance of presentation commensurate with its rigour.[6]

Writing to his friend and former pupil Marcus Herz in 1781, soon after the initial publication of the first *Critique*, Kant thanks Herz for his determination to read this book thoroughly, complaining that he 'can count on such effort only from a very few readers'.[7] He goes on to remark that

> one cannot expect a way of thinking to be suddenly led off the beaten track into one that has heretofore been totally unused. That requires time, to stay that style of thinking little by little in its previous path and, finally, to turn it into the opposite direction by means of gradual impressions.[8]

As we shall see over this chapter, the notion that genuine philosophy necessitates *work*, that it is not a form of *historical cognition* able to be transmitted verbatim, in propositional form, from one mind to another – in short, as Theodor Adorno puts it, that 'philosophy is not a subject like law, for instance, where the lecturer tries to impart a body of knowledge that students then have to reproduce' – remains a recurrent feature across Kant's oeuvre.[9] The proper aim of philosophy, from his point of view, is 'to allow all of the steps of reason to be seen in the clearest light', and this means those who wish to philosophize must be inducted in a particular manner, quite distinct from other fields of knowledge.[10] Assuming they follow this path, any human being (since they are a rational being) should, in theory, be able to develop a genuinely *rational cognition* – and, to speak with an appropriate tone when addressing speculative philosophical problems about which they will never attain any cognition. And yet, Kant's emphasis upon the work ethic appropriate to philosophizing also allows him to call into question the possibility that *all* humans are capable of such philosophical insight.

Historical and rational cognition

Kant begins his critical project with the premise of needing to construct 'a system of caution and self-examination out of the nature of reason and the objects of its pure use', imposing impassable limits upon speculative reason, a circumscription one achieves through procedures of *discipline*, which he defines as the limitation and eventual eradication of 'the constant propensity to stray from certain rules'.[11] Reason must restrain itself, in a perpetual process of self-limitation, lest its enthusiasm tempt it to try grasping beyond the boundaries of the objects of experience, unleashing swarms of sophistic inferences exceeding the extremities of human insight.[12] This discipline, however, is needed for neither empirical nor mathematical concepts, since the former are tested continuously according to the 'touchstone of experience' (via the natural sciences) and the latter 'must immediately be exhibited *in concreto* in pure intuition, through which anything unfounded and arbitrary instantly becomes obvious' (reflecting Kant's postulation of mathematical cognition as founded upon a *construction of concepts*).[13] Hence why only speculative reason, which in its transcendental use of concepts cannot rely upon either empirical or pure intuition to keep its hyperbole in check, requires such a regimen.

The distinction Kant draws between metaphysics and mathematics – and his concomitant claim that 'it is not suited to the nature of philosophy [. . .] to strut about with a dogmatic gait and to decorate itself with the titles and ribbons of mathematics' – is common across much of his oeuvre, even as he upholds mathematics as an exemplary science (confirming the necessity of synthetic *a priori* judgements).[14] It is also unsurprising, given the dogmatic rationalists' habitual and spurious privileging of mathematical reason as a model for metaphysical thought.[15] Kant believes that mathematics' grounding in definitions, axioms and demonstrations is entirely unsuited to philosophical enquiry: 'by means of his method the mathematician can build nothing in philosophy except houses of cards, while by means of his method the philosopher can produce nothing in mathematics but idle chatter'.[16]

In the 'Announcement' of the programme for his 1765–6 lecture course – a self-published pamphlet advertising said course to prospective students – we witness another iteration of this distinction, inherited from Christian Wolff, with Kant setting *mathematics* and *history* on the one side apart from *philosophy* on the other. In this instance, though, he separates them based on their distinct modalities of transmission. The difficulty inherent in the instruction of young minds, Kant submits, is that a teacher is compelled to impart knowledge their students are not yet mature enough to grasp in full. As a result, the former must help the latter progress through three stages of development: 'firstly the man of *understanding*, then the man of *reason*, and finally the man of *learning*'.[17] This means beginning with intuitive judgements (drawing comparisons based on sensible data), and then slowly and carefully moving towards higher judgements and concepts, making no injudicious leaps. The goal of the teacher here is to not just transmit *thoughts* but to cultivate a certain kind of *thinking* or understanding, leaving the pupil in good stead to tackle future problems on their own. If the teacher does not follow such a method, 'then the pupil picks up a kind of reason, even before his understanding has developed', the result being that 'his science is a borrowed science which he wears, not as something which has, so to speak, grown within him, but as something which has been hung upon him', an imitative acquisition that may testify to a certain rote learning (to the extent that he has pursued a course of study), but does not bear out any genuine understanding.[18]

The 'peculiar nature of philosophy itself demands such a method of teaching', Kant suggests, but it also presents unique difficulties, relying upon a peculiar, *zetetic* method of instruction.[19] 'The youth who has completed his school instruction has been accustomed *to learn*. He now thinks that he is going to *learn philosophy*. But that is impossible, for he ought now to learn to philosophize'.[20] Hence Kant's aforesaid separation of the philosophical sciences from the historical and mathematical. In the latter two disciplines, it is possible to learn – that is, 'it is possible to impress either on the memory or on the understanding that which can be presented to us as an already complete discipline' – precisely because both are able to furnish a positive knowledge immediately assimilable by the understanding: history (under which Kant also includes fields such as jurisprudence) documents the facts of others' testimonies and experiences, all of which are founded upon empirical data whereas mathematics relies upon self-evident concepts and infallible demonstrations.[21] One can thus integrally transmit historical circumstances and mathematical propositions to an audience, via reference to evidence, without anything significant being lost in the process.

Philosophy, however, is markedly different, because it is not possible to point to a single text (like Polybius' *Histories* or Euclid's *Elements*) that, simply by reading and grasping the knowledge within, will enable one to become a proficient philosopher. The integral transmission of philosophy would require the existence of an integral, fully realized philosophy:

> one would be betraying the trust placed in one by the public if, instead of extending the capacity for understanding of the young people entrusted to one's care and educating them to the point where they will be able in the future to acquire a more mature insight *of their own* [. . .] one were to deceive them with a philosophy which was alleged to be already complete and to have been excogitated by others for their benefit. Such a claim would create the illusion of science.[22]

Or, as reiterated in notes taken from his 1782–3 lecture series (the *Metaphysik Mrongovius*), undertaken soon after the first publication of the *Critique of Pure Reason*:

> the whole of metaphysics is nothing other than a chain of built-up and overthrown systems. No book has yet appeared where there is something permanent. It is not a science which has the fate to be permanent. [. . .] It will be objected that Wolff and Crusius have published metaphysics. Without checking the matter itself, look only at the success. They have all collapsed already. A few propositions were true, but not the whole.[23]

Kant thus draws a sharp line between authentic and inauthentic transmission of philosophical knowledge. While one can project the appearance of philosophical sagacity through the mechanical repetition of prior thinkers' propositions, this can only remain *cognitio ex datis*, a historical form of cognition in philosophical guise (i.e. a cognition *objectively* philosophical but *subjectively* merely historical), a repetition of data without substantive insight. The latter can only be cultivated through rational cognition, *cognitio ex principiis*, arising from the free use of reason.

The interesting consequence of this is that, for Kant, a concrete philosophy does not actually exist, remaining merely an idea of a possible science towards which we might aspire in our philosophizing. Moreover, the philosopher – if we regard them not just as someone skilled in reason (a *Vernunftkünstler*, such as a mathematician, logician or naturalist) but as a 'legislator of human reason', who uses the various methods of philosophy to further the essential ends of said reason – cannot be found anywhere, but must be regarded as an ideal towards which we must orient our philosophizing.[24] Pupils should thus stop looking towards the philosophical writer, the author of books, as the paragon of philosophical judgement, from whom they might gain knowledge; rather, they should start seeking their own 'proficiency in the method of reflecting and drawing inferences'.[25] In developing such a proficiency, said pupils would end up capable of forming their own judgements about an author's arguments, instead of just passing off these arguments as their own.

'As far as reason is concerned', Kant propounds, we can never really learn philosophy, 'we can at best only learn *to philosophize*'.[26] And most people, he implies, do not even get that far, instead 'remain[ing] students their whole lives'.[27] As he puts in the first *Critique*, in a passage worth quoting at length:

> however a cognition may have been given originally, it is still historical for him who possesses it if he cognizes it only to the degree and extent that it has been given to him from elsewhere, whether it has been given to him through immediate experience or told to him or even given to him through instruction (general cognitions). Hence he who has properly *learned* a system of philosophy, e.g., the Wolffian system, although he has in his head all of the principles, explanations, and proofs together with the division of the entire theoretical edifice, and can count everything off on his fingers, still has nothing other than a complete *historical* cognition of the Wolffian philosophy; he knows and judges only as much as has been given to him. If you dispute one of his definitions, he has no idea where to get another one. He has formed himself according to an alien reason, but the faculty of imitation is not that of generation, i.e., the cognition did not arise *from* reason for him, and although objectively it was certainly a rational cognition, subjectively it is still merely historical. He has grasped and preserved well, i.e., he has learned, and is a plaster cast of a living human being.[28]

The aforementioned distinction between historical and rational cognition (into which one can sort all forms of subjective cognition) is thus figured in terms of a chasm between a subjective interiority and objective exteriority, with the locus of this division being the role one's *own* reason plays (or does not play, as the case might be) in the respective imitation or generation of cognition. Anticipating the dualism of heteronomy and autonomy that would come to guide his moral philosophy from the *Groundwork of the Metaphysics of Morals* onward, Kant presents integral transmission (typified in this case by the Wolffian corpus) as a kind of alien cause guiding one's learning, offering an outward appearance of knowledge which turns out to be hollow and unphilosophical. Rational cognitions lose their status as such when they are objectified, cast off from the reason that originally engendered them, and committed to memory by others. And by taking on these cognitions as their own without bringing reason to bear upon them, the philosophical pupil adopts a lifeless, almost inhuman mask of knowledge (a *Gipsabdruck*).

The congenital inability to philosophize

Kant furnishes a striking theory of communication, conceiving of philosophical knowledge, and the manner in which one must convey it in order to preserve its properly philosophical character, as distinct from that of other sciences, resisting any straightforward transmission. And on the basis of this theory, it would not be inordinate to infer that Kant would regard a large segment of the human population as incapable of ever learning to philosophize. In *Observations on the Feeling of the Beautiful and Sublime* (1764), published a year prior to the lecture announcement mentioned earlier, Kant asserts that although women possess as much understanding as men, the former hold a *beautiful* form of understanding, and the latter a deeper, *sublime* understanding. He explains this differentiation as follows:

> for the beauty of all actions it is requisite above all that they display facility and that they seem to be accomplished without painful effort; by contrast, efforts and difficulties that have been overcome arouse admiration and belong to the sublime. Deep reflection and a long drawn out consideration are noble, but are grave and not well suited for a person in whom the unconstrained charms should indicate nothing other than a beautiful nature. [. . .] The beautiful understanding chooses for its objects everything that is closely related to the finer feeling, and leaves abstract speculation or knowledge, which is useful but dry, to the industrious, thorough, and deep understanding.[29]

When educating women, he suggests, one will 'seek to broaden her entire moral feeling and not her memory, and not, to be sure, through universal rules, but rather through individual judgment about the conduct that she sees about her', offering 'never a cold and speculative instruction, always sentiments and indeed those that remain as close as possible to the relationships of their sex'.[30]

Kant thus praises women's natural inclination towards the sentimental, while simultaneously foreclosing from them the higher ends that make up philosophy proper.[31] Any loftier aspirations in the education of women, it would seem, are not only unbecoming but doomed to failure, for women cannot progress beyond holding up a mere superficial appearance of knowledge (equivalent to the 'borrowed science' referenced earlier):

> a woman who has a head full of Greek, like Mme Dacier, or who conducts thorough disputations about mechanics, like the Marquise du Châtelet, might as well also wear a beard; for that might perhaps better express the mien of depth for which they strive.[32]

And lest one assume such attitudes are just misbegotten relics of his incipient, immature writings, Kant makes an almost identical claim decades later, in *Anthropology from a Pragmatic Point of View* (1798), snidely opining that scholarly women 'use their *books* somewhat like their *watch*, that is, they carry one so that it will be seen that they have one; though it is usually not running or not set by the sun'.[33]

The implication of all this is that while reason impels man to direct his thought towards the latter's essential ends, woman remains by natural necessity in a state of philosophical neoteny, never capable of truly reaching the 'mature and manly [*männlichen*]' power of judgement that 'has at its basis firm maxims of proven universality'.[34] Woman is excluded from the critical project proper, insofar as her facile and sentimental use of reason is not suited for *a priori* cognition. We witness, in his lecture course of 1775–6, a similar characterization of the so-called oriental nations, which he claims are 'completely incapable of judgment in accordance with concepts', and hence are 'capable neither of a philosophy nor of mathematics', relying upon shape, appearance and intuition in order to form their judgements.[35] And we can assume – given that, in paraphrasing David Hume, he insists that among the thousands of Africans transported as slaves, 'not a single one has ever been found who has accomplished something great in art or science or shown any other praiseworthy quality' – he would likely extend the same lack of generosity to other races and nations as well.[36]

In one especially stark passage from the *Observations*, after recounting a misogynistic remark supposedly made by an African carpenter to the French missionary Jean-Baptiste Labat, Kant opines that the carpenter's comments might be worthy of consideration, 'except for the fact that this scoundrel was completely black from head to foot, a distinct proof that what he said was stupid'.[37] Even though Kant may actually be of the same mind with respect to this carpenter's opinion (in short, that white men afford their wives too much autonomy), he still feels confident in rejecting them out of hand ('*a priori*', we might say) based on a preexisting prejudice regarding the cognitive abilities of this man's race. The content of the proposition is not enough, it would seem, to be afforded validity, for Kant seems to believe this man could have only arrived at such a judgement by accident. The foreclosure of integral transmission thus, in this case, plays into what Achille Mbembe describes as 'the daily work [. . .] whose goal was to produce the Black Man as a racial subject and site of savage exteriority, who was therefore set up for moral disqualification and practical instrumentalization'.[38]

One could, of course, argue that such anthropological anecdotes, which put Kant's offensive (but at the time he was writing, fairly unremarkable) chauvinism on full display, do not impinge upon the coherence of his critical project in the main (and in many cases precede the full elaboration of said project), and instead simply demonstrate Kant's failures in living up to the critical attitude that he himself wishes to instil, which would demand an unequivocal respect for all human beings. But such anecdotes and asides correspond to a perspective traversing both his pre-critical and critical works, premised upon the notion that the ability to recite philosophical arguments (i.e. propositions that are *objectively philosophical*) is not the same as the capacity to philosophize, for the latter involves using one's reason to furnish concepts and judgements that are also *subjectively philosophical*, rather than historical. Propositions are not enough to demonstrate a philosophical thought orientation, because anyone is able to display them conspicuously, with no actual cognition sitting behind.

The effect of such a notion is to proscribe the straightforward transmission of philosophical propositions without the corresponding cultivation of a properly philosophical mode of enquiry. This proscription enables Kant, at certain moments, to dismiss the apparent philosophizing of certain groups of people as *a priori* inauthentic, excluding them from the philosophical enterprise. But it also enables him, with a broader horizon and in a much more unconventional manner, to exclude anyone who believes themselves to be a philosopher. To speak philosophically demands that one self-effacingly dissimulate this position of mastery. Kant believes it important to 'discourage the self-conceit of someone who ventures to claim the title of philosopher', but this affected humility only serves to alter the criteria by which the authenticity of philosophical speech can be measured.[39]

A superior tone

In the same passage from the *Observations* discussed earlier, Kant contends that 'laborious learning or punctilious pondering, even if a woman could get very far with them, destroy the merits that are proper to her sex', and although they might earn her a 'cold admiration', they will also 'weaken the charms by means of which she exercises her great power over the opposite sex'.[40] To some degree, Kant is just passing off his barely sublimated recourse to a banal misogynistic trope (viz. that men are not attracted to bookish women) as an incontestable sign of some deeper gendered scission between men and women's respective faculties of understanding.[41] There is another aspect to these comments, however, which merits further attention. In both Kant's writings on the gendered division of reason and those on the correct method for learning to philosophize, we can discern a kind of *work ethic* at play, whereby he underscores the formidable investiture of effort serious philosophical enquiry requires.

This focus upon an arduous exertion of reason is less surprising when considered in relation to Kant's moral philosophy, in which he repeatedly emphasizes the unabated labour demanded by practical reason:

> the proposition about the moral vocation of our nature, that only in an endless progress can we attain complete conformity with the moral law, is of the greatest usefulness, not merely in regard to the present supplement to the incapacity of speculative reason but also with respect to religion. In default of it, one either quite degrades the moral law from its *holiness* by making it out to be *lenient* (indulgent) and thus conformed to our convenience, or else strains one's calling [*Beruf*] as well as one's expectation to an unattainable vocation [*Bestimmung*], namely to a hoped-for full acquisition of holiness of will, and so gets lost in enthusiastic *theosophical* dreams that quite contradict self-knowledge; in both cases, constant *effort* to observe precisely and fully a strict and inflexible command of reason, which is yet not ideal but true, is only hindered.[42]

The moral destiny of human reason, therefore, lies not in happiness, nor in any other empirical state or object of being, but in the recognition of a *duty*, following a *calling*, striving *ad infinitum* in our attempts to approximate a practical *idea* of holiness our finitude as human beings prevents us from ever attaining in full. Moral philosophy 'is not properly the doctrine of how we are to *make* ourselves happy but of how we are to become *worthy* of happiness.'[43] Hence why Hunter argues that Kant's account of practical reason is built upon an ascetic rite, an 'exoteric instrument for a practice of speculative self-purification' calling on his audience 'to pursue an abstract universal principle of morality' as 'the means by which they will purify their insight and come to full participation in the community of rational beings'.[44] If one does not subscribe to this notion of an unending progression towards adequation with the moral law, Kant claims, then one will end up either conceiving of this law as lenient and forbearing, conforming itself to *our* needs, or conceiving of one's calling as directed towards the impossible goal of attaining holiness in its full plenitude, leading one down the blind alley of mysticism.

This latter point – the Kantian rejection of any mysticism that would claim to furnish an immediate intuition of the supersensible – is of especial interest here. I wish, therefore, to shift focus towards one of Kant's late essays, 'On a Recently Prominent Tone of Superiority in Philosophy' (1796), a polemic whose principal target, although left unnamed, is J. G. Schlosser, Goethe's brother-in-law, who had developed a curious, esoteric form of mysticism, influenced by his translation of Plato's epistolary apocrypha, which rejected rational intellection in favour of feeling and intuition as the primary means of knowledge, and who viewed such intuition as only obtainable by a select few, opposing any kind of holistic or popular education instructing all students in matters extending beyond the mere exigencies of the labour to which they are inevitably destined (although unnamed as well, Kant is likely also directing his opprobrium at F. H. Jacobi, who similarly appealed to an immediately apprehensible truth foreclosed to reason).[45] Such thinkers are, for Kant, emblematic of the decline of philosophy from a science of wisdom, as the ancients envisioned it, to a mere mystery cult, the unveiling of a hidden truth to the understanding of certain privileged thinkers. And these most recent possessors of such a mystery 'are those who have it *within them*, but are unfortunately *incapable* of uttering and disseminating it generally, by means of language', hoarding the ineffable for themselves.[46]

Throughout his critical philosophy, Kant is adamant that human beings do not possess any kind of *intellectual intuition* – within the sphere of speculative reason, one cannot *cognize* objects not given via sensible intuition.[47] One may *think* such objects, to the extent that they are logically non-contradictory, but such thoughts will never correspond to our concepts of understanding, and one will never gain any genuine knowledge (i.e. cognition) of them.[48] At best, they can only function as *noumena* in the negative sense of this term, regulative principles used to remind reason of its innate limitations.[49] Now, if our faculty of cognition did possess the capacity for intellectual intuition, then this direct grasp of the supersensible would, as a matter of course, come to seem superior to any conceptual knowledge of this derived from practical reason, for by means of the latter 'the discursive understanding must employ much labor on resolving and again compounding its concepts according to principles, and toil up many steps to make advances in knowledge', whereas the former 'would grasp and present the object immediately, and all at once'.[50] And since people 'who *have enough to live on*, whether in affluence or penury' are inclined to 'consider themselves *superior* in comparison with those who must work in order to live' – a superiority Kant attributes, as illustrative, to Arab and Mongolian nomads, who treat city dwellers contemptuously because 'wandering about in the desert with his horses and sheep is more pastime than work' – those who claim to possess an immediate intuition of a higher truth will invariably look down upon those who have worked hard to gain their knowledge.[51]

One of the scandalous aspects of Schlosser's mysticism then, in Kant's estimation, is that it makes a mockery of the work ethic proper to philosophical enquiry:

> an alleged philosophy is openly proclaimed to the public, in which one does not have to *work*, but need only hearken and attend to the oracle within, in order to gain complete possession of all the wisdom to which philosophy aspires. And this, moreover, in a tone which shows that the proponents of this philosophy are not at all inclined to align themselves with those who – *like schoolmen* – consider themselves obliged to proceed slowly and circumspectly from the critique of their cognitive powers to dogmatic knowledge, but are able, rather – *like men of genius* – to accomplish by a single piercing glance within them everything that industry can ever hope to achieve, and a good deal more besides.[52]

Such an approach does not operate merely with pride but also with *superiority*. Rejecting the 'Herculean labor of self-knowledge', whereby one methodically climbs towards higher concepts, it instead soars immediately to an apotheosis from which the philosopher is just 'speaking from his own observation, and is not obliged to be answerable to anyone else'.[53] One can only attain solutions to the problems posed by reason through concepts. And transcendent concepts, which exceed the bounds of all possible experience, cannot ever bring us true knowledge of an object; rather, they can only supply an ersatz substitute, the delusive glimpse of a *mystery*, by which problems for which reason has no answer are mistaken for an arcane knowledge accessible only via supernatural illumination. The mystical philosopher 'finds, in the very fact that he is brooding inwardly upon an idea, which he can neither make intelligible to himself, nor communicate to others, the true philosophy', and is inclined to view such speculation as 'far more inviting and splendid than the law of reason, to earn oneself a possession by work'.[54] This philosopher speaks in the superior tone of one who has not had to work for their knowledge.

Kant's distrust of mystagogues (as well as those who wish to return to philosophizing in poetry, rather than prose) – that is, philosophers of *feeling*, rather than ratiocination – stems from their appeal to an immediacy of knowledge (intellectual intuition), claiming access to an oracle within themselves the insights of which cannot be expressed, and thus figuring philosophy as an art of rarefied genius rather than a possession of human reason *tout court*. His concerns relate once again (following his distinction between objectively and subjectively philosophical propositions) to the *form* of philosophizing, rather than its content. He is not interested in whether or not these mystical philosophers' claims are correct; he instead reflects upon the means by which their propositions are *grounded* (with the premise that one can only achieve such grounding through the gradual and laborious process of learning already enumerated earlier, by which one's reason is both cultivated and disciplined, gaining a maturity that is never simply connate in its speculative mode). Philosophy, we learn, demands work. And when he determines that propositions are *not* grounded (i.e. they refer to transcendent concepts of reason rather than immanent concepts of understanding, residing outside any relation to possible experience and sensibility in general) he then turns to the question of tone.

Kant had already alluded to this peculiar positioning of tonal dispute in the first *Critique*: although there can be 'no real polemic in the field of pure reason', for within this domain disputants can only tussle with their own shadows, with no object upon which they might grasp, there is still value, he contends, in engaging in such speculative sparring, as long as one adopts the right manner of speaking.[55] For this conflict 'cultivates reason by the consideration of its object on both sides, and corrects its judgment by thus limiting it', helping to further sharpen the disputants' thinking by allowing them to see a problem from other perspectives and to formulate new objections unanticipated by their opponent. Crucially though, in dispute here 'is not the *matter* but the *tone*', for the reason that 'enough remains left to you to speak the language, justified by the sharpest reason, of a firm *belief*, even though you must surrender that of *knowledge*'.[56] With respect to pure reason, tone is not an issue when dealing with apodictic claims, for these do not depend upon any kind of external support whatsoever. In this way, argues Nancy, 'philosophy installs itself thus *not as merely another tone* [...] but as *the absence of tone*, the absence of the seductive, contagiously affect-laden voice, the absence of the veiled voice – and thus as an atonal exposition'.[57] But for Kant, tone *is* an issue in matters that do not possess such certainty – after all, the proclivities of human reason ensure such matters will continue to be discussed and debated, and thus, we must attempt to do so in a calm and modest manner, without the pretence that this will lead to us gaining any knowledge.

'Reason must subject itself to critique in all its undertakings', Kant propounds, 'and cannot restrict the freedom of critique through any prohibition without damaging itself and drawing upon itself a disadvantageous suspicion'.[58] It is in the interests of reason to follow its own paths, testing every hypothesis without hindrance, and it is the right of every free citizen to raise objections or express misgivings without reservation. It is not only inevitable but useful for reason to be granted this freedom, allowed to discover its own limits rather than having them enforced by some outside force. But this can only occur once its hubristic tone has been quelled. Tone is crucial in such discussions because when one makes claims to *knowledge* (as opposed to belief) built upon the shaky ground of transcendent concepts of reason, one is making claims unverifiable by either *a priori* certainty *or* empirical experience, and therefore unsuitable for public exhibition and judgement.

This belief in a free and egalitarian practice of philosophizing motivates Kant's hostility towards mystagogues, who by comporting themselves '*in a superior fashion*' seek to elevate themselves above other philosophers, and in doing so 'violate the inalienable right of the latter to freedom and equality in matters of mere reason'.[59] Those who refuse any recourse to justification of their concepts and instead appeal to an inner *feeling* (especially when they posit this feeling not as a subjective sentiment but that of an object apprehended through intellectual intuition) are able to hold themselves above their peers by laying claim to a knowledge which is not universally attainable through the hard work of rational excogitation, making themselves the arbiters of who can gain access to it – 'the mystagogue, who not only raves on his own behalf, but is simultaneously the founder of a club, and in speaking to his adepts, rather than to the people (meaning all the uninitiated), plays the *superior* with his alleged philosophy'.[60] They hold themselves unanswerable to the tribunal of public judgement, safe in the conviction that the truth that they harbour within themselves will always remain incommunicable.

These concerns regarding the rhetorical means by which the act of philosophizing is conducted, forming a substantial part of the Transcendental Doctrine of Method, reflect the extent to which Kant views common reason – that is, the reason possessed by all finite, rational beings – as the foundation of critical philosophy, the corollary of which is that he encourages us to put propositions forward so that they might 'defend themselves before a jury drawn from their own estate (namely the estate of fallible human beings)'.[61] The content of metaphysics (i.e. *a priori* cognition) must be communicable, for it does not belong merely to a select few minds, but to human reason as a whole, and it is only thanks to such a universal communicability that reason is able to sharpen itself by submitting its judgements for public scrutiny and debate. By the same token, though, Kant's concerns here also reflect the extent to which he regards reason as unavoidably susceptible to the sophistic inferences of speculative reason – he worries that the false sophistries arising from the dogmatic usage of pure speculative reason embolden people to *speak rapturously and interminably* about topics of which they can possess no knowledge.[62]

Listening to the voice of reason

As much as Kant touts the labour inherent in authentic philosophizing, he must also deal with the fact that most of this labour has, in the past, been directed towards dead ends, reaching for noumenal objects always slipping from one's grasp. He thus comes to the conclusion that 'there must somewhere be a source of positive cognitions that belong in the domain of pure reason', and that these cognitions 'in fact constitute the goal of the strenuous effort of reason', providing a cause to which 'the unquenchable desire to find a firm footing beyond all bounds of experience' can be ascribed.[63] This source is the realm of practical reason, which furnishes an *a priori*, supersensible and universally valid principle (viz. the moral law) that guides the human will based on an unshakeable duty. And while human beings might be led towards concepts of duty via moral *feelings*, which are themselves empirical and contingent, these feelings 'are aroused only by the *voice of reason*, which speaks clearly to everyone and is capable of being scientifically known'.[64] The goal of Kant's moral philosophy, then, is to elucidate and reinforce the moral law, making apparent the unquestionable authority from which said 'voice' of reason speaks, and in doing so to expose the inadequacy of any would-be philosopher who professes to be guided by an inner *oracle*, unattached to any universal law.[65]

This commanding voice of reason has always spoken to human beings, long before any philosophers attempted to articulate it. As Kant writes in the second *Critique*, its 'heavenly voice' is 'so distinct, so irrepressible, and so audible even to the most common human beings', it can overcome even the lure of the desire for one's own happiness (and indeed, he suggests, only professionalized philosophy has managed to close its ears to this voice).[66] Humans have always shown a capacity to know what is right (and to recognize their obligation to act in a principled manner, though one may receive no apparent material reward for such action), even if they have never heretofore formulated it as a pure, apodictic law. The voice of reason, as Mladen Dolar puts it, 'is a purely formal voice, the form of a voice, imposing pure formality, submission to form'.[67] Devoid of empirical content, it speaks nothing other than an injunction to submit to the moral law.

This emphatic voice's message, in Kant's words, 'makes even the boldest evildoer tremble and forces him to hide from its sight'.[68] It is not only the patently ignoble, however, who fear its sublime power; on the contrary, 'every man finds in his reason the idea of duty, and trembles on hearing its brazen voice'.[69] As rational beings, painfully aware of our own finitude, we find ourselves awed by the moral law's capacity to overrule all external inclinations that tempt us, by the fact that this law is prescribed by our own reason (and yet enjoins us with the certainty of a divine command) and by the awareness that our will is, by virtue of its conformity with this law, capable of overcoming all heteronomous desires and drives. The voice of reason speaks louder and more adamantly than all the other determinations pressing upon us, with a terrifying power that can only come from within us, and yet seems to possess a divine authority.

Most fundamentally though, our respect for the moral law, and for the voice of reason delivering its message, comes from our 'astonishment at the magnitude and sublimity of the inward disposition in mankind, and at the same time the impenetrability of the mystery that veils it'.[70] A mystery exceeding all possible expression: not the moral law itself (which is articulable as an *a priori* principle), but the postulate or inner Idea of *freedom*. This mystery concerns the capacity of man to pursue his duties in spite of the seemingly limitless might and continual resistance of the laws of nature as given in time and space; a capacity to act that does not yield to the powers of nature; the determination of one's will independent of all natural necessity.[71] But although it comes from within us, this mystery or secret is not just the issuance of some mystical inner oracle, grasped in its fulgurant immediacy, as the mystagogues might have it; rather, it is a 'secret which can become *possible to feel* only after slow development of the concepts of the understanding, and of carefully tested principles and thus *only through work*'.[72] The feeling of freedom is not the basis of moral knowledge; instead, through clear, sedulously refined cognition, this feeling (and not just its ersatz, speculative sentiment) can be attained within the realm of practical reason.

Once this cogitation has been accomplished, Kant intriguingly asserts, one will inevitably speak in a different manner. 'The tone of one who considers himself possessed of this true secret', he reckons, 'cannot be superior: for only dogmatic or historical cognition is puffed up.'[73] 'Chastened by critique of his own reason', the philosopher who has pursued this felicitous path of enquiry, tempering and circumscribing his claims rather than incautiously extending them into hazy speculative territories, is obliged to an unpretentious 'moderation in his claims'.[74] For Kant then, we might say, it is less that a particular way of speaking enables one to gesture towards the incommunicable – after all, tone only pertains for him to disputes regarding that which one can have no genuine cognition; all propositions grounded upon firm, objective knowledge have no need for any rhetorical accoutrements – and more that an individual's recognition of their own freedom, via the unwavering injunction of the voice of reason, is not only fostered by a peculiarly philosophical mode of transmission (and the demanding labour involved in deriving clear concepts from this law commanded within us) but actually encourages a particular way of speaking, especially when discussing issues for which no definitive answer will ever be possible. And at least on the face of it, this appropriate tone of voice would seem to be attainable by all human beings, to the extent that they are by definition rational beings.

Kant's critical philosophy, and above all his moral philosophy, establishes that propositions must be communicable to all rational minds, even though a quite particular *form* of communication is needed in order to foster an authentic, philosophical way of thinking (and speaking). The voice of reason speaks on equal terms to all human beings, and it is exactly this universality philosophy itself must emulate, lest it fall back into an undemocratic elitism – hence his frequent emphasis in the first *Critique* upon the need to defend freedom of public expression, whereby anyone's thoughts and doubts can be put forward, debated and adjudicated without prejudice. In fact, this sacred right to free expression is a necessary component of human reason, 'which recognizes no other judge than universal human reason itself, in which everyone has a voice'.[75] Decrying the assumption that 'a cognition that pertains to all human beings should surpass common understanding and be revealed to you only by philosophers', which would render the reason possessed by ordinary people opaque to itself, Kant instead declares that in regard to those principles applicable to all human beings 'nature is not to be blamed for any partiality in the distribution of its gifts', and with respect to human nature's essential ends 'even the highest philosophy cannot advance further than the guidance that nature has also conferred on the most common understanding'.[76]

In the indictment presented within Kant's 'Superior Tone' essay, Derrida suggests, 'professional philosophers are not pardoned when they take on an overlordly tone because, in raising the tone thus, they elevate themselves above their colleagues or peers, and wrong the latter in their inalienable right to freedom and equality for all that relates to mere reason'.[77] And they do this by conflating the voice of reason with the voice of the oracle residing within each of us, the oracle that speaks to us in private, that speaks of subjective feelings, pleasures and desires. To speak in conformity with the voice of reason, by contrast, is to speak of the objective truths accessible to all human beings, and one who speaks in such conformity will never speak in the haughty manner of those who listen and appeal instead to their inner oracle. The egalitarian tenor of the critical project seems to contrast markedly with the previous examples laid out in this book, for which a philosophical manner of speaking is something not necessarily available to common human reason.

At the same time though, it is hard not to be reminded of Kant's own superior tone when he patronizingly minimizes the cognitive capacities of women, or when he crudely condescends people of colour (on the basis of little more than anecdote and conjecture). Although such slights become less common in his later work, and would seem to contradict both the letter and spirit of so much of his practical philosophy, they certainly do not vanish, and thus a lingering question remains: Does Kant really believe that all human beings – even if one must, in accordance with the categorical imperative, regard them as free beings – can speak and think in the manner of a philosopher? Or are there substantial segments of humanity who do not possess the kind of sublime reason that would allow them to elevate their thought towards this level of abstraction, and can at best parrot philosophical propositions in the same way one might retell historical narratives? And if the latter determination is made on the basis of their sex, or race, or some other apparently innate trait, does this mean Kant is still, in effect, using the notion of a properly philosophical way of speaking as a means of arbitrarily circumscribing the exercise of philosophical reason? The conditions of possible discourse, with respect to the rational cognition of concepts by which he defines the philosophical enterprise, would seem to be narrower than Kant's liberal universalism would, on paper, allow.

4

Speaking from the heart
J. G. Fichte on the role of the scholar

Reception to the first edition of the *Critique of Pure Reason*, although often cautiously complimentary about its breadth, ambition and erudition, was not as effusive as Kant anticipated. The anonymous Feder-Garve review – which Kant justifiably considered a hatchet job, motivating him to write both the *Prolegomena to Any Future Metaphysics* and the second edition of said *Critique* – begins by describing the book as a work 'which always exercises the understanding of its readers – even if it does not always instruct it – which often strains their attention to the point of exhaustion'.[1] In spite of the sedulous attention it gives to the pedagogical exigencies of philosophy (and the proper means by which one should disseminate philosophical knowledge), the consensus among contemporaries (shared to some degree even by Kant himself) was that the presentation of the critical project adequately conveyed neither its premises nor its goals.

Even J. G. Fichte, whose essays and lectures are fervid in their praise for Kant, characterizes the latter's writings, in a letter to K. L. Reinhold, as '*absolutely incomprehensible* to anyone *who does not already know what they contain*', explaining that this fact 'in no way detracts from Kant's merits as a *thinker*, although of course it completely disqualifies him as a *teacher*'.[2] Reinhold had already become well known for his *Letters on the Kantian Philosophy*, published as journal articles between 1786 and 1787, spreading the good news of a system which, in his opinion, responded to the 'most pressing philosophical needs' of his time, even if many prominent philosophers remained baffled by it.[3] Largely because of these attempts to popularize Kant's transcendental philosophy, Reinhold was offered the chair of philosophy at the University of Jena, and his subsequent attempts to develop an Elementary Philosophy, supplementing the Kantian approach with a heretofore lacking first principle, would prove a decisive influence upon Fichte, who, in 1794, took over his position at the university.[4]

Whereas Reinhold built his philosophy upon the foundation of a principle of consciousness, the 'original, unexplainable and simple concept of representation' which both precedes consciousness and is presupposed by the latter, Fichte builds his instead upon the first principle of an absolute freedom which supplants substance or essence as the core of the self.[5] This principle, expressing a primacy of practical over theoretical reason, is inspired by his reading of Kant's *Critique of Practical Reason*. But what he gains from this book is not just a convincing argument but a fundamental change in outlook. Kant's claims move Fichte in a way that exceeds any mere relaying of knowledge, as he makes apparent in a letter written to an old friend in 1790, soon after this epiphany:

> I have been living in a new world ever since reading the *Critique of Practical Reason*. Propositions which I thought could never be overturned have been overturned for me. Things have been proven to me which I thought could never be proven – for example, the concept of absolute freedom, the concept of duty, etc. – and I feel all the happier for it. It is unbelievable how much respect for mankind and how much strength this system gives us![6]

Fichte's reading of Kant transforms him. He does not simply discover a new way of conceptualizing freedom; rather, he is led to discover this freedom within himself.

Fichte's *Wissenschaftslehre* (the Doctrine of Science that constitutes his project in the main) would eventually aim at encouraging the same kind of epiphany within others, instead of travestying this constitutive freedom through dogmatic forms of representation. He conceives of freedom as a principle that cannot just be encountered but must be enacted for oneself within oneself:

> philosophy is not something that floats in our memory or is printed in books for us to read; instead, philosophy is what has stirred and transformed our spirit and has ushered it into a higher, spiritual order of things. Philosophy is something which has to exist within us. It must be our entire being.[7]

The job of the scholar (i.e. the philosopher, the two terms being synonymous for Fichte) is to help lead individuals towards the truth within themselves instead of dispensing a set of propositions to be memorized and repeated. For although 'all men have a sense for what is true', this truth must be 'developed, scrutinized, and purified', and this is precisely the scholar's duty, who can then disseminate it among the 'uneducated', who cannot recognize these concepts for themselves.[8] The scholar is tasked with the education of humanity.

The attention that Fichte pays towards the question of education, and the scholar's role as an educator, is tightly bound up with his equal interest in the question of intersubjectivity, whereby he underscores the social and communal functions of philosophy. Education for Fichte is about much more than conveying knowledge; it is about building a society and improving the lot of those who live within it. But when coupled with his concern with identifying a uniquely philosophical standpoint distinct from ordinary experience, this dual focus upon intersubjectivity and education affords him the opportunity to delimit who can and cannot be taught (or teach) philosophy. Frustrated by those who do not seem to find the same epiphanic clarity in his guiding notion of freedom, he declares that it is pointless trying to educate certain audiences (most prominently, dogmatists and women) in philosophy, and that these same audiences will never be able to speak in an authentic philosophical manner, arbitrarily circumscribing the boundaries of philosophical communicability from the outset.[9]

Egoism and intersubjectivity

In a letter to Jacobi, written in 1795, Fichte complains that his early work has been misinterpreted by 'offended courtiers and irate philosophers' who conflate his foundational concept of the *absolute I* with that of the *individual*, unfairly attributing 'the disgraceful theory of practical egoism' to him.[10] Fichte's contemporaries tended to view his idealism as absolutizing a transcendental self or I for whom all external objects are mere subjective projections of its own ceaseless activity, reducing the external world to the status of a self-imposed limit waiting to be overcome.[11] Hence his persistent reputation to this day as a solipsistic idealist, conceiving of the world as nothing more than the product of subjective thought. And yet, Fichte's first lectures, delivered soon after his arrival in Jena in 1794, indicate that his philosophical premises are anything but egoistic. As Alexis Philonenko contends, 'the question of the existence of others' is 'crucial in the development of Fichte's philosophy', and indeed, 'the problem of intersubjectivity is the chief question of Fichte's first philosophy'.[12] But it is also key to understanding the conception of the scholar (*Gelehrter*) mobilized within this philosophy, and how Fichte positions their vocation (*Bestimmung*) in relation to broader society.

Such is the central concern of Fichte's *Lectures Concerning the Scholar's Vocation*, a series of public presentations delivered in 1794, acting as both a prelude to and advertisement for his private courses on the *Wissenschaftslehre* in which he would unpack the full content of his transcendental system. The scholar, Fichte argues, possesses a particular talent: namely, an ability to become acquainted with man's originary drives and needs, and the means by which they can be satisfied. Scholars seek a knowledge of man in totality – 'a complete survey of his entire nature' – and apply this knowledge for the benefit of society, eliciting within others a sense of their true needs and how to serve them, without requiring the rest of society to comprehend the arduous enquiries undertaken in order to reach these conclusions.[13] After all, acquiring such knowledge is no easy task: 'if there is any common need which urgently demands that a special class of persons be dedicated to its satisfaction, it is this one.'[14] The scholar dedicates his life to obtaining this knowledge of man, with all its attendant difficulties and demands. Not everyone has the aptitude or inclination to engage in scholarly enquiry, and it would not be of much service to anyone if they tried – 'other things also have to be done, and this is why there are other classes of men'.[15]

What exactly it would mean to know man in his totality is left unanswered in these precursory lectures, but we are told such knowledge presupposes 'philosophy in its entirety – and moreover a well-grounded and exhaustive philosophy'.[16] In other words, it would only be in Fichte's full lectures on the *Wissenschaftslehre* (and their various written accompaniments) that he would elaborate the scholar's task. In the latter works, this distinction between the scholar and other classes of people is thematized in terms of the distinction between a speculative or transcendental point of view (i.e. philosophy proper) and an ordinary point of view (i.e. common sense), the former of which 'observes how there must come to be things for the individual', understanding that everything exists does so on the basis of and for an I, whereas the latter 'is confronted with things, men, etc., that are independent of him', conferring an existence upon the world such that it is presumed to always exist, even in the absence of all cognition.[17] Although the scholar, occupying as he does a higher, transcendental standpoint, must be able to account for the origin of this common sense, the inverse is not necessarily true.[18] He deduces and explains the ordinary person's sincere belief in a reality existing independent of thought, recognizing the ultimate harmony between the transcendental and ordinary standpoints, one conditioned by the other.

For Fichte, the scholar can comfortably shift between the mundane and the speculative. 'One has not yet achieved a clear understanding, has not yet obtained the true philosophical view of things, and has not yet reached the correct standpoint', he propounds, 'so long as one continues to think and to expect that daily life is something altogether different' from the transcendental standpoint.[19]

'Something that does not occur as such within ordinary consciousness is thus present within the consciousness of the philosopher': namely, the latter is able to raise his consciousness above all experience, intuiting something which cannot be apprehended within sensibility (i.e. space and time) via pure thinking.[20] This something is the activity of the pure, non-empirical I, which is identical with the human mind itself, the ultimate foundation of all thought (and thus of the world also, insofar as it is posited by thought). The scholar lifts himself above the ordinary point of view, which focuses upon the mind's immediate representations of the physical world, reflecting upon (and thus representing) the very process by which these representations are produced.

Such reflection – described as a 'pure intuition of the I as a subject-object', grasping the flux of pure self-activity which Fichte regards as constitutive of all existence – is effectuated through the *intellectual intuition* that Kant derided as a mere delusion of dogmatic metaphysics.[21] Intellectual intuition is, for Fichte, the highest form of possible thought for a finite being; the apogee of the transcendental standpoint; a mode of thought detaching itself from all empirical givens in order to seize the self-determination of the I as the condition of possibility for all such empirical experience. And it is precisely the hard-earned access to this standpoint, and an understanding of how it remains in harmony with that of everyday experience, which distinguishes the scholar from other classes and professions. Indeed, 'if one does not want to take upon oneself the effort of penetrating into philosophy by the thorny path of speculation, then it is futile to expect those benefits which philosophy can guarantee'.[22]

The scholar's duty to educate

The scholar must not, however, hoard the fruits of such reflection for himself alone. It is his ethical duty to continually use and pass on his knowledge for the betterment of humankind. Indeed, within these initial lectures, Fichte describes the role of the scholar as primarily *social* and *communicative*, situating their position within the context of a broader *social drive* belonging to all men. Fundamental to man's existence, he declares, is a drive to recognize the existence of other free, rational beings like himself, and enter into society with said beings. 'It is man's *destiny* to live in society; he *ought to* live in society.'[23] This social drive sparks within us a desire not just to dwell among others but to improve the lot of humanity as a whole. This takes place not unilaterally but as a joint effort, enriching others' intellects as we ourselves are enriched by them. It 'requires us to share the good that we possess with those who need it and to receive what we lack from those who have it', in an endless quest to cultivate the talents of all rational beings.[24]

This reciprocal exchange ensures 'every individual obtains *indirectly from the hands of society* that complete education which he could not obtain *directly from nature*'.[25] Individuals' advantages accumulate in 'a common store for the free use of everyone', so each person's peculiar deficiencies might be collectively ameliorated and humanity's talents more equitably distributed, contributing to the constant struggle of reason to overcome nature.[26] In the end, 'the final aim of all society is *the complete equality of all of its members*', and this aim entails an equal education and cultivation for all involved.[27] The scholar's principal role is to furnish such education, dedicating himself not only to the acquisition of knowledge but to the transmission of this knowledge, as a means to promote and supervise the progressive development of human talents and thus the continual progress of humanity in general.

The scholar must, by definition, communicate what he has learnt. He must 'apply for the benefit of society that knowledge which he has acquired for society', both making his audience aware of their true needs and furnishing them with the means for satisfying them.[28] This communication is necessary because not all men (and certainly not all *people*) have the time, inclination or intelligence to philosophize. Clearly, 'all men have a sense for what is true', but it is the scholar who has 'developed, scrutinized, and purified' this sense, guiding all people towards the truth he has discerned.[29] Philosophy, then, as a science capable of apprehending both the ends of man and the ways in which they can be fulfilled, is for Fichte not a frivolous or impractical discipline and certainly is not one involving isolation or solitude. Philosophical knowledge 'is supposed to be useful to society'.[30] And indeed, 'the concept of the scholar arises by comparison and by reference to society', for one can only identify the scholar in distinction from those who are not scholars.[31]

And yet, possessing only a finite, empirical consciousness, even the scholar is incapable of describing the foundational principle of all experience – namely, the productive activity of freedom, which posits both itself and the world in a single motion – in itself, as a unified, synthetic act. In representing the act of representation, 'he freezes this process, holding still for examination that which is changeable and transient within the mind'.[32] In something of a rejoinder to Reinhold's Elementary Philosophy, Fichte positions the pure I above and in excess of all possible representation.[33] To reduce the workings of the human soul to mere representation is, for Fichte, to disregard the absolutely free and unconditioned self-positing which lies at the origin of all consciousness, and without which one cannot account for freedom.

Fichte and Reinhold agree that the first principle of philosophy (and thus of broader human experience) cannot manifest within the sphere of empirical consciousness, given it is, in fact, the explanatory ground for said consciousness. 'Every philosophy', Fichte suggests, 'presupposes something, something that it does not demonstrate and on the basis of which it explains and demonstrates everything else'.[34] But for him, the first principle is not the fact (*Tatsache*) of representation but an act (*Tathandlung*) which precedes and exceeds all representation and thus cannot be brought under the yoke of theoretical determination. This principle is the free activity of the pure I:

> every act of representing is an act of self-positing. Everything begins with the I. The I is not a component part of the representation; instead, all representation proceeds from the I. All possible consciousness presupposes immediate consciousness and cannot be comprehended in any other way. [. . .] Immediate consciousness is itself the ultimate reason or foundation upon which everything else is based and to which everything else has to be traced back, if our knowledge is to have any foundation.[35]

The I's immediate consciousness of itself – the absolute positing of its own existence – explains all that is present within consciousness, but it cannot itself be explained, let alone given within the sensible intuition of space and time; rather, it can only be intuited intellectually.[36]

Specifically, the act in question here consists in letting one's I act internally and observing what takes place. This is an act of *intuiting* (a *pure, intellectual* intuiting, since it involves no sensible content), and through its self-reversion (since one's thought is directed back towards the I as it acts upon itself), a *concept* of the I arises. Fichte does not postulate this self-reverting activity as a product of the I; on the contrary, this activity *is* the I, insofar as the I posits itself as an I – at once the subject and object of consciousness.

Putting aside the complexity and ambiguity of Fichte's account of intellectual intuition – a term he employs frustratingly multifariously[37] – the crux of the matter is that this first principle, insofar as it is an act rather than a fact, exceeding representation and the determination of empirical consciousness, 'can only be *sought out*; it can be neither *proven* nor *determined*'.[38] The intuition 'required of the philosopher: an act of intuiting himself while simultaneously performing the act by means of which the I originates for him', cannot be proven by concepts, nor can an understanding of it be imparted via concepts;

rather, it is 'something everyone has to discover immediately within himself'.[39] Such recognition – unable to be established through argumentation and yet necessary for all *bona fide* philosophical knowledge (and the social hierarchy it engenders) – is what typically comes to be described, in the absence of ample and comprehensive education, as 'philosophical genius'.[40] The irony being that the scholar, in possession of a transcendental standpoint elevating their thinking above mundane experience and commensurately elevating their social status above that of most other men (let alone women, as we shall soon see), is still incapable of adequately describing the ground of this elevation. But Fichte does not view this incapability as a deficiency on the scholar's behalf but a mark of those endowed with a genuinely philosophical way of thinking.

The incommunicability of freedom

Fichte's peculiar characterization of philosophy's first principle (and the means of its intellection) has considerable ramifications for the manner in which he believes the scholar should disseminate philosophical ideas. If the scholar's calling is not merely to accumulate knowledge for its own sake (or for his own ends) but to disseminate it for the benefit of all humanity, this means he must work within the realm of discursive concepts. The genetic explanation of the workings of the mind, and thus of man's inner nature, is governed by the same empirical determinations of which it hopes to describe the origin, and is encumbered by the baggage of the language in which one must express it. The scholar is, for Fichte, condemned to furnish accounts of experience that can only partially reconstruct the originary activity of the I's absolute self-positing, which makes up this experience's genesis.

Perhaps the key insight furnished by intellectual intuition is the understanding that the I's autonomy – its freedom, its pure willing, its absolute selfhood – is ultimately incomprehensible, even while it remains a necessary postulate for all genuine philosophical enquiry: it 'cannot be grasped by our representations, nor can it be grasped by our language'.[41] In particular, although this activity is postulated as a single, unified action, whereby the I posits itself as self-positing, and in doing so, also posits a world in opposition to itself – 'in a single stroke, I exist and the world exists for me' – the scholar, like all rational (i.e. finite) beings, experiences it in accordance with the forms of space and time, and must therefore treat it as a linear sequence of discrete, interconnected actions.[42] 'The idealist's cognition is, and can never be anything but, discursive; that is to say, he develops his concepts little by little and infers one from the other', the result being 'he develops his system step by step, even though this constitutes but a *single* act within our consciousness'.[43] He becomes acquainted with this single action of the I only by 'disassembling and dissecting it', rendering it in a serialized rather than simultaneous form, precisely because he is only capable of thinking within the strictures of time – and this is how he manages to systematically present this foundation of all cognition.[44]

To say the scholar can only think discursively is to say his thinking, as a finite being, can only think within sequential time; he cannot simply apprehend all activity in one fell swoop. 'The finitude of rational beings consists in having to explain things', and this explanation occurs by making connections between things, proceeding from one thing to the next.[45] Accordingly, since it is the scholar's job, so to speak, to explain the inner workings of man, he must inevitably figure the intuitive in discursive terms, reconstructing through concepts a free activity that remains stubbornly irreducible to any such representation.

All the discursive arguments in the world, regardless of how clear and precise they might be, cannot be substituted for one's own intellectual intuition. Philosophizing must commence with the *act* designated as its postulate, and one must literally enact this first principle, rather than analysing it as an already-given fact: 'the reader or student of philosophy [must] begin by doing something'.[46] Given this postulate is, in Fichte's conception, the only possible ground by which one might prove all possible philosophical propositions – even though it itself cannot be proven – all those who wish to philosophize need to possess it. And since they can only gain possession of it by enacting it themselves, the act of intellectual intuition constitutes not only the ground of philosophizing but the only means by which one can be inducted into the philosophical enterprise. 'If one wants to communicate this philosophy to someone else, one has to ask the other person to perform the action in question.'[47] Put simply, philosophical argumentation begins with a principle which is itself unable to be demonstrated through any kind of argument or discursive concept – and therefore is, of course, unable to be communicated *as such*. A principle one must grasp within oneself.

The fact one cannot communicate this principle as such (i.e. any conceptualization of it, by means of which some aspect of it is rendered transmissible, cannot act as a substitute for one's own intuition of it, and will remain philosophically inert, serving no real cognitive function, unless it is connected to said intuition) does not make the scholar's task futile though. Fichte cogently lays out his aims for the dissemination of his philosophy in a letter to Reinhold from 1795:

> what I am trying to communicate is something which can be neither *said* nor *grasped conceptually*; it can only be *intuited*. My words are only supposed to guide the reader in such a way that the desired intuition is formed within him. I advise anyone who wishes to study my writings to let words be words and simply try to enter into my series of intuitions at one point or another. I advise him to go on reading even if he has not completely understood what went before, until at some point a spark of light is finally struck. This spark of light, if it is whole and not half, will suddenly place him in that position in the series of my intuitions from which the whole must be viewed. For example, the heart of my system is the proposition 'The I simply posits itself'. These words have no meaning or value unless the I has an inner intuition of itself.[48]

The scholar might not be able to transmit the principle to other people, but he can assist them in intuiting it within themselves.[49] And if he succeeds in this, all the propositions following from this principle will become explicable, even if the principle itself remains only intuitable.

The ramifications of this foreclosure of the *Wissenschaftslehre*'s first principle to discursive reason are legion, and first spelt out in detail in a series of lectures immediately following those *Concerning the Scholar's Vocation*, during Fichte's first semester at the University of Jena. In these lectures (*Concerning the Difference between the Spirit and the Letter within Philosophy*), Fichte argues that one can assiduously study the propositions of philosophy, employing them in an entirely level-headed manner, without ever seizing upon the essential truth of their first principle. One might very well be fully conversant in the *letter* of philosophy, without ever getting one's head around its *spirit*. And in neglecting this latter aspect, one risks falling into a formulaic expression of the first principle, blindly accepting and reciting it (for either naïve or pragmatic reasons) without ever actually acquiring it for oneself. And regardless of how competent one might appear in making use of it, 'so long as one has not had the intuition of what is expressed in this formula, then one possesses no more than a formula'.[50]

The scholar, in his role as an educator of humanity, is hence limited to distributing enervated, objectified manifestations of his own philosophical insights, by which others might also develop an authentic philosophical mentality. Philosophical discourse, as important as it might be, is only ever really useful as a propaedeutic to one's own philosophical discoveries, which all occur within the depths of one's own being. Philosophy is *lived*, and any attempt to communicate the knowledge gained from it – whether by spoken or written word – can only be an exteriorized adjunct. Fichte makes no attempt to communicate the spirit of philosophy *qua* spirit; rather, he strives to furnish a *systematic* (and thus scientific) account in accordance with this spirit.⁵¹ A systematic account, in his eyes, is one in which all propositions share in one and the same certitude, derived from a single principle, established prior to all the others.⁵² It requires, in other words, a sound foundation upon which its scientific structure can be built and from which the certitude of all subsequent claims can be inferred, but one can only seek this foundation in a first principle indemonstrable within the confines of this science.

Philosophical wisdom will never be attained, Fichte believes, by just listening to or reading about the experiences of others – at best, one will arrive at a kind of pseudo-wisdom, bandying about received knowledge. Yet it is still the scholar's responsibility to help people intuit this principle for themselves, and this entails a particular mode of address: one which does not claim to capture the foundational truth of philosophy but which exhorts its audience to find this truth within their inner being. The *Wissenschaftslehre* is a system, Fichte declares, 'for persons who are able to think for themselves', and it 'cannot be grasped merely by reading and study'.⁵³ His refusal to adhere to a fixed terminology (or to develop a special terminology of his own, as Kant did) – a choice almost certainly contributing to the confusion and misconstrual that has long plagued the reception of his philosophy – is, he claims, meant to oblige his students to think for themselves, rather than proceeding by mere imitation:

> one can grasp the truth of this system only by reproducing these actions for oneself and producing these self-observations within one's own consciousness. Consequently, it is a system suited only for independent thinkers – though it can also serve to promote independent thinking, especially among young men.⁵⁴

Once again, we witness a philosopher using the problem of communicability in order to circumscribe the appropriate audience for his system, and thus to determine who can truly philosophize. The question we need to therefore ask is: Who does Fichte specifically exclude from this domain of 'independent thinkers', and thus from the circle of philosophical communicability? What is the position, for instance, of those who are not neither 'young' nor 'men', let alone those who, from his perspective, are not capable of 'independent thinking' in relation to the philosophical enterprise? What if they were deemed incapable of raising themselves to the transcendental standpoint, and thus of speaking properly philosophically? Surely then, could one not dismiss all apparent insights they put forward as nothing more than repetitions of others' observations? This is precisely how Fichte's second circumscription of his audience takes place.

Inveterate dogmatists

Fichte insists certain people, thanks to their education and upbringing, are constitutionally incapable of taking up the idealist mentality. He directs his greatest opprobrium in this respect at dogmatists, who have obstinately 'made up their minds about everything', making them unfit for idealist philosophy.[55] Unlike Kant, for whom the imputation of dogmatism refers chiefly to those who make use of *a priori* principles as a foundation for metaphysical cognition without bothering to interrogate the limits of pure reason, Fichte instead regards dogmatists as those who posit a thing in itself which precedes the free activity of the I, and to which the latter must conform. Thus, while Fichte himself does not perceive Kant as being a dogmatist (because he cannot bring himself to imagine this philosophical luminary would *really* believe in something as specious as a thing in itself outside the sphere of cognition), he does perceive of many Kantians as dogmatists, against whom he counterposes his own idealist interpretation of transcendental philosophy.

Whether consciously or otherwise, Fichte argues, all prospective scholars adopt a certain standpoint, which then becomes the foundation of all their subsequent arguments. And the standpoint one adopts is not determined purely on rational grounds but by an originary *act*. Everything thus stems from the freedom of thinking. One's philosophy is decided by a free choice, albeit one that, like all such choices, finds its footing in one's own peculiar concerns and inclinations. Fichte thus distinguishes the idealist from the dogmatist on the basis of a 'difference of interest'.[56] Dogmatism arises in those who have not fully discovered their own freedom, and as a result project their self-consciousness onto objects, lending the latter a certain self-sufficiency that in truth belongs to the subject alone. These thinkers possess only an indirect, dispersed and specular conceptualization of their own selves as the products of objects. Idealism, by contrast, arises in those who have not been deceived into perceiving themselves as dependent upon external things, but instead immediately recognize their own self-sufficiency – a direct conceptualization of their own selves. Idealism casts its gaze towards freedom; dogmatism towards facticity and determinism. And this interest is reflected in how the (prospective) scholar communicates: the dogmatist defends himself with 'vehemence and bitterness', in large part because something of his inner self already discerns the truth of the idealist's arguments, whereas the idealist 'is quite unable to prevent himself from looking down upon the dogmatist with a certain amount of disrespect', his coolness and condescension brought on by the fact he has already passed through the stage of dogmatism and come to appreciate its inveracity.

While, as we shall see, Fichte wishes to disabuse his audience of the notion that philosophy is the exclusive product of 'genius', he also warns them against the idea that, through hard work or contrivance, an individual can overcome the obstruction of an unshakeably dogmatic soul. The dogmatist's interests and positions are so tenacious, one is unlikely to ever overturn them. A lot of prospective scholars will never be able to escape the shackles of dogmatism:

> a philosophical system is not a lifeless household item one can put aside or pick up as one wishes; instead, it is animated by the very soul of the person who adopts it. Someone whose character is naturally slack or who has been enervated and twisted by spiritual servitude, scholarly self-indulgence, and vanity will never be able to raise himself to the level of idealism [. . .] one can point out to the dogmatist the inadequacy and inconsistency of his system; one can confuse and worry him on every side; but one cannot convince him, for he is incapable of calmly and coolly listening to and evaluating a theory that he finds to be simply unendurable. If idealism should prove to be the only true philosophy, then from this it would follow that in order to philosophize one must be born a philosopher, must be reared as a philosopher, and must educate oneself as a philosopher. But no application of human art or skill can make one into a philosopher. This science, therefore, does not expect to make many converts among people who are *already firmly set in their ways*.[57]

Whence follows his hope of raising a new generation of philosophical students who have not been forced to learn prefabricated principles but have been prepared in such a fashion that they might discover for themselves the freedom residing within them. And who can in turn assume the mantle of the scholar, using this discovery for the benefit of broader society.

Whence also follows Fichte's staunch refusal to entertain those who would demand the universal communicability of philosophical propositions. In this respect, Fichte's refusal hangs on his central claim that all demonstration must be based upon something entirely indemonstrable: in the same way that any philosophical proof must be built upon and fortified by a fundamental ground that itself cannot be proven conceptually (but must be intuited by each person), in order to prove something to someone else, we must show that person how the truth of our given proposition is supported by a principle to which they have already assented. In short, 'any communication of conviction by means of proof presupposes that both parties agree upon at least something'.[58] And as a consequence, it would seem that it is in fact impossible to communicate the

Wissenschaftslehre to a dogmatist, 'since it *simply not agree with him upon a single point* concerning the *material* of cognition, and thus there exists no common ground from which they could jointly proceed'.[59] The dogmatist might be able to recite various ideas drawn from the *Wissenschaftslehre*, but one will invariably fail in trying to convey the *spirit* of this project to them.

Given the impossibility of seeing into an interlocutor's soul (meaning one must trust in an other's free self-activity, for one cannot actually *know* of its existence), 'one cannot provide another person with a specific set of thoughts, but can do no more than offer him the guidance that will help him to think these specific thoughts on his own'.[60] In fact, Fichte suggests, the reason his dogmatic opponents are so tireless in their demand for universal communicability is that they cannot conceive of any form of relationship between beings aside from that which conforms to a mechanistic model of efficient causality, transporting ideas directly from one mind to another. Since they 'do not possess enough mental agility and dexterity' to observe their own free acting, they have no capacity for grasping, let alone facilitating, the kind of free interaction that allows them to be inducted within the sphere of philosophical speculation.[61] Hence, it would be a waste of time and effort for one to bother engaging with them. Dogmatists are, for all intents and purposes, a lost cause.

Fichte does admittedly offer the prospect that his opponents might succeed in 'overcoming the very incapacity' with which he reproaches them.[62] The coherence of his system demands this: by virtue of their status as a free being, even the most ardent dogmatist contains within themselves the possibility of coming to appreciate this freedom. But his rhetorical focus is, in the main, fixed upon their inveteracy: 'we do not wish to convince these opponents, because one cannot will to do something impossible. We do not wish to refute their system for them, because we are unable to do this.'[63] Fichte regards it as fruitless, in the general run of things, to try and overcome the 'original sin of dogmatism'.[64] Scholars who have already inherited a dogmatic standpoint have little chance of ever grasping the spirit of the *Wissenschaftslehre*.

A gendered economy of the will

Fichte does not wish philosophizing to be viewed as a rarefied activity, but he nevertheless holds it to be distinct from ordinary thought and speech. Whereas the scholar can fluently transport himself between the ordinary standpoint and the transcendental standpoint (which does not allow him to transcend his worldly existence, just explain its genesis), many others possess little aptitude for venturing beyond the familiar realm of everyday experience. The scholar must permit such people 'to remain peacefully within the circle of ordinary experience', as long as they do not

> try to pull down to their own level everything which they cannot themselves reach: if, for example, they demand that everything which is published should be as easy to use as a cookbook or an arithmetic book or a book of rules and regulations, and if they decry everything which cannot be employed in such a manner.[65]

These non-philosophers are probably skilled in many other areas and the cultivation of their peculiar talents will assist in the improvement of society; what distinguishes them from the scholar is that they are not charged with supervising and promoting the progress of the human race in general.

Fichte is at pains to highlight that all human beings are, by definition, rational beings, with no innate differences in their capacities for thinking and learning. 'Reason is the common possession of everyone and is entirely the same in every rational being. The same talent possessed by any one rational being is also possessed by every other rational being.'[66] The universality of his philosophy depends upon such a claim. This means all human beings are, at least in principle, capable of acting as *philosophical* beings: the concepts of the *Wissenschaftslehre* are not restricted to the purview of a privileged scholarly class, for they are actually and necessarily operative within every rational being, constituting the *a priori* basis for all consciousness. Or in other words, 'the pure *I* underlies all of their thinking and is present in their every act of thinking, for otherwise no act of thinking could occur at all'.[67] And yet, in a rebuke to his dogmatic critics, for whom 'every conviction [. . .] must be communicable through concepts', such that it must also be possible to 'force one's conviction upon anyone else purely by means of concepts', Fichte insists this conceptual universality does not in itself guarantee access to the transcendental standpoint philosophizing proper demands.[68] Philosophizing requires a kind of knowledge one cannot transmit integrally and systematically but can only find within oneself, through an intimate and conscious exercise of one's own freedom.

In his appeal to this knowledge (viz. intellectual intuition) and consequent foreclosure of its communicability, Fichte does not intend to imply that philosophizing necessitates some kind of connate talent, gifted only to certain people; on the contrary, by cultivating such knowledge we might finally quash the notion that philosophy requires possession of an exceptional 'philosophical genius':

> the *Wissenschaftslehre* will become universally comprehensible and easy to understand just as soon as it becomes the main goal and deliberate aim of all education. [. . .] Education of the whole person from earliest youth: This is the only way to propagate philosophy.[69]

The first principle of his system may not be communicable as such, but all rational beings possess it. And yet, as we have already witnessed, it is apropos of such questions of education – in particular, the question of *who* is indeed deserving of such an education – that the sphere of communicability comes to be circumscribed, and these egalitarian goals severely compromised. For Fichte uses his philosophy to exclude, from a transcendental point of view, those who might, in an empirical sense, still have access to it – specifically, women.[70]

Although outright misogyny has been a perennial feature within Western philosophy, Le Dœuff submits that 'references to women's incapacity for theory begin to proliferate from the eighteenth century onwards' – that is, only in the past three hundred or so years do we begin to see women explicitly disbarred from the philosophical enterprise.[71] For instance, although Plato is often dismissive towards women, he nevertheless advocates in *The Republic* for them to receive the same education as men, a posture quite distinct from that of Kant, who, as we have seen, at certain points seems to regard women as unsuitable for instruction in philosophy. In fact, such sentiments are common among the German idealists, Schelling excluded: as Dale Snow remarks, 'Kant, Fichte, and Hegel are remarkable for the low esteem, even for their day, in which they held women', warning that we cannot simply excuse them as being products of their time, given their views on women are often significantly *less* egalitarian than those of their contemporaries.[72]

Fichte's analysis of sexual difference in the *Foundations of Natural Right* is a forthright attack on the rights of women. 'The question of whether the female sex is as entitled to every human and civil right as the male sex', Fichte observes, 'could be asked only by someone who doubted that women are full human beings', and yet, he nevertheless questions 'whether and to what extent the female sex *can even will* to exercise all its rights'.[73] Woman cannot, in Fichte's estimation, rationally will her own autonomy; rather, in marriage she submits to the will of her husband as a result of 'her own enduring, necessary wish to be subjected', and this wish constitutes the basic condition of her moral outlook.[74] Man wills his own freedom (in accordance with the moral law), whereas woman wills her own subordination to man, marriage being the natural unity of active masculinity and passive femininity, a union 'necessarily and completely determined by nature and reason', producing a gendered economy in which marriage entails the surrendering of the woman's will to that of her husband.[75]

These reflections upon marriage typify a particular pattern of argumentation within Fichte's work: woman's freedom is affirmed but then qualified. And this is evinced also in his account of education. If it is through the *conscious* enactment of his freedom that an individual can intuit his own self-positing, and 'thereby raises himself to the point where he acquires the need for a philosophy', we are compelled to ask whether, from Fichte's perspective, all human beings, in spite of whatever freedom they are guaranteed to possess, can actually raise themselves to this standpoint.[76]

In fact, while the truths of philosophy, according to Fichte, undoubtedly apply to women (and are communicable to women via specific means), these women are not themselves capable of discovering such truths for themselves. Responding to the charge that women are 'cunningly kept in a state of ignorance' by being denied access to education, Fichte retorts that men of learning do not study only for themselves but for others, and resultantly must be conversant not only in the content but the *form* of what they learn.[77] The scholar 'must know *how* this stock of learning is discovered and developed out of the human soul'.[78] Women, by contrast, are not expected to teach and accordingly have no need to study these formal elements of intellection that make up speculative reason; instead, they require only the 'results of intellectual culture' for practical usage, and they 'obtain these results in society'.[79]

Although one 'cannot claim that women are *inferior* to men in terms of intellectual talents', Fichte explains, one can certainly claim that 'the minds of men and women are, by nature, very different'.[80]

> Man reduces everything that is in him and for him to clear concepts, and makes his discoveries through reasoning alone. [. . .] Woman has a natural feeling for determining what is true, proper, and good [. . .] when something is given to her from an external source, it is easy for her to judge whether or not it is true or good, based on mere feeling, without clear insight into the reasons for her judgment.[81]

The consequence is that while woman is already innately rational, for her 'fundamental drive immediately and originally merges with reason' and 'her entire system of feelings is rational and geared towards reason', man 'must first, through effort and activity, subordinate all of his drives to reason'.[82] Fichte regards woman as always already rational inasmuch as she makes only a practical, never a speculative use of reason. 'She cannot, and ought not, go beyond the limit of her feelings and into the interior of things.'[83]

We thus find at the core of this supposedly universal account of consciousness a fundamental rupture. Regardless of Fichte's desire to foster a philosophical attitude among all humanity, no longer restricted to certain privileged individuals, he makes it readily apparent that, while women may well be indirect beneficiaries of this general uplift in knowledge, they themselves will never truly philosophize, and hence do not need to receive such education directly. Women may possess a natural talent for divining the truth of things, but this comes at the expense of, not in addition to, access to the speculative viewpoint which defines philosophical activity. As long as she is unmarried or widowed, a woman may well take part in various crafts and professions, but thanks to her very nature, philosophy remains foreclosed. More specifically, since a woman is destined for neither scholarship nor public office, she has no need to probe into the causes of intellectual culture (and its genesis in the human soul) and can remain content in gaining the overall benefits of this culture, receiving its results within society.

In short then, transcendental speculation – the basis of the philosophical enterprise – is a task lying beyond the reach of women, who can make use of the products of philosophy within a social context, but cannot contribute to its ever-growing body of knowledge, having as they do an entirely practical, rather than theoretical, grasp of truth.[84] Women might be able to recite the *Wissenschaftslehre* to the letter, but they will never be able to enact its *spirit*. The significance of this cannot be understated. Fichte stresses that although 'one can indeed manage the ordinary business of earthly life' without engaging in philosophical enquiries, 'it would be difficult to be considered a rational, free, and suprasensuous being' in the absence of such intellectual activity.[85] The uncomfortable implication, which Fichte comes very close to spelling out explicitly, is that women are not *really* rational beings. The inner workings of their own minds remain at least somewhat opaque to them (although apparently not to men, since Fichte seems to have abundant confidence in his observations regarding womankind).

An arbitrary circumscription

Writing at a time when, as Helen Watanabe-O'Kelly notes, thinkers were beginning to discard theological explanations of sexual difference, and instead 'deduced the subordinate position of women from nature, a position that prevented them from playing a role in the state [. . .] and from enjoying the benefits of higher education and participation in the public sphere', Fichte denies women the speculative functions he ascribes to scholars, thus delimiting the discipline of philosophy as something valid for and applicable to women (inasmuch as they fall under the universal descriptor of *man*), and yet which they cannot take part in themselves (inasmuch as the additional descriptor of *woman* tempers the aforesaid universality).[86] The possibility that in Fichte's system, 'the universal truth of his science of knowledge' is, as Karen Kenkel puts it, in fact 'an exclusionary truth for men and about men', provides us with a conspicuously frank philosophical justification for women's exclusion from this discipline (and from education, and thus intellectual life more generally).[87] And this justifies a delimitation of women's communicative social role as well.

Ruminating upon the intellectual pursuits he deems suitable for women, Fichte opines that there have been women geniuses in languages, mathematics (or at least in those aspects of it demanding only rote learning), and fictional and historical writing, and yet 'we have not had female philosophers or mathematical innovators'.[88] This, he argues, is because women 'cannot make new discoveries'.[89] Their writing is only suited as a means 'to disseminate, through popularization, what is already known and settled':

> popular writings for women, writings about women's upbringing, moral teachings for the female sex in particular, can all be best written by women; first, because they know the female sex better than any man ever will, since they themselves are members of it (assuming, of course, that they are also capable of raising themselves above it to some extent); and secondly, because – as a *rule* – it is easier for them to find acceptance from a female audience. Such writings can teach even an educated man a great deal about the nature of woman. This assumes, of course, that these female authors also write as women, and want to appear in their writings as women and not poorly disguised men.[90]

If these women chose to write for a male (or indeed, *universal*) audience, their writing could be understood as nothing more than 'an instrument of their coquetry', and the greater independence they could gain would likely weaken or dissolve their marriages.[91]

For Fichte, men are capable of producing universally communicable (and thus universally applicable and valid) philosophical concepts, whereas women are not. Women can only guarantee the validity of their writings when they restrict their applicability to the domain of other women and their interests. Men might learn something about women from these writings, but the writings do not speak to or for them in the same way as a man's writings (which are, of course, communicable to both men *and* women). Since they should not be educated in philosophy (and indeed, *cannot* be properly educated in it), and have no right to contribute to such education, women are kept outside the sphere of philosophical communicability. And this allows one to dismiss a woman's writings as *a priori* unphilosophical, not on account of their content but simply because they have been authored by beings who, by definition, are unable to do more than affect the appearance of philosophizing. Fichte's emphasis upon the incommunicability of philosophy's first principle – insofar as it can only be intuited intellectually, as opposed to being represented in a discursive concept – and his accordant claim that understanding philosophy by the letter is not the same as understanding its spirit, is intended to ward off sophistic, dogmatic arguments, but it also provides a means of expeditiously dismissing those he deems heterogenous to the philosophical enterprise: any claims to their possession of the same knowledge can be denied offhand, since they are merely reciting the ideas of others – they have not *really* grasped any principles within themselves.

In contrast to his attack on dogmatists, Fichte offers little concession, however halfhearted, to the possibility that women might overcome their purported intellectual limitations. Women, he informs us, cannot make properly philosophical discoveries, cannot enquire into the inner nature of things (including themselves) and cannot in good faith profess themselves capable of transmitting knowledge in the universal manner demanded of a scholar. Congenitally deprived of conceptual thinking, women will never truly grasp the first principle of philosophy, let alone assist others in the same, and are thus denied the opportunity to play any real role in humankind's progress. The aim of the educator is 'to communicate to others what he has learned and to augment it through his own discoveries, so that the culture will not come to a standstill', suggesting women's role, at best, is to not impede such a process, since they cannot contribute positively to it. In fact, observes Bärbel Frischmann, women would seem to have little agency with respect to their own destiny, let alone that of humanity:

> behind the veil of a positive characterization of what women ought to become – i.e. loving wives – Fichte actually tells us what they ought not and even cannot become: women cannot become public officials, scientists, teachers, physicians, sextons, innovators, philosophers, mathematicians and so on. Although women are supposedly 'supremely practical', they are not actually free beings capable of deciding, determining or controlling their own futures.[92]

There is a sharp disparity between the egalitarian thrust of Fichte's ethical project and the way he excludes women, in a contrived and convoluted manner, from any positive role within it. The Fichtean account of intersubjectivity is premised upon the recognition of beings outside of oneself as free beings, limiting one's freedom in relation to the concept of their freedom. Yet when it comes to women, their freedom is understood only in terms of a freedom to submit, to relinquish their willing – an argument that seems to jar with his confident aspirations towards social equality. Whereas for men, the *Wissenschaftslehre* is intended to allow for their continued becoming, their ceaseless self-improvement (and accordingly, that of the entire species also), for women, it works to keep them in their place, to submit them to a static essence acting as the support for man's becoming.

Fichte's repeated denunciations of dogmatism appear to stem from a genuine frustration that the epiphany he experienced while reading Kant's *Critique of Practical Reason* (viz. that absolute freedom *does* exist) is not quite as easily replicated in others.[93] But what is notable about his approach is the extent to which he sublimates this frustration by reframing it in transcendental terms. In doing so, he further draws in and secures the boundaries of philosophical communicability, creating a philosophical community – both ideal and empirical – from which certain groups of people are *a priori* excluded. The *Wissenschaftslehre* supervenes upon a first principle no one, least of all Fichte himself, can communicate. To claim to be able to do so (or to stipulate that one's interlocutors must do so) straightaway betrays one's failure to grasp it. All Fichte's system can do is gesture towards this principle, and the manner in which this gesturing occurs is, for him, of vital importance.

This emphasis upon the intransmissibility of the spirit of philosophy, rather than affirming each person's claim to freedom, supplies Fichte with a means for determining, on an *a priori* basis, who is and is not to be deemed worthy of philosophical instruction and allows him to dismiss certain individuals' claims to philosophical wisdom as being not in the *spirit* of philosophy. This is why his observations regarding women, although a minor part of his overall output, are anything but extraneous. For it is in these observations that the outright arbitrariness of this circumscription is revealed. His rationale for precluding women from philosophizing (and brushing off any sign they might be capable of doing so) is structurally homologous to that which he deploys against dogmatists, but while the latter exclusion at least has some kind of empirical basis to it, the former is an entirely arbitrary decision, premised not upon any systematic and rigorous deduction or necessary truth, but derived from anecdote, conjecture and engrained social norms. Fichte is content to put forward a model of 'equality' positioning women as passive, subservient and silent in the face of philosophical reason. He hopes to 'encourage independent thinking in others by providing them with material for thought', but he has already decided in advance who can benefit from such material.[94]

5

A new breed of philosophers
Friedrich Nietzsche's tyrannical impulse

Like all the thinkers discussed in this book's foregoing chapters, Friedrich Nietzsche underscores the limits and limitations of philosophical discourse, scolding those who presuppose the universal communicability of their own ideas. Unlike these prior thinkers, however, he seldom gestures towards a hidden reality beyond such limits; on the contrary, he views any such distinction between reality and mere appearance as a theological relic, corruptive to philosophical thinking. He does, however, remain steadfast in the conviction that there is a particular mode of comportment proper to philosophizing: namely, the continual invention and legislation of concepts. Where the rabble *communicate*, sharing clichés and banal propositions among themselves, drawing from a long-standing amassment of stock concepts held in common, the philosopher – a higher type of man – *creates* and *imposes* his own concepts. In this way, the latter speaks in accordance with the will to power rather than with a fabricated object of knowledge (a thing in itself).

Any attempt to produce a systematic account of the Nietzschean philosophy, even within the confines of a single book (let alone his entire oeuvre), will involve egregious but inevitable exceptions, omissions and distortions. His books actively resist formalization. He does not wish for his writings to be treated like typical philosophical treatises, as storehouses of facts and propositions for others to passively study and comment upon:

> Scholars who spend basically all their time 'poring over' books [. . .] ultimately become completely unable to think for themselves. When they are not poring over books, they are not thinking. When they think, they are responding to some stimulus (– a thought they have read about). In the end, all they do is react. Scholars spend all their energy saying yes and no, criticizing what other people have already thought – they do not think for themselves any more . . .

Their instinct for self-defence has worn out, otherwise they would be defending themselves from books.[1]

Rather than offering us yet another new philosophy, a new set of concepts (let alone a new 'system', in the typical manner of nineteenth-century German philosophy), Nietzsche, submits Gianni Vattimo, 'wants to propose a new way of understanding and doing philosophy'.[2]

Accordingly, in this chapter I will stick to two main themes that recur often throughout Nietzsche's otherwise capricious and heterogeneous body of work: first, the inadequacy of language, especially to the extent that it congeals into concepts and customary ways of speaking; and second, the true philosopher as a creative, destructive and even tyrannical force, far removed from the comfort and security of ordinary existence. With these themes in mind, I will argue that in his repudiation of communication (in the most literal acceptation of this term), Nietzsche offers an ostentatious staging of the problem of integral transmission, but one which quickly comes to be defined by a virulent (albeit at least somewhat figurative) validation of dominance and exclusion as the basis of the philosophical endeavour. Denigrating commonality and propinquity, values he regards as alien to true philosophizing, he finds the justification for continued dissemination of philosophical concepts in a demand for an undemocratic, inegalitarian form of thought predicated upon the recognition of a difference in rank between the philosopher and the herd-like rabble (the *pathos of distance*).

The limitations of conceptual reasoning

Nietzsche's early work, preceding publication of the first volume of *Human, All Too Human* (1878), is tremendously indebted to the philosophy of Arthur Schopenhauer. He sees in Schopenhauer the epitome of a truly philosophical mindset, counterposed against the staid abstractions and pedantic disquisitions of the Academy:

> Kant clung to his university, submitted himself to its regulations, retained the appearance of religious belief, endured to live among colleagues and students: so it is natural that his example has produced above all university professors and professorial philosophy. Schopenhauer had little patience with the scholarly castes, separated himself from them, strove to be independent of state and society.[3]

The Kantian project, Nietzsche suggests, falls short of the profound, life-transforming impact its adherents ascribe to it. In most cases, it furnishes the same kinds of anodyne, undemanding teaching that have always characterized academic philosophy:

> the 'truth' of which our professors speak so much, seems to be a more unassuming [*anspruchsloseres*] being from which no disorder and nothing extraordinary is to be feared: a self-contented and happy creature which is continually assuring all the powers that be that no one needs to be the least concerned on its account; for it is, after all, only 'pure science'.[4]

And even if it did have a transformative effect, this would likely prompt nothing more than scepticism, relativism and an undermining of all confidence in one's own knowledge, culminating in an unabating incertitude occasioned by the distinction between the appearance of things and the thing in itself.[5] By contrast, Schopenhauer 'leads us from the depths of sceptical gloom or criticizing renunciation up to the heights of tragic contemplation, to the nocturnal sky and its stars extended endlessly above us'.[6] Nietzsche urges us to 'pursue the great ideal of the Schopenhauerean man', for it is 'the fundamental idea of culture [. . .] *to promote the production of the philosopher, the artist and the saint within us and without us*'.[7]

While Schopenhauer's influence upon Nietzsche's early philosophy manifests in a variety of ways, most important for our purposes is the former's distinction between intuitive and abstract cognition. Through a radicalization of this distinction, Nietzsche develops his own incipient theory of communication, doing away with the conceptual abstraction that persists in Schopenhauer's account of the same. Intuitive cognition, as Schopenhauer would have it, is the domain of real objects, whereas abstract cognition is the domain of concepts. More specifically, intuitive representation 'presents itself with naïve truthfulness as just what it is', given to the senses and the understanding in an immediate presence, in accordance with the forms of space and time and governed by the principle of sufficient reason.[8] As such, it 'arouses neither scruple nor doubt in the beholder who remains with it', remaining untouched by concerns regarding truth and falsity.[9] It is only through abstraction and reflection (i.e. the activities of *reason*) that these latter kinds of judgements arise. Reason, which belongs to human beings alone (unlike intuition), is conceptual in nature: its function is to form universal concepts, the content of which is derived from intuitive data. Abstract cognition serves to 'fix the immediate cognition of the understanding for reason by setting it down in abstract concepts, that is, by making it clear, i.e. putting it into a state to be interpreted for others, to make it meaningful'.[10] It allows humans to form judgements and put these to practical use – above all else, it allows them to *communicate* their thoughts through language.

Together, these two forms of cognition make up, for Schopenhauer, the world of representation. And although for him this world is, in turn, fundamentally grounded in the will, this does not call its validity into question (though it does indicate a fundamental absence, insofar as the will remains unrepresentable). The world, he explains, 'is not a lie or an illusion: it presents itself as what it is, as representation, and in fact as a series of representations bound together by the principle of sufficient reason'.[11] It is from this certitude, by which Schopenhauer attempts to head off the assertions of both dogmatists and sceptics, that Nietzsche's own account of conceptual reasoning, and language more generally, diverges. In several early essays and notes, Nietzsche begins to question the notion that the intellect, as a faculty of categorization and denomination, might have any purchase on the world at all (let alone the thing in itself, were such a thing to exist). Language, conceptual reasoning and the whole apparatus of truth they carry with them seem to him a hindrance to genuine philosophizing – exactly the kind that Schopenhauer, in his view, epitomizes.

The philosopher's intellectual drive, their inclination to truth and certitude, argues Nietzsche, leads them down the wrong path: it 'forces him into *communication* [*Mittheilung*] and the communication in turn into logic', which brandishes its self-declared supremacy over other modes of knowledge – love, art and so forth.[12] 'Logic is merely slavery in the bonds of language', and it is precisely the illogicality of language – its recourse to metaphor; its predilection for equating the unequal – that allows logic to claim said supremacy, producing universal concepts to *express* the singularity of their experience.[13] These concepts can be nothing more than inadequate metaphors – a problem reaching back to the very origins of Western philosophy:

> every profound philosophic intuition expressed through dialectic and through scientific reflection is the only means for the philosopher to communicate what he has seen. But it is a sad means; basically a metaphoric and entirely unfaithful translation into a totally different sphere and speech. Thus Thales had seen the unity of all that is, but when he went to communicate it [*mittheilen*], he found himself talking about water![14]

Schopenhauer's postulation of conceptual reasoning via abstract cognition as an unproblematic, albeit derivative, means of communicating thoughts (providing the basis for shared judgements of truth) therefore starts to be questioned.

Nietzsche harnesses the former's positing of an intuitive knowledge to radicalize his position, challenging the equation of knowledge with conceptual abstraction, and expunging from him the traces of conventional academic philosophy.

Nietzsche *contra* communication

Nietzsche's early positions on language are most fully fleshed out in 'On Truth and Lie in an Extra-Moral Sense' (1873), unpublished during his lifetime. As becomes a frequent theme in his later work, Nietzsche situates the philosopher's will to truth in relation to the herd mentality he believes humankind has developed in order to stave off the conflict inherent in the state of nature. Once this peace treaty between individuals has been established, 'what is henceforth to be called "truth" is fixed, i.e. a universally valid and binding designation of things is invented and the legislation of language supplies the first laws of truth'.[15] Language becomes the arbiter of all things: not just a determinant of truth and falsity but the logical foundation upon which such a distinction becomes meaningful. While Nietzsche would not disagree with the Hobbesian conviction that without the capacity for speech society would not have been possible, he views this originary prioritization of communication as involving a crucial trade-off, insofar as it convinced humans of the inimitable superiority of their intellect – and in particular, led them to the false belief that there could ever be an adequation between things and their linguistic designations.[16]

'Only through forgetfulness', argues Nietzsche, 'can man ever come to believe that he is in possession of a truth', the latter referring to a direct correspondence between language and all realities.[17] Humans have forgotten this primordial trade-off, this compromise whereby they incapacitate an immediate relation to their own singular experience through the mediation of language and conceptual reasoning, substituting a hallucinatory relation between concepts and things in themselves for it. Indeed, we habitually believe that, in speaking of the world outside of us, we are drawing upon some knowledge of these things in themselves, 'and yet we possess nothing but metaphors for things which do not correspond in the slightest to the original entities'.[18] We use language in this way so customarily, so *unconsciously*, we no longer question its validity.

Nietzsche wants to tear the suture between language and truth open:

> what then is truth? A mobile army of metaphors, metonymies, anthropomorphisms, in short, a sum of human relations which have been poetically and

rhetorically intensified, transferred, decorated and which, after lengthy use, seem firm, canonical and binding to a people: truths are illusions that are no longer remembered as being illusions, metaphors that have become worn and stripped of their sensuous force.[19]

The problem Nietzsche identifies in this passage is not the use of metaphor itself, which he posits as a fundamental human drive, but the way in which truth's status *as* metaphor has been blotted out. While every metaphor, in its original state, is the direct, irreducible index of a unique sensuous impression, eluding all classification, in order to provide themselves a sense of comfort and security in their selective truth, humans have consistently chosen to allow these metaphors to ossify, converting them into rigid, generalizing concepts:

> only oblivion of that primitive world of metaphors, only the congealment and solidification of what was originally a hot and liquid mass of images pouring out of the primal force of human imagination, only the invincible belief that *this* sun, *this* window, *this* table is a truth in itself – in short, only forgetting that he is himself a subject, and an *artistically creative subject* at that, enables man to live with a degree of peace, certainty and consistency.[20]

Humans have forgotten that our relation to the world was, is and can only ever be *aesthetic* in nature, mediated by our 'freely poetic [*dichtenden*] and freely inventive' faculties.[21] Language can only furnish a tenuous translation of the singular experience it attempts to capture.

The consequence of this forgetting is that the irrepressible fecundity of our intuition, of that which is specific to our individual existence, is concealed beneath a coagulated layer of conceptual abstractions, each of which seeks to fabricate identity out of the non-identical. Any given concept, by virtue of the fact it must apply not only to the singular instance from which it was first derived but to a host of other instances, all of which may be similar but are in no way identical, acts as an instrument of forgetting, occluding one's memory of the real, individual experience that gave rise to it. Man 'submits his actions as a *rational* being to the rule of abstractions: he is no longer prepared to be carried away by sudden impressions, or intuitions, but he generalises all these impressions to form less colourful, cooler concepts', for it is in the latter that he finds a safer, firmer, foundation for thought, both more familiar and more peremptory.[22]

In later works, Nietzsche does not retain the level of scepticism articulated in this early essay (nor does he keep up his veneration for Schopenhauer); he becomes much more open to the possibility of truth, albeit a decidedly individual and perspectival version of truth. He does, however, in spite of the variances across (and indeed, within) his published and unpublished works, hold firm to the view that we must 'free ourselves from the seduction of words', wishing to pull philosophy away from its reliance upon stale designations and mummified concepts.[23] 'Convictions', he suggests, 'are more dangerous enemies of truth than lies', and it is through conviction – erroneous beliefs, illusions and fantasies that have, through generations of accretion, built up a patina, lending them an appearance of objective truth – that we end up with essences, things in themselves, and categorical imperatives: specious claims to objective truth which obscure the original arbitrariness of their formation.[24] Nietzsche decries *customary* uses of language, which rely upon delusive ideas that have had a 'substratum of reality' foisted upon them, lending them an underserved authority.[25] And philosophers are very much complicit in this linguistic sclerosis, transforming their own preconceptions into abstract concepts, shorn of all evidence of such crude motivations, which they can then rationalize and defend after the fact:

> the last thing in metaphysics we'll rid ourselves of is the oldest stock, assuming we *can* rid ourselves of it – that stock which has embodied itself in language and the grammatical categories and made itself so indispensable that it almost seems we would cease being able to think if we relinquished it. Philosophers, in particular, have the greatest difficulty in freeing themselves from the belief that the basic concepts and categories of reason belong without further ado to the realm of metaphysical certainties.[26]

Philosophers typically act, complains Nietzsche, as 'sly spokesmen for prejudices that they christen as "truths"', spurring on and justifying this conceptual atavism which seeks refuge in time-worn arguments and hackneyed certitudes.[27] Hence his pertinacious enmity towards all customary ways of speaking, and the value he accords to the singularity of individual experience. The pivotal question, though, is how he reconciles this attitude with a desire to promulgate his own philosophy – an act that would, one must assume, risk it also becoming just another set of prejudices masquerading as eternal truths. The answer, as we will see, lies both in the prominence he places upon ongoing creativity, demanding from the philosopher a continual conceptual upheaval, and in the distinction he posits between those who impose concepts and those who merely adhere to them.

Perspectivism and interpretation

Nietzsche remains steadfast in his stance towards communication, which, although a necessary feature of human existence, cannot and should not be treated as a means of adequation. Through the abstractions of language (alongside logic, mathematics, physics, etc.), philosophers distance themselves from the complexities of experience:

> the significance of language for the evolution of culture lies in this, that mankind set up in language a separate world beside the other world, a place it took to be so firmly set that, standing upon it, it could lift the rest of the world off its hinges and make itself master of it. To the extent that man has for long ages believed in the concepts and names of things as in *aeternae veritates* he has appropriated to himself that pride by which he raised himself above the animal: he really thought that in language he possessed knowledge of the world.[28]

The problem is not so much communication itself but the anthropocentric notion that language involves more than designation, that one can use words to express a direct knowledge of things. Abstract reasoning constructs a world amenable to its own judgement (and hence its own mastery), bearing no relation to the world as lived – the chaotic, protean world of sensations, impressions and drives. It is just another metaphorical construction, dealing in fictions gradually rendered 'true' through familiarity. Language is crass: it speaks of identity where in fact we can find only individuality and difference; it speaks in black-and-white dualisms and oppositions (and above all else, of the 'true' and the 'false') where in fact we can only find various shades of grey; and most fatally, it speaks of an objective external reality, projecting one's simplified judgements, valuations and desires outside of oneself and reifying them as 'things'.

The thinker, suggests Nietzsche, 'knows how to make things simpler than they are'.[29] They conceptualize the world, and in doing so, they rob it of its nuance, intricacy and indeterminacy. They schematize and abbreviate, reducing it to a set of received wisdoms. They make communication – the mediation of the world via linguistic concepts – the measure of the world, eliding the way in which it springs from their fundamental 'capacity to create (fashion, fabricate, invent)', and treating it instead as a faculty for knowledge *about* the world.[30] Hence why Nietzsche celebrates a mode of philosophizing that does not valorize or prioritize such mediation:

> our true experiences are completely taciturn. They could not be communicated [*mittheilen*] even if they wanted to be. This is because the right words for them do not exist. The things we have words for are also the things we have already left behind. There is a grain of contempt in all speech. Language, it seems, was invented only for average, mediocre, communicable things. People *vulgarize* themselves when they speak a language.[31]

The word *mittheilen*[32] (literally 'to share with'), like its English equivalent *communicate* (deriving from the Latin *communicare*, 'to share'), emphasizes the shared aspect of such communication, which draws upon a reserve of terms and concepts held in common and able to be exchanged. In order to be communicated, a sensory impression must be rendered 'fixed, simplified, specifiable' by the intellect, translating it into a familiar, recognizable (and banal) form.[33] Communication and intellection, more generally, remind us that humans are at least partly herd animals, to the extent that their usual attempts to understand themselves as individuals instinctually revert to what is non-individual. 'At bottom, all our actions are incomparably and utterly personal, unique, and boundlessly individual, there is no doubt; but as soon as we translate them into consciousness, *they no longer seem to be*.'[34]

Hence Nietzsche's appeal to a *perspectivism* which eludes all such schematism, resisting extrapolation from the individuality of a singular point of view.[35] 'Inasmuch as the word "knowledge" has any meaning at all', Nietzsche argues, 'the world is knowable: but it is variously *interpretable*; it has no meaning behind it, but countless meanings'.[36] One must not conflate such interpretation with mere subjectivism, for the positing of a subject (or even just of an interpreter) is just one more interpretation, a fiction we impose upon the world. Nietzsche does not deny the possibility of knowledge per se, but he refuses any recourse to the positivist notion of objective 'facts' shorn of their perspectival partiality – in other words, he rejects any appeal to either things in themselves or knowledge in itself. Hence, 'the demand for an *adequate mode of expression is nonsensical*: it's of the essence of a language, of a means of expression, to express only a relation'.[37]

This perspectivism forms part of Nietzsche's broader attempt to proffer a naturalistic account of the origins of knowledge, morality and conceptual reasoning, viewing these as evolutive adaptations of the human species, rather than *a priori* principles providing a secure grounding for cognition.[38] Humankind, he suggests, 'desires the pleasant, life-preserving consequences of truth; he is indifferent to pure knowledge without consequences, and even hostile to harmful and destructive truths', developing the concept of 'truth' as a kind of useful fiction, valorizing security, comfort, caution and so forth. What we habitually regard as true thus emerges out of a value judgement, an interpretation, determining what is or is not propitious for the species' survival. Like all value judgements, these truths are born of instincts and desires: 'physiological requirements for the preservation of a particular type of life'.[39] Nietzsche is even inclined to suggest that 'the falsest judgments (which include synthetic judgments *a priori*) are the most indispensable to us', arguing that 'without measuring reality against the wholly invented world of the unconditioned and self-identical, without a constant falsification of the world through numbers, people could not live'.[40] These 'truths' are errors, but they are useful errors, and this explains why they linger. The problem for philosophy, however, is that these 'useful and species-preserving' errors have so often hardened into articles of faith, passed down from generation to generation, their expedient and perspectival origin having been forgotten.[41] Philosophers have gradually confused their effects with their truth value, projecting the contingent predicates of our own preservation onto being in general. 'The *strength* of knowledge lies not in its degree of truth, but in its age, its embeddedness, its character as a condition of life.'[42]

Much of Nietzsche's project involves elucidating the instinctual drives and desiderata underpinning these errors – operating under the assumption that 'our world of desires and passions is the only thing "given" as real, that we cannot get down or up to any "reality" except the reality of our drives'.[43] At root, our existence as human beings, our experience of the world and the goals, purposes and meanings we ascribe to it are nothing other than multitudinous expressions of our *will to power*. Again, for Nietzsche, it is not the subject that makes the initial value judgements (i.e. the perspectives) from which our thoughts and feelings arise, even though we might customarily attribute them to this fictitious entity; rather, 'it is our needs *which interpret the world*. [. . .] Every drive is a kind of lust for domination, each has its perspective, which it would like to impose as a norm on all the other drives'.[44] The will to power itself interprets, and this interpretation, above all else, strives for *mastery*, as much in the world of organisms as that of ideas and concepts.

The need for creation

Philosophers, Nietzsche believes, have forgotten that their will to truth functions in service of the will to power: the real task of the former is 'to help a certain kind of untruth to victory and permanence, to take a connected whole of falsifications as the basis for preserving a certain kind of living things'.[45] Indeed, as much as Nietzsche resents the unquestioned predominance of traditional metaphysical concepts, he nonetheless remains impressed by the sheer strength of force of those thinkers who were able to *impose* such abstractions, transforming arbitrary designations into concrete laws:

those law-giving and tyrannical spirits capable of *tying fast* the meaning of a concept, *holding fast* to it, men with that spiritual force of will, who know how to turn the most fluid thing, the spirit, to stone for long periods and almost to eternalise it, are commanding men in the highest sense.⁴⁶

To take a single point of view – a single value judgement or interpretation – and decree that it applies to all events, under all circumstances, is an audacious act of falsification, a brazen claim to mastery. An audacity which, in Nietzsche's estimation, is the fundamental basis of all philosophy. After all, 'every drive craves mastery, and *this* leads it to try philosophizing', striving to 'present *itself* as the ultimate purpose of existence and as rightful *master* of all the other drives'.⁴⁷

So the problem, from Nietzsche's standpoint, is not the domineering impulses of metaphysics but the fact their dominance has been left unchecked. To remain forceful, concepts and values need to be challenged:

> even if we were mad enough to consider all our opinions true, we should still not want them alone to exist – I cannot see why it should be desirable that truth alone should rule and be omnipotent; it is enough for me that it should possess *great power*. But it must be able to *struggle* and have opponents, and one must be able to *find relief* from it from time to time in untruth – otherwise it will become boring, powerless and tasteless to us, and make us the same.⁴⁸

The interminable endurance of our metaphysical bequest is the stigma of a decadent culture, given in to its herd mentality. The comfort and security putatively stable, immutable truths bring with them might well help preserve the species, but it does so at a considerable cost, stultifying and infantilizing society. Our desire for truth is precisely 'this need for the familiar, the will to uncover among everything strange, unusual, and doubtful something which no longer unsettles us', seeking out the familiar and commonplace, that which 'makes us feel at home', expelling or domesticating anything anomalous and unprecedented.⁴⁹ It arises from a fear of the unknown. The philosopher then, as Nietzsche conceives of their role, must 'acknowledge untruth as a condition of life', and this means 'resisting customary feelings of value in a dangerous manner', placing themselves beyond good and evil (and indeed, true and false).⁵⁰

If logic, mathematics, metaphysics and even language furnish nothing more than fictions (albeit oft-useful ones), then one can surely also invent other fictions. In contrast to the workmanlike practices of philosophical labourers (such as Kant), who take dominant truths and convert them into signs and formulas, rendering them 'clear, obvious, comprehensible, and manageable',

Nietzsche argues that *'true philosophers are commanders and legislators'* – they create values, and just as importantly, they *impose* these values.[51]

> True philosophers reach for the future with a creative hand and everything that is and was becomes a means, a tool, a hammer for them. Their 'knowing' is *creating*, their creating is a legislating, their will to truth is – *will to power*.[52]

If Plato conceives of philosophy as consisting in the recollection of primaeval truths inscribed within the soul, Nietzsche conversely conceives of it as a recovery of human beings' creative capacities – the possibility of erasing the palimpsest of received truths inscribed over many generations and starting anew, opening up new horizons and perspectives. And in fact, this is exactly what Plato himself did, in spite of what his own statements might suggest: in 'throwing drab, cold, gray nets of concepts over the brightly colored whirlwind of the senses', he displayed a certain 'type of *enjoyment* in overpowering and interpreting the world', construing experience via a perspective that was, at the time, genuinely novel in its confident expression of mastery over the sensuous and its unilateral proclamation of the all-embracing validity of this perspective.[53]

This emphasis upon creation manifests in variegated ways across Nietzsche's oeuvre. In 'On Truth and Lie', he speaks of 'the drive to create metaphors, that fundamental drive of man', which is 'not truly defeated but barely tamed by constructing for itself, out of its own evaporated products, the concepts, a world as regular and rigid as a prison fortress', arguing that this drive 'continually confuses the conceptual categories and cells by introducing new transferences, metaphors and metonymies', wishing to render our waking world as enigmatic and mercurial as our dreams.[54] The intellect, 'that master of deception', can in this account be liberated from the restrictive metaphysical armature that 'needy man clings all his life in order to survive', smashing it up and reassembling it in countless ways, deceiving in a fruitful rather than harmful manner, guided by intuitions rather than concepts.[55] Embracing one's intuitions in such a fashion also involves a rejection of the norms of communication:

> from these intuitions there is no regular road leading to the country of ghostly schemata, of abstractions: the word is not made for them, and man falls silent when he sees them, or he speaks in nothing but forbidden metaphors and outrageous combinations of concepts.[56]

The 'intuitive man' breaks the social contract lending security and prudence to our everyday lives, refusing to allow his experiences to be confined within the strait-lacing of customary language.

In Nietzsche's later work, we see such an approach to philosophy tied to the will to power – to the need for philosophers who, through their ability to create and legislate new perspectives, might curb the 'degeneration and diminution of humanity into the perfect herd animal'.[57] In *Beyond Good and Evil* (1886), he announces the 'arrival of a new breed of philosophers, ones whose taste and inclination are somehow the reverse of those we have seen so far – philosophers of the dangerous perhaps in every sense', a higher type of person who will accord a greater value to 'appearance, the will to deception, and craven self-interest' than they will to truth, honesty, selflessness or any other principles to which we are heir.[58] Philosophy needs 'a bit *more* strength, flight, courage, artistry', and this means abandoning the quest for knowledge in favour of invention – a kind of fecund ignorance.[59] These new philosophers will not dwell for too long, settling down within a single, safe viewpoint; rather, they will be tirelessly on the lookout for new, unexplored perspectives. Genuine philosophizing entails 'a life lived freely in ice and high mountains – visiting all the strange and questionable aspects of existence, everything banned by morality so far'.[60]

Philosophers of the future

Nietzsche situates the true act of philosophizing within a mode of expression that, in overturning the clichés of customary communication, grounding itself in invention rather than pre-established coherence and generalized abstraction, dismisses the reciprocity central to dialogue. Hence his depiction of the titular character in *Thus Spoke Zarathustra*, who perceives in the market square only 'the noise of the great actors and the buzzing of poisonous flies', a space wherein the rabble demand simple, unconditional answers from showy performers spruiking tired concepts.[61] 'Away from the market place and fame', he declares, 'all greatness takes place; away from the market place and fame the inventors of new values have lived all along'.[62] It is hardly surprising that Nietzsche's hatred of the vulgar, the popular and the common would lead to this pursuit of solitude. But what accompanies it as well is an increasingly domineering, inegalitarian demand for the philosopher to not only elevate themselves above the rabble but to impose themselves upon it as well. Given his dismissal of communication (in the sense of a shared or consensual construction of meaning) as a legitimate end of philosophy, he needs to devise another justification for continuing to disseminate his concepts among a populace he so despises. As Vattimo explains:

> the philosopher finds himself with nothing left to rely on: whatever kind of evidence he adduces will cause him to lapse back into the world of fiction he wishes to criticize, making him a spokesman for the same instincts from which metaphysics arises and which it is his business to refute. The only possibility is for him to tear himself (violently in a certain sense) free of the world of the prevalent fiction.[63]

Nietzsche locates this possibility in the will to power, and the need for the philosopher, as a higher type of man, to impose their will – and in particular, the values they have invented – upon others. This willed creativity must, as Seán Burke puts it, 'fill the void opened by a vanquished conceptuality'.[64]

'I am always driven anew to human beings', Nietzsche affirms, 'by my ardent will to create; thus the hammer is driven toward the stone'.[65] True philosophy, philosophy that believes in itself, 'always creates the world in its own image, it cannot do otherwise; philosophy is this tyrannical drive itself, the most spiritual will to power, to the "creation of the world", to the *causa prima*'.[66] In his valorization of this tyrannical drive, Nietzsche does more than posit a particular kind of philosophical discourse as superior to quotidian *doxa*; instead, he celebrates those philosophers capable of joyfully bringing their own singular concepts to bear upon others. Disavowing the pursuance of '*equal rights* and ultimately *equal needs*', insofar as this 'brings with it the exclusion and slow extinction of the higher, more dangerous, stranger and, in short, *newer* men' capable of such experimentation, bringing culture to a standstill, he grounds philosophy in a despotic relationship between a *higher type* of men and their herd-like unequals.[67] He does not want to just establish a new mode of philosophical communication but places his hopes in a new breed of men, a new philosophical aristocracy, who will overcome the drive to communicate (to the extent it entails having something *in common*). After all, 'it would offend their pride, as well as their taste, if their truth were a truth for everyone'.[68]

Nietzsche furnishes a thoroughgoing account of the environmental conditions under which we might breed and raise this higher type of man. He emphasizes that invention, fabulation and even deception are basic aspects of human experience: that 'to experience is to invent', constantly extrapolating and fabulating from the ever-changing intuitions given to us and the drives impelling us.[69] But he also emphasizes, much more strenuously, that the ability to harness these for loftier ends depends on a certain pedigree:

> you need to have been born for any higher world; to say it more clearly, you need to have been *bred* for it: only your descent, your ancestry can give you a right to philosophy – taking that word in its highest sense. Even here, 'bloodline' is decisive. The preparatory labor of many generations is needed for a philosopher to come about; each of his virtues needs to have been individually acquired, cared for, passed down, and incorporated.[70]

To truly philosophize, one needs more than just hard work and an appropriate education; one needs to be bred for such activities. 'Everyone *possesses inborn talent*, but few possess the degree of inborn and acquired toughness, endurance and energy actually to become a talent', to become who they really are, to affirm themselves as creators and legislators in their own right.[71] Humanity must prepare itself for a 'wholesale attempt at breeding and cultivation' that will 'put an end to the gruesome rule of chance and nonsense that has passed for "history" so far', and it is in large part down to philosophers to clear this path.[72]

At many different points, Nietzsche enumerates the requisite qualities for such philosophers (talents, men of intuition, free spirits, higher types, heroic human beings, *Übermenschen* or whatever other honorifics he bestows upon them) – those endowed with 'the dangerous privilege of living *experimentally*'.[73] And while there is, given this experimental orientation, little consistency in the qualities he sets forth, certain motifs endure. First, a kind of nobility, a desire for individuality, to become what one truly is, to differ from others and to affirm this difference – and accordingly, a decided solitude. Second, a self mastery, self-discipline and possession of a certitude in one's own works. In short, a positive self-reverence, free from any enervative *ressentiment*. Third, a peculiar health or strength gained not from a sheltered, comfortable upbringing but from exposure to chance, risk and danger in all their forms, spurning 'the universal, green pasture happiness of the herd, with security, safety, contentment, and an easier life for all'.[74] He seeks the courage of those 'who are strengthened by wars and victories, for whom conquest, adventure, danger and even pain have actually become a necessity'.[75] And lastly (though there are no doubt many others), an innate cunning, a desire to not only take part in deception (as we all do) but to affirm it, and a willingness to inflict pain:

> who will attain something great if he does not feel in himself the power to *inflict* great pain? Being able to suffer is the least; weak women and even slaves often achieve mastery at that. But not to perish of inner distress and uncertainty when one inflicts great suffering and hears the cry of this suffering – that is great; that belongs to greatness.[76]

Nietzsche's political worldview, contends Daniel Conway, is characterized by an idiosyncratic 'perfectionism', locating 'the sole justification of human existence in the continued perfectibility of the species as a whole, as evidenced by the pioneering accomplishments of its highest exemplars'.[77] This perfectionism becomes increasingly inegalitarian and anti-democratic in nature, expressed in the hope of breeding a higher class of man by affirming humanity's 'evil, terrible, tyrannical, predatory, and snakelike'.[78] Nietzsche pushes vigorously against the degeneration of humanity into 'stunted little animals with equal rights and equal claims' – a trend that he views as a negation of life; a crude sentimentality inhospitable to the cultivation of higher types.[79] For 'life itself', he propounds, 'is *essentially* a process of appropriating, injuring, overpowering the alien and the weaker, oppressing, being harsh, imposing your own form' – actions unfairly slandered by moralists, who wish to lower humanity to the level of their own mediocrity.[80] Life is will to power, and thus to affirm life is to proliferate, predate, dominate, capture, master and exploit.

This appeal to breeding does not imply the innate superiority of a given race or people; on the contrary, as Kofman observes,

> his concern is the struggle for power, the submerged play of wills in a fight to survive or predominate, and the see-saw shifts of power in the course of history, since one group's domination over another is never definitively won or assured. Over and above all 'racial limitations', Nietzsche postulates a universal principle of intelligibility – the will to power – which explains, regardless of the differences, the will to be a 'chosen people', to be first in everything everywhere. [. . .] Thus substituting an economic reading of kinship for a physiological one – a reading of inheritance where the line is not transmitted through blood but rather through instinctive drives, forces cultivated for centuries by the preeminent, finally exploding in the genius – Nietzsche creates a fantastic genealogy for himself, going back to the very highest and most ancient: all the way to Dionysus.[81]

Nietzsche counterposes the democratic impulse against these '*new philosophers* [. . .] who are strong and original enough to give impetus to opposed valuations and initiate a revaluation and reversal of "eternal values"': the former is not merely a particular form of political organization but 'an abased (more specifically a diminished) form of humanity', the cessation of which these incipient philosophers herald.[82] Philosophy in this sense is thoroughly aristocratic, insofar as the fundamental belief of any aristocracy 'must always be that society *cannot* exist for the sake of society, but only as the substructure and framework for raising an exceptional type of being up to its higher duty and to a higher state of *being*.[83] Crucially, such higher beings do not belong to a community; like all aristocrats, they instead perceive themselves as giving meaning and justification to this community by the very fact they transcend it. We of modernity suffer from the fact that 'the ancient slave is absent from our sensibility' – which is to say, the problem is not so much a literal lack of slavery as it is a cultural deprivation stemming from the absence of the *mindset* afforded by slavery.[84] And philosophy suffers from this deprivation as well:

> the Greek philosopher went through life feeling secretly that there were far more slaves than one might think – namely, that everyone who was not a philosopher was a slave; his pride overflowed when he considered that even the mightiest men on earth might be his slaves. This pride, too, is foreign and impossible for us; not even metaphorically does the word 'slave' possess for us its full force.[85]

This is not just a lament for social difference, or even hierarchy, but for *distance* – a noble haughtiness (in the most literal sense of the word) from which one looks down upon the rabble.[86]

Rather than equality (which can only be expressed in terms of similitude, and which can only signal decline), Nietzsche wishes to foster a return to the *pathos of distance* – 'the continuing and predominant feeling of complete and fundamental superiority of a higher ruling kind in relation to a lower kind, to those "below"'; 'the rift between people, between classes, the myriad number of types, the will to be yourself, to stand out' – which he believes has conversely been a characteristic feature of every strong age.[87] If the new philosopher is an exemplar of the higher type of man Nietzsche valorizes, he can only emerge from a milieu suffused with this pathos:

> every enhancement so far in the type 'man' has been the work of an aristocratic society – and that is how it will be, again and again, since this sort of society believes in a long ladder of rank order and value distinctions between men, and in some sense needs slavery. Without the *pathos of distance* as it grows out of the ingrained differences between stations, out of the way the ruling caste maintains an overview and keeps looking down on subservient types and tools, and out of this caste's equally continuous exercise in obeying and commanding, in keeping away and below – without *this* pathos, that *other*, more mysterious pathos could not have grown at all, that demand for new expansions of distance within the soul itself, the development of states that are increasingly high, rare, distant, tautly drawn and comprehensive, and in short, the enhancement of the type 'man', the constant 'self-overcoming of man'.[88]

In his later work, from *Beyond Good and Evil* (1886) and *On the Genealogy of Morality* (1887) onward, Nietzsche underscores that through this aristocratic mindset, a superabundance of life might once again be able to flourish. The possibility might arise of 'rearing a master race [...] a new, tremendous aristocracy built upon the harshest self-legislation, in which the will of philosophical men of violence and artist tyrants is made to last for thousands of years'.[89]

Esotericism

As uncomfortable as his frequent appeals to violence, conquest, discrimination (including a distinct, albeit inconstant misogynistic streak, the details of which I have not even attempted to survey) and even eugenics might be when one scrutinizes them more than a century after the fact, Nietzsche's writings are variegated and contradictory enough to resist the kinds of reductive readings to which critics have often subjected them.[90] Against my selective practice of quotation in this chapter, one could equally point towards passages like the following, that frame this desire for a cultivation of the human species rather differently:

> the thirst for equality can express itself either as a desire to draw everyone down to oneself (through diminishing them, spying on them, tripping them up) or to raise oneself and everyone else up (through recognizing their virtues, helping them, rejoicing in their success).[91]

Nietzsche's fragmented, aphoristic and often contradictory style of writing makes his own viewpoint quite difficult to pin down. His claim that 'there is no "correct" interpretation' of a text, which follows naturally from his emphasis upon the perspectival nature of knowledge, experience, morality, desire and even reality itself, of course applies to any text, not just his own.[92] But he makes a particular effort to ensure that, while individual statements and aphorisms might well be cogent, their situation within a larger corpus always remains indeterminate. His writings disrupt any attempt to attribute a definite position to him, or indeed, to take any of his statements seriously.[93]

Nevertheless, Nietzsche explicitly and portentously frames the possibility of rising above the morass of conceptual clichés, of philosophizing in a truly *living* manner, in accordance with the will to power, in terms of domination and exclusion.[94] Philosophizing, in his estimation, demands both a resistance to communication *qua* commonality, ennobling the individual perspective over shared concepts and ideas, and a rejection of equality *qua* propinquity, extolling a conscious maintenance of the distance between the philosopher (as an outstanding individual; a higher type of man) and the masses. And though Nietzsche does not reject expression of philosophy through language as such (because it fulfils a necessary pragmatic function), he does view communication, when understood in terms of conceptual abstraction, as enervating philosophical activity. In this respect, Nietzsche fits neatly within a tradition which views the letter as deadening the spirit of philosophy. He reminds us that we should take care not to 'limit our notion of the "philosopher" to the philosophers who write books – or put *their own* philosophy into books!'.[95] But it is not just the written or printed word to which his complaints apply; rather, he condemns *all* communication, regardless of its medium.

Nietzsche is not bothered by philosophers disseminating their ideas (as long as these are original ideas, *created* rather than merely recycled); he *is* bothered, however, by the notion that philosophy must consist in conceptual transmission, passing an idea or value intact from one individual to another. For this transmission takes the equivalence between the philosopher and their audience for granted, presupposing that these individuals are roughly equal in nature and rank, able to share in the same experiences and ways of thinking. Communication is an instrument of levelling, a deplorable erasure of the individual as such. The very intimation of such equivalence elides the singularity of experience and sutures the gap between higher types and their subordinates, demanding a psychological and social propinquity that can only end up stifling the philosopher's creative instincts.

Thus, as with all the thinkers discussed in this book, it all comes down to the problem of integral transmission. Concepts are always impositions for Nietzsche, moulding our singular experiences into crude, preformed categories handed down over generations. Concepts impose individual perspectives and valuations upon others. Concepts can certainly be transported from one mind to another, but this is only possible because they are abstracted from the individual qualities of experience. They are exchangeable precisely because they are detached from the drives and sense impressions giving rise to them. They are inclusive because they are *generic* rather than *specific*. A true philosopher – drawn from the new breed of philosophers upon whom Nietzsche pins his hopes – philosophizes in accordance with the will to power, and this means they must *impose*, instead of allowing themselves to be imposed upon. Such imposition takes place not under the delusive guise of communication, with its presumptions of equality and propinquity, but with a cultivated attunement to *distance* – the unbridgeable separation between the philosopher in their creative action and the rabble in their vapid conformity:

> the higher *ought* not to abase itself as the tool of the lower, the pathos of distance *ought* to ensure that their tasks are kept separate for all eternity! Their right to be there, the privilege of the bell with a clear ring over the discordant and cracked one, is clearly a thousand times greater: they alone are *guarantors* of the future, they alone have a *bounden duty* to man's future.[96]

And this peculiar duty, connected to the pathos of distance, carries with it implications for how the philosopher should express their ideas.

'Our highest insights must – and should! – sound like stupidities, or possibly crimes', Nietzsche suggests, 'when they come without permission to people whose ears have no affinity for them'.[97] He wishes to recover the ancient distinction between exoteric and esoteric thought – which, he purports, 'was found everywhere that people believed in an order of rank and *not* in equality and equal rights' – perceiving in it a relation of verticality (i.e. hierarchy), whereby 'the exoteric sees things up from below – while the esoteric sees them *down from above*'.[98] True philosophy is, for reasons that should now be self-evident, esoteric. It is not made for mass consumption; it should be aimed at those who have the courage to follow its lead, not in the sense of adhering to its postulates but of using it as a springboard for their own acts of creation and legislation. The manner in which this philosophy is expressed may well therefore be unintelligible to those lower types lacking in such impulses:

> one does not only wish to be understood when one writes; one wishes just as surely *not* to be understood. It is by no means necessarily an objection to a book when anyone finds it incomprehensible: perhaps that was part of the author's intention – he didn't *want* to be understood by just 'anybody'. Every nobler spirit and taste selects his audience when he wants to communicate [*mittheilen*]; in selecting it, he simultaneously erects barriers against 'the others'.[99]

Few philosophers have made this latter point as percipiently as Nietzsche, paying attention to the presumed audience of his writing, and who this presumption might exclude, deliberately or otherwise. He does not, however, just concern himself with scrutinizing such exclusions, but validates them as the very basis of the authentic philosophical enterprise. As Joanne Faulkner suggests, his proclaimed pursuit of a different, higher type of man as the bulwark against cultural decadence and philosophical stagnation becomes a means of helping those in his audience who might aspire to such an ideal recognize this desire within themselves, suppressing their less productive impulses:

whereas on the surface this proclamation refers to a difference between types of 'men' – those equal to the challenge of his philosophy, and those who are not – at another level the annunciation divides each and every reader in two, thus exploiting the schism at the heart of identity itself. This in turn prepares the reader to be interpellated to Nietzsche's project; to play her part according to the imperatives of Nietzsche's text, as either what will prevail or what must be overcome to produce the new human type.[100]

Nietzsche makes it readily apparent, however, that he believes most readers are unlikely to heed such a call. Any philosopher aspiring to greatness will ensure the exclusionary character of their work. A genuine philosophy, in Nietzsche's conception, is an undemocratic, inegalitarian philosophy, which does not seek to share insight with those who are unworthy but to impose itself upon them. The philosopher speaks philosophically (i.e. esoterically) only to those who have suitably cultivated the pathos of distance.

The question remaining is: Should we understand this as a sardonic and playful call for a blossoming of creative philosophies neither swayed by popular prejudice nor beholden to atavistic traditions (an exclusion of those reactionaries and moralists who impede the full flourishing of individuals' creative potential)? Or rather, as a serious, albeit fanciful, call for an aristocratic mode of philosophy actively opposed to principles of democracy and equality (an exclusion of the masses and their supposedly insipid, cowardly, uninventive ways of thinking)? And can the former – in its stringent individualism – be realized without some recourse, however unwitting, to the latter?

6

The mark of a true Christian
Søren Kierkegaard on solitude

For all their differences (and there are many – not least, in their attitude towards Christianity), Søren Kierkegaard and Friedrich Nietzsche are, in some respects, cognate thinkers. Both celebrate the sovereignty of the solitary individual, both are dismissive of all authorities and institutions hindering said individual's becoming, and both are derisive of modern culture and its dependence upon ossified traditions passed down over generations. More than anything else, though, both Kierkegaard and Nietzsche consider the exchange of ideas, reified in the form of abstract, objective knowledge, as an enervation of the subjective or perspectival forces from which these ideas originate. For these two thinkers, as Vattimo observes, 'truth is not an objective fact to be recognized in a cold and detached manner' but is 'rather a question of personal decision, of commitment'.[1] Kierkegaard maintains that the paradoxical *truth* of Christianity (the incarnation of an infinite God as a finite, mortal being) and the possibility of *faith* (the condition of receptivity for such truth) cannot simply be learnt from others; one instead encounters them in a personal, internal solitude, requiring a withdrawal into subjectivity, a turn inward. This truth is, in some sense, identical to this inward self-activity. 'Even if one were able to convert the whole system of faith into conceptual form', he declares, 'it does not follow that one has comprehended faith, comprehended how one entered into it or how it entered into one'.[2] A theologian rather than a philosopher, Kierkegaard views the very act of philosophizing, built upon conceptual and discursive reasoning, as ineffectual (and, in most cases, actively counterproductive) for articulating the truth of Christianity. Philosophers 'exist precisely in order to transform the preternatural into the ordinary and trivial'.[3] Every individual must instead encounter the profundity of this truth – which is, in the end, the only genuine, eternal truth – for themselves.

Given one cannot transmit truth as such by means of objective knowledge, Kierkegaard – taking up Socrates' maieutic method, at least in broad strokes – perceives his role as facilitating what he calls *indirect communication*, nudging the reader towards this truth without candidly spelling it out. His own writing reflects this approach: circuitous and elliptical in its style, dissimulating both its aims and its objects of critique, and often written under the guise of various pseudonymous personae, it inhibits any straightforward assimilation into an existing body of objective knowledge.[4] '*The objective accent*', he argues, '*falls on what is said, the subjective on how it is said*', to the extent that 'in the mouth of such and such a person what is true may become untrue' – to orient a reader or listener towards their own subjectivity, and thus towards the truth, requires an attentiveness to the way one communicates.[5]

Kierkegaard is, alongside Plato, the key exemplar of the mentality I have been trying to describe in this book: since every individual must come to the truth subjectively, it is impossible, in his estimation, to transmit the content of the faith that would lead them down this path integrally; any attempt to do so risks deluding one's audience into believing they are Christians when they are not. To avoid such a scenario, the thinker must gesture towards the truth indirectly, refraining from overt explicitation. It might seem peculiar, then, that Kierkegaard receives a somewhat restricted treatment in this chapter. The fact is his strategy of indirect communication is so manifest across his work – even if its particularities are still fervently debated – and such a central concern in the secondary literature that any extended precis I can give is likely to just be going over well-trodden ground.[6] Instead, I wish to make a fairly modest observation: namely, that Kierkegaard's unwavering focus upon the singular individual, and his polemical reproach of the crowd in all its forms, alongside his emphasis upon subjectivity and denigration of objective knowledge, finds its logical conclusion in his demand that Christian thinkers communicate indirectly, and that this becomes a mechanism by which he can denigrate and dismiss the religious proclivities of the masses – for while he stresses that he does not wish to judge who is or is not truly a Christian, this injunction nevertheless supplies a means for calling their faith into question.

A passionate interest

Kierkegaard's theology presages an increased fascination, beginning around the turn of the twentieth century, with the unrepresentable and incommunicable aspects of experience, and an increased hostility directed towards rationalized, conceptual thought.[7] Kierkegaard does not seek to describe experience nor to map out its conditions schematically but to *cultivate* a properly religious (i.e. Christian) attitude among the individuals his theology addresses – and as he makes abundantly clear, it addresses individuals *qua* individuals alone:

> the problem is not about the truth of Christianity but about the individual's relation to Christianity, that is, not about the indifferent individual's systematic eagerness to arrange the truths of Christianity in §§, but about the infinitely interested individual's concern regarding his own relation to such a teaching.[8]

Speculative philosophy, personified more than anything else by the Hegelian system in its concern with objectivity, methodical systematicity and its quest for absolute knowledge, remains wholly indifferent to the eternal happiness a genuinely religious perspective offers. 'If the truth is spirit, then the truth is a taking to heart, not an immediate and utterly unconcerned relationship of an immediate *Geist* to a sum of propositions.'[9]

Christianity 'wants to make the single individual eternally happy', but this demands a *passionate interest* in such happiness on the part of the individual – exactly the kind of heartfelt resolve and introspection which objectivity forecloses.[10] Indeed, 'Christianity does not lend itself to objective observation, precisely because it wants to intensify subjectivity to the utmost', the expression of this utmost exertion being an infinitely and unconditionally impassioned interest in one's eternal happiness, a happiness founded upon one's faith.[11] Such faith will never issue from the dispassionate, disinterested equanimity of objective scholarship. Those who pursue the latter may well think, in their careful, diligent deliberation, that they have touched upon some kind of elementary truth regarding Christian faith. But this can only be a delusive edifice, with little bearing upon Christianity as such. In fact, 'anyone who has an objective Christianity and none other is *eo ipso* a pagan, for Christianity is precisely an affair of spirit, of subjectivity and inwardness'.[12] Where objectivity, unreflectiveness, is directed outward, always striving towards a finite goal, the passion of subjective reflection moves infinitely inward, such that 'the truth is the subject's transformation in himself'.[13] The objective thinker always 'remains outside'.[14]

Kierkegaard wants to counteract the accumulation of knowledge constituting the usual desideratum of science and philosophy. His project is subtractive, stripping away the congealed layers of custom, convention and received wisdom deflecting the individual from any passionate interest in the infinite – that is, from any real *decision*.[15] Which also means stripping away the honorifics and appellations of authority that so often mark intellectual pursuits:

> Christianly, one does not proceed from the simple in order then to become interesting, witty, profound, a poet, a philosopher, etc. No, it is just the opposite; here one begins and then becomes more and more simple, arrives at the simple. This, in 'Christendom', is *Christianly* the movement of reflection; one does not reflect oneself into Christianity but reflects oneself out of something else and becomes more and more simple, a Christian.[16]

Such reflection does not, therefore, have any effect upon one's external status as a philosopher, or a theologian, or any other such social category, but only upon one's own internal faith. 'The first condition of all religiousness [is] to be an individual human being', Christianity firmly placing its emphasis upon the individual subject and their singular relationship with God, the corollary being that this relationship must, in order to ensure its singularity (and thus its authenticity), be grounded not in the shibboleths and dogma of religious authority (e.g. Scripture, the Church and inherited traditions) but in a decisive, personal and infinitely interested passion for one's eternal happiness.[17]

This subtractive standpoint with respect to Christianity, rejecting all worldly authority, demands self-denial from the individual, continually paring down one's self-conceit. And such self-denial can categorically 'be understood neither by a noisy assembly nor by an esteemed public, nor in a half-hour', for 'much fear and trembling, quiet solitude, are required, and for a long time'.[18] In stressing the benefits to subjective introspection afforded by solitude, Kierkegaard can be situated not only within a long lineage of Christian asceticism but also among a group of philosophers (e.g. Heraclitus, Plato and Nietzsche) who regard philosophizing as necessitating a separation from a public who are liable to lead one astray. Furthermore, one of the striking features he shares with these three thinkers is an intense scepticism not just towards the public in general but the public as it manifests in his age. Kierkegaard, in other words, is a seminal critic of mass culture.

A derision for the tendencies of the time in which he lives saturates Kierkegaard's work, beginning with his master's thesis, *On the Concept of Irony with Continual Reference to Socrates* (1841), wherein he complains that the era in which he lives, in its fascination with the momentous and extraordinary, 'does not permit one to stand still and to concentrate', an age which 'hates isolation' and 'lives for the idea of community'.[19] He worries that 'knowledge not only about the secrets of the human race but even about the secrets of God is offered for sale at such a bargain price today that it all looks very dubious', remarking that 'in our joy over the achievement in our age, we have forgotten that an achievement is worthless if it is not made one's own'.[20] Although he finds many other faults with contemporary attitudes, it is these two basic points that remain of most interest to me. A dichotomous contrast between the inward-looking solitude of the religious thinker and the outward-looking, communal-oriented knowledge acquisition of contemporary scholarship informs Kierkegaard's perspective. As he describes in *Fear and Trembling* (1843, published under the pseudonym Johannes de silentio), he lives in 'an age when passion has been abandoned in order to serve scholarship', when 'every lecturer, tutor, student, every outside and insider in philosophy does not stop at doubting everything but goes further', relentlessly pushing beyond the boundaries of faith.[21]

Kierkegaard juxtaposes a passionate interest in eternal happiness against the relentless forward march of knowledge characteristic of scholarship. Where the subjective thinker, who continually tasks themselves with becoming subjective (the individual's highest task), lives their life in accordance with an endless repetition (the realization of Christianity's eternal truth), one that 'lasts as long as life itself', the objective thinker 'goes further, and further, and scorning repetition's deepening in the one thought, never repeats himself but astonishes the age first by being systematician, then world-historian, then astronomer, veterinarian, waterworks inspector, geographer, etc.'.[22] Put another way, objectivity involves a never-ending accretion of facts wholly distinct from Christian repetition, the latter of which locates truth not in isolable, articulable propositions but in a ceaseless becoming, an exercise of *appropriation* by which individuals encounter and make this truth their own, and in turn make and remake themselves in view of the highest good of the infinite. Objective accretion will *never* touch upon the eternal truth decisive for one's eternal happiness but can only distract from it. And it is for this reason that Kierkegaard considers his age especially susceptible to objective delusions – after all, 'the more culture and knowledge, the greater the difficulty in becoming a Christian'.[23] The gradual accumulation of inherited viewpoints, passed down from generation to generation, inevitably leads to a more objective (and thus less passionately interested) society. Hence, he believes himself to live at a time devoid of genuine faith:

> if we were to express in a single sentence the difference between ancient times and our own, we should most likely have to say that in ancient times only a few knew the truth, while now everyone knows it, but that inwardness stands in the inverse relation.[24]

Modernity, overburdened by its accrued knowledge and single-mindedly focused upon the linear temporality in which this accrual takes place, has forgotten the meaning of inwardness, subjectivity, eternity and thus existence itself.

'So much is it a matter of course that the individual is a Christian, a believer, etc.', observes Kierkegaard, 'that it is foppery to make a fuss about it, or even a freak of fancy'.[25] His writings both presume and inveigh against a ubiquitous European Christendom, a society in which Christianity is an unquestioned norm, an unshakeable, insipid set of social conventions. An individual's Christianity, he complains, is, in his time, taken as given – a far cry from the painful risks the early converts and martyrs took in professing themselves to be Christians, having to sever ties with friends and family, and even jeopardizing their own lives. And this givenness nourishes the temptation to push further into fanciful speculation. As he stridently declares,

> it would [...] be a huge injustice should any later generation be able safely, that is objectively, to enter Christianity and thus secure a share in what the first who did so had bought in subjectivity's direst mortal danger and had acquired, subject to the same danger, through a long life.[26]

Instead of merely being a matter of course, a disinterested way of living in which one's status as a Christian stems from one's parents, in their responsibility for baptizing their children, and one's activities are conducted along the lines of socially conditioned formality, Christianity demands decisiveness, the kind of radical decision that one can only make in the zeal of the utmost subjective passion, faced with an awareness of one's eternal responsibility, acting for oneself alone.[27] In the need to peel away all these layers of conventional religious thinking, Kierkegaard's strategy of indirect communication comes to the fore.

The strategy of indirect communication

'How can you believe', Christ asks his accusers in the Gospel of John, 'when you accept glory from one another and do not seek the glory that comes from the one who alone is God?'.[28] Congruent with this, faith, as Kierkegaard conceives of it, is a gift bestowed upon us by God alone; we cannot acquire it from other mortal beings, however earnest their intentions. After all, relationships between finite individuals are, at least in broad strokes, easily understood and articulable, whereas the secret of our free, spiritual relationship to God, the basis of all such faith, remains inexpressible and singular. Thus, the fact that one individual cannot integrally transmit faith to another is not in itself a sign that these individuals lack receptivity to faith in their own right, nor does it show a contingent deficiency relating to their communicative capacities or the affordances of a particular language; entirely to the contrary, the paradoxical relationship between human finitude and the infinite, or eternal truth and the transitory time of existence, *is* the very object of faith, such that any attempt to render it communicable between individuals can only transform it into something redolent of, but not the same as faith as such:

> Christianity has proclaimed itself as the eternal, essential truth that has come about in time; it has proclaimed itself as *the paradox* and has demanded the inwardness of faith in respect of what is a stumbling-block to the Jews and foolishness to the Greeks, and to the understanding the absurd.[29]

Christianity is by nature paradoxical, founded as it is upon the absurd premise that God was incarnated as a mortal being, indistinguishable from any other such being, at a particular historical moment, and thus, that the eternal truth has come to be within time. And in this paradox, which repels all objective enquiry, the inwardness of faith finds its confirmation.

Christianity does not want to be understood. Trying to understand it will never, under any circumstances, allow one to penetrate its truth. It proffers a secret one does not need to understand, and which, in fact, one should not make pretences to understanding. A secret in which one must simply and purely have faith. To become receptive to such faith, all one needs to understand is that it cannot be understood. And therefore, one cannot convert this secret into the kind of discursive reasoning amenable to communication in its typical philosophical, theological, scientific or vernacular modalities. Christianity, as the sole source of truth, abhors the 'untruth that has but one aim and aspiration, to disseminate'.[30] It is on this basis, caught between two seemingly conflicting desiderata – the need to evangelize, to spread the good news of Christianity on the one hand, and the need to avoid falling into any kind of straightforward dissemination that would lead his audience astray – that Kierkegaard develops his quite sophisticated theory of communication, premised upon the distinction between direct and indirect communication.[31]

Direct communication, the ordinary, everyday mode of transmitting information, the mode proper to objective thinking, begins, as Kierkegaard would have it, 'with individuals, a few readers, and the task or the movement is to gather a large number, to acquire an abstraction: the public'.[32] It is a form of mass communication, tailored to an imagined audience in which concrete individuals are homogenized and generalized into a crowd. Even when speaking one-to-one, direct communication does not recognize its interlocutors' individual existence – their singularity – treating them instead as just one among many others. It makes no attempt to help them look inward, to grapple with the fundamental decisions defining their existence. It does not arouse fear and trembling. It delivers an accessible, agreeable message, premised upon knowledge and understanding, applicable to all. Modern Christianity exemplifies such a mentality: it relies upon the strength of authority of the Church, Scripture, the state and so forth in order to foster belief; it broadcasts its message to the broadest possible audience, constituting an imagined communion of believers; and, it distils this message down to a set of bland, digestible platitudes, and then delivers it in a propositional form that presumes both its objective veracity and the inevitability that all will accept it as such.

An immediate mode of address, direct communication allows people to share the details of their immediate existence. It takes for granted a certitude that might be suitable for the banalities of everyday conversation but has no place when discussing the endless becoming which religious fidelity comprises. It presupposes a simple model of shared understanding, whereby one interlocutor's acknowledgement of a message suffices to signal both their comprehension and agreement. There is no consideration of the *form* the communication takes – that is, of the relation between the author or speaker and the ideas that they put forward – but only of the words used to *express* these ideas. And it expects these ideas can be learnt and repeated by rote, without the recipient having any experience of what they signify. At bottom, direct communication neglects the act of appropriation, in which this recipient must incorporate what they have heard or read into the particularities of their own life as an individual, using it to reflect upon and shape their subjective existence, rather than treating it as a brute fact or foregone conclusion applicable to all. This direct approach, as widespread as it might be, is, in Kierkegaard's estimation, at best fruitless, and in most cases, actively counterproductive when it comes to religious matters.

'Just as important as the truth, and the more important of the two', Kierkegaard explains, 'is the manner in which the truth is accepted, and it would help only very little if one got millions to accept the truth if they were translated by their very manner of acceptance into untruth.'[33] One can easily fool oneself into believing that an audience's willingness to listen, applause and polite displays of admiration somehow indicate their acceptance of the truth one has tried (and failed) to disseminate; likewise, one can easily lead an audience away from the truth (or perhaps teach them to contrive a false outward impression of possessing this truth) by resorting to various tricks of persuasion or appeals to sympathy, kindness, popular biases and so on, however well-intentioned their use might be. 'There is no direct or immediate transition to Christianity', and no 'rhetorical push' is ever going to give one an entry point into genuine religious experience.[34] No direct communication will ever be able to direct its audience inward, to turn them towards the fundamental questions of their own existence (and thus their eternal happiness), not as a social being but as a solitary, unique individual. Hence Kierkegaard's espousal of an indirect communication via which he hopes to 'shake off "the crowd" in order to get hold of "the single individual".[35] After all, he asserts, 'there is in a *religious sense* no public but only individuals, because the religious is earnestness, and earnestness is: the single individual' – not one particular individual but every human being, unconditionally, in their individuality.[36] Sociality and community have no purchase upon the inwardness of one's self-activity, for in the latter nothing is shared out or held in common; to orient oneself passionately towards the prospect of one's eternal happiness is to work towards the plenitude of an irreducible, entirely self-possessed individuality.

Communicating indirectly, in conformity with subjective thinking, involves foregoing the hierarchy of authority underpinning the direct route, according to which the teacher or author is presumed to possess knowledge (or in some cases, the awareness that they do not possess certain knowledge) that they must impart to the student or reader.[37] Further, one must keep in mind that truth can only be found by turning inward, never through appeal to objective externalities. This inwardness or appropriation does not occur in a single act but is repeated in an endless becoming: to find the truth is to remake oneself continually in conformity with such a principle. An indirect communication does not aim to be passively received but to spark something within the recipient, to encourage such an appropriation. Most importantly, one must avoid starting from the presumption that one is already a good Christian – and one must certainly not loudly declare confidence in one's own Christianity. The point of such an approach is not to compel or coerce one's audience to adopt a specific belief or conviction (which would travesty their subjective individuality) but to treat them as an individual, to release them from the fetters of objective thinking and their ingrained deference to authority, to make them aware of their own inner subjectivity, and thus open the possibility of genuinely free decision.

Pivotal to all of this is what Kierkegaard refers to as *double reflection*, in which, as already alluded to earlier, the thinker who seeks to free another individual in this manner reflects not only upon their message's *expression* (the first stage of reflection) but also its *form*, which concerns 'the relation between the matter to be imparted and the imparter, and reflects the imparter's own relation to the idea' (the second stage of reflection).[38] This double reflection is key to the fruitful contrivance of indirect communication, designed to prevent the straightforward assimilation of ideas and to encourage the process of appropriation within the reader or listener. It is guided by the principle that 'subjectivities must be kept devoutly apart from one another, and not allowed to run together and coagulate into objectivity', resisting the temptation to render one's utterances too comfortably assimilable.[39] At the heart of Christianity lies a secret: namely, the nature of a person's relationship to God:

> ordinary communication, objective thinking, has no secrets; it is only with doubly reflected subjective thinking that secrets arise, i.e., all of its essential content is essentially secrecy because it cannot be imparted directly. The fact that the knowledge in question is not to be said directly, because the essential thing with the knowledge is the appropriation, makes it a secret for everyone who is not in the same way doubly reflected within himself. But the fact that this is the essential form of such truth makes it impossible to express it in any other way. So anyone wanting to impart it directly is dull-witted; and if another person asks him to do so, he too is dull-witted.[40]

Again, this secrecy – and its concomitant incommunicability by all direct means – is not accessory to its truth but constitutes the latter's essential form.

As already noted, appropriation is not a single act, valid once and for all, but a perpetually repeated task, a lifelong becoming. Human existence is an endless coming-to-be, and 'the genuinely existing subjective thinker simulates this existence of his constantly in his thinking and invests all his thinking in becoming'.[41] Subjective thought does not depend upon universal concepts and necessary, *a priori* conditions as objective thought does; instead, it is always being reshaped by the thinker, attuned to the particularities of their own existence in a persistently redoubled self-reflection.[42] Likewise, its becoming does not have a fixed goal in mind, in the sense of a finite and plausible reachable end-point; rather, the thinker strives infinitely, and thus comes to be infinitely. The same goes for style, Kierkegaard suggests, for 'the only writer who really has style is the one who never has anything finished, but "troubles the waters of language" every time he begins'. Hence why indirect communication is always, in part, an artistic endeavour: it can never be mindless or conventional but must always seek to upturn established ways of expressing oneself.

The desire for 'an authorship whose every word must be watched and every sentence undergo double reflection' of course becomes the point of departure for Kierkegaard's own writing, which is renowned for its laboured, oblique articulation of its subject matter, and the convoluted dialogue that takes place between his various conflictual pseudonymous personae.[43] Curiously though, this authorship, like all indirect communication, turns out to be only a microcosm of a much greater authorship: viz. that of God himself. After all, 'no anonymous author is able to hide himself more cunningly, no maieutic artist able to avoid the direct relation more painstakingly than God'.[44] God is in all his creations, but only indirectly – his work is directly present, but he himself is not. The book of nature may well be legible in the realm of objective scholarship, but proof of God's authorship remains elusive. When one has properly turned inward, however, one starts to see God everywhere. And in this way, one discovers that a genuine relationship with God can only ever be indirect.

God dissimulates his presence within nature in order to prevent any misleading suggestion of a possible direct relationship between himself and human beings. He forces us to find him for ourselves, by looking within ourselves:

> the spiritual relationship to God in truth, i.e. inwardness, is first made possible precisely by the breakthrough of inwardness that corresponds to the divine artfulness that God has nothing, absolutely nothing about him that is striking; indeed, far from being conspicuous, he is invisible, so that one would never dream he was there, although his invisibility is in turn his omnipresence.[45]

God's inscrutability in nature finds its counterpart in the outward imperceptibility of genuine Christian faith. In a manoeuvre not dissimilar to that deployed by Fichte vis-à-vis freedom, Kierkegaard forecloses the possibility of *ever* objectively determining whether someone else is truly a Christian (or just displaying the socially acceptable embellishments of a nominally Christian life), but at the same time, deploys this foreclosure as a mechanism for calling others' Christianity into question.

Identifying the authentic Christian

Kierkegaard is, by his own description, exclusively a religious thinker, whose authorship bears upon Christianity and the question of becoming a Christian. He does not try to sublate religious thought into a greater systematic unity in the manner of the German idealists; on the contrary, he takes no interest in any aspect of knowledge that will not help himself or others find the path towards a genuine Christianity. And a central aspect of this project is his taking 'direct and indirect polemical aim at that enormous illusion, Christendom, or the illusion that in such a country all are Christians of sorts'.[46] As already observed, Kierkegaard takes exception to the *default status* of Christianity in his time, its nationwide (and indeed, continent-wide) ubiquity, which ensures that the public never call their own faith into question:

> What does it mean, after all, that all these thousands and thousands as a matter of course call themselves Christians! These many, many people, of whom by far the great majority, according to everything that can be discerned, have their lives in entirely different categories, something one can ascertain by the simplest observation! People who perhaps never once go to church, never think about God, never name his name except when they curse! People to whom it has never occurred that their lives should have some duty to God, people who either maintain that a certain civil impunity is the highest or do not find even this to be entirely necessary! Yet all these people, even those who insist that there is no God, they all are Christians, call themselves Christians, are recognized as Christians by the state, are buried as Christians by the Church, are discharged as Christians to eternity![47]

This fierce attack upon the very concept of Christendom goes hand in hand with his equally polemical attack upon any numerical agglomeration of human beings: the crowd, the public and so on. More specifically, he finds it appalling that matters of truth could be treated as settled by dint of number of adherents, transforming truth into a mere question of agreement or an argument from authority. The 'tyranny of the numerical', as he puts it, must be counterposed against the single individual, for in a religious sense there is nothing other than such an individual.[48] Truth has no meaning outside a personal interest in the infinite. It belongs to the single individual, and to them alone. And all properly religious communication must therefore also be personal, not only in the sense that truth must relate to the individual in their singularity but also in that it 'can neither be communicated nor be received without being, as it were, under the eyes of God, without the help of God, without God's being a participant, the middle term' – exactly the kind of *personal* interchange the *im*personal relationships fostered by the crowd or public preclude.[49] It is not just that truth should not be assessed numerically, but that such agglomerations actively impede this kind of personal relationship with God. Whereas faith demands individual responsibility in the face of the absurd – the radical freedom of decision – the crowd disperses such responsibility among a multitude of individuals, resulting in thoughtlessness and impenitence.

The crowd, in Kierkegaard's eyes, is synonymous with untruth. It is a denial of God. In fact, he argues, 'even if [. . .] all individuals who, separately, secretly possessed the truth were to come together in a crowd (in such a way, however, that "the crowd" acquired any *deciding*, voting, noisy, loud significance), untruth would promptly be present there'.[50] Of course, such a gathering might perform a useful function in a political or cultural context, but this is of no interest to Kierkegaard, for it does not pertain to religious matters. Crowds pursue only mundane, worldly goals. They look outward, not inward. One's faith, premised as it is upon kinship with divinity, will never be bolstered by kinship with other human beings: 'everyone should be careful about becoming involved with "the others", essentially should speak only with God and with himself'.[51] And while the crowd is not a new phenomenon, Kierkegaard regards the press, the exemplar of abstract, direct, impersonal communication, as exacerbating its worst proclivities:

> in our day, when that which is the secret of evil has become wisdom – namely, that one is not to ask about the communicator but only about the communication, only about 'what', about the objective – in our day what does it mean to be an author? It means, often even when he is identified, to be an *x*, an impersonal something that, by means of printing, addresses itself abstractly to thousands upon thousands but itself is unseen, unknown, living as secretly, as anonymously, as impersonally as possible, presumably so that the contrast between the enormous means of communication and being an individual human being does not become obvious and glaring.[52]

The press, as an almost unprecedented form of mass media, depersonalizes, and thus de*moral*izes, both its authors and the audience they address, providing an anonymity that can only work to diminish individual responsibility.

There is something quite liberating about Kierkegaard's iconoclastic take on Christian faith: censuring outward displays of religious devotion, and seeking to escape the rigid pieties and institutionalized instruments of obedience that have shaped European consciousness ever since Christianity was first elevated to the status of a state religion, he repositions religiousness (which he connects solely to Christianity) as something belonging to ourselves alone, involving no external compulsion but only an inner striving. He constructs his project with the exigency of respecting all others' individuality, and not reducing them to mere constituents of a larger congregation. To love one's neighbour is to honour 'every individual human being, unconditionally every human being', and thus to express 'human equality unconditionally'.[53]

At the same time though, the overall effect of Kierkegaard's project, despite its lofty aspirations towards such equality, is to dismiss the faith of almost all his contemporaries, ring-fencing Christian faith as a rarefied mode of introspection. Of course, Kierkegaard himself claims he is attempting no such thing:

> I certainly do have faith in the rightness of my thought despite the whole world, but next to that the last thing I would surrender is my faith in individual human beings. And this is my faith, that however much confusion and evil and contemptibleness there can be in human beings as soon as they become the irresponsible and unrepentant 'public', 'crowd', etc. – there is just as much truth and goodness and lovableness in them when one can get them as single individuals. Oh, to what degree human beings would become – human and lovable beings – if they would become single individuals before God![54]

Since God created man in his own image, every human being, regardless of their intellectual capacities, is capable of becoming a genuinely Christian, subjective thinker. Stressing that most purported Christians are not *actually* Christians does not lead by necessity to the conclusion that these people, as misled or deluded as they might be, do not possess the capacity to *become* Christians.

Notwithstanding such assurances though, it is apparent throughout his work that even if Kierkegaard is not trying to pass judgement upon individuals themselves, his critiques of mass culture amount to the same thing, presenting the image of a decadent, injudicious age devoid of responsibility and dispossessed of an authentic inner life. Part of this is a product of his polemical tone, which seeks to both set forth an image of an ideal Christian existence others might, in moments of quiet solitude, compare against their own lives, and to provoke them, aggressively shaking them out of their unquestioned assumptions and entrenched velleities, pushing them towards decision. But part of it is also his seemingly sincere contempt for what he views as the banality of *everyday* existence: the fact that, as he sees it, 'habit and routine and want of passion, and affectation, and gossiping with neighbours next door and opposite little by little ruin most people so that they become thoughtless – and base their eternal happiness on one thing and then another and then something else', living lives bereft of passion.[55] Despite any of his protestations, claiming his polemic 'does not lean toward any decision in the external, in the secular world', there is undoubtedly still a profane, sublunary politics at work within his writings, decrying objective truth claims, institutional authority, inherited tradition, outward affectation and prioritization of one's social existence, and instead valorizing the solitary individual, whose freedom is directed only inward, towards themselves.[56]

Indirect communication consists in 'making it difficult for people to become Christian by putting them off', rendering it insusceptible to being straightforwardly propagated via social dissemination.[57] It calls his audience's attention to the arduous and unremitting task becoming a Christian involves, at the risk of making it thoroughly unappealing. In fact, it makes it so difficult 'that the number of Christians among the cultivated in Christendom may not be very large'.[58] So the imperative, for the authentically religious thinker, of communicating indirectly is, from the outset, a mechanism of exclusion, for even if the difficulty it fosters is not meant to preclude any particular individual taking part in this task, it does fulfil a gatekeeping function, demanding both a certain comportment from those who seek to impart the truth of Christianity and a specific type of reflection from those who hope to receive said truth. And this gatekeeping is achieved precisely by rendering this truth incommunicable: posited as paradoxical, an absurdity from the perspective of objective cognition, Kierkegaard strips the Christian message of its semantic content, such that its form of communication *is* effectively its message. This message's truth value is indexed to the communicative traits and foibles of a particular author or speaker, and ultimately to a personal relationship mediated by God, to the extent that a truth can be converted into untruth merely based upon the context and manner in which someone puts it forward.

Even more significantly though, Kierkegaard's articulation of the strategy of indirect communication, as ambiguous as it might often be, reveals the point at which an individual's inner life bleeds into their social existence, complicating his strict delineation between a subjective interiority and objective exteriority. For while this divide is meant to ensure that others cannot question one's faith on the basis of objective criteria, remaining wholly personal, the importance Kierkegaard places upon the manner in which thinkers communicate their faith just creates a new criterion, within the context of sociality, by which the overt manifestation of one's faith can be assessed. Not only does the prospect that an individual's faith might be nothing more than an affectation or ingrained custom constantly hang over them – Kierkegaard himself is certainly more than willing to judge vast swathes of the population in these terms – but any propensity for conversation, gossip, proselytization or any other sort of 'direct' communication regarding religious matters becomes a telltale sign of their inauthentic faith. For anyone who would speak of faith in such a manner, or who would attempt to disseminate the Christian message, as they understand it, to a wide audience clearly does not grasp it in the first place. Opacity becomes the marker of the true Christian, and transparency that of the untruths of Christendom.

7

Aspiring to a higher good
Speaking of affliction with Simone Weil

In the prior chapters of this book, I have examined a series of philosophers who, with diverse means and motivations, have sought to circumscribe the boundaries of philosophizing by upholding a specifically philosophical manner of speaking. Need the latter function as a mechanism of exclusion though? In Chapters 7 and 8, I wish to place two philosophers side by side, in what is likely to be seen as a somewhat odd pairing. After all, even if they might share certain reference points, Simone Weil and Michel Foucault would rarely be viewed as cognate thinkers. In the examination of two specific texts, however – viz. Weil's 'Human Personality' and Foucault's *History of Madness* – the former a short polemical essay, and the latter a sprawling, sometimes ponderous tome of historical research, we can detect, *mutatis mutandas*, an unmistakable affinity, inasmuch as both concern themselves with the ways in which the pained cries of the oppressed have been silenced, and the methods by which we might make these cries audible without speaking for them. In other words, both deny the possibility of integrally transmitting the words of such groups via institutional, juridical or pathological discourses, and offer alternative approaches whereby the philosopher might allow them to be heard.[1] The question, however, is whether these approaches really do signify an inclusive procedure distinct from those covered elsewhere in this book, or whether they merely provide the opportunity for the philosopher to speak in the name of those hitherto positioned as external to the philosophical enterprise proper.

Like Kierkegaard before her, Weil is suspicious of the institutions of religious orthodoxy, viewing them as inimical to the human individual's spiritual life.[2] Both see the prospect of salvation as lying in an ascetic relationship to divinity – in the former, a passionate *interest* oriented wholly inward; in the latter, an *attention* that fixes its gaze upon higher, impersonal principles – that cannot just be taught (as the church attempts to do) but must be enacted as a fundamental part of one's being, and which has no correlation with abstract, objectified conceptualizations of the individual or the collective. But Weil's suspicions extend far beyond just religious institutions: occupied as she is with a number of pressing political concerns, she is equally dubious when it comes to nationalism, political partisanship, trade unions and even modern science. And, writing in large part during the ravages of the Second World War, she is especially damning about those who glorify war.[3]

One of the noteworthy features of Weil's philosophy (which is, by any standard, idiosyncratic) is her view of language as something that, in its use and misuse, has profound consequences – and in some cases, literal human costs. In her 1939 essay, 'The Power of Words', an anti-war tract, she expounds in disquietingly grisly detail upon the devastating effects that careless deployment of words – and more specifically, the elevation of vague abstractions to the status of proper nouns – can have:

> when empty words are given capital letters, then, on the slightest pretext, men will begin shedding blood for them and piling up ruin in their name, without effectively grasping anything to which they refer, since what they refer to can never have any reality, for the simple reason that they mean nothing.[4]

For instance, Weil argues, the word *nation* and all its derivations, in their contemporary acceptation, are devoid of meaning. 'Their only content is millions of corpses, and orphans, and disabled men, and tears and despair.'[5] As evoked in the original French title of this essay (*Ne recommençons pas la guerre de Troie*), she worries that the world is about to be embroiled in another Trojan War – which is to say, a long-drawn-out, pointless conflict fought in the name of an empty, albeit personified ideal:

> the Greeks and Trojans massacred one another for ten years on account of Helen. Not one of them except the dilettante warrior Paris cared two straws about her; all of them agreed in wishing she had never been born. The person of Helen was so obviously out of scale with this gigantic struggle that in the eyes of all she was no more than the symbol of what was really at stake; but the real issue was never defined by anyone, nor could it be, because it did not exist.[6]

In the *Iliad*, the Achaeans wage war against the city of Troy for the sake of a woman whose beauty means nothing to any of the actual soldiers involved and cannot measure up to the inordinate violence taking place; in her time, Weil worries, wars are being fought over similarly abstract and meaningless nouns. For her contemporaries, 'the role of Helen is played by words with capital letters'.[7]

At a time when superstition is no longer afforded a rightful place within thought, Weil is convinced that it has taken its revenge under the guise of abstract verbiage: fixed and isolated signifiers that cannot do justice to the concrete facts of our lives, the latter of which we experience as 'changing, varying realities, subject to the casual play of external necessities, and modifying themselves according to specific conditions within specific limits'.[8] Such vacuous words 'stupefy the mind; they not only make men willing to die but, infinitely worse, they make them forget the value of life'.[9] They render the citizenry compliant, making problems in need of solutions seem like inevitabilities that must be endured.[10] Hence the need, as Weil would have it, to cleanse them from social and political life, analysing and clarifying the words that we use and jettisoning those that turn out to be meaningless. For 'when a word is properly defined it loses its capital letter and can no longer serve either as a banner or as a hostile slogan; it becomes simply a sign' with a clear referent and concrete, pragmatic usage.[11] This process of analysis, clarification and expurgation, 'strange though it may appear, might be a way of saving human lives'.[12] Accordingly, as I will explore in this chapter, Weil places her hopes in a manner of speech aspiring towards the higher ideas of justice, truth and beauty. 'With three such beautiful words', Weil declares, 'we have no need to look for any others'.[13]

The person and the human being

This theme of the far-reaching power of language is also of chief importance in 'Human Personality', an essay written about three years later, in the final months of her life. In this work, Weil takes aim at the philosophical school of Personalism (principally the version espoused by Jacques Maritain) and its centring of the 'human person', and her critique hinges upon what she perceives as an endemic abuse of language within this school.[14] 'Something is amiss', Weil declares, 'with the vocabulary of the modern trend of thought known as Personalism'.[15] And it all comes down to an obsession with this very word 'person', which she decries as a mere empty abstraction with no bearing upon the fundamental ideas with which she is concerned: justice, truth, beauty and above all, the *sacred*. To speak of oneself or others as persons, or of the human person as such, is to efface all these ideas, these higher goals:

> There is something sacred in every man, but it is not his person. Nor is it the human person. It is this man; no more and no less. [. . .] It is neither his person,

nor the human personality in him, which is sacred to me. It is he. The whole of him. The arms, the eyes, the thoughts, everything.[16]

The very notion of the human person, suggests Weil, is premised upon a meaningless proper noun, not only incapable of being defined in words (a characteristic applicable to many nevertheless clear ideas) but of being conceived by the mind. A concept alien to the everything (*tout*) of all human beings, their integrity and wholeness. Setting up 'as a standard of public morality a notion which can neither be defined nor conceived', Personalism constitutes just another extension of the untenable discourse of 'rights' codified in the wake of the French Revolution.[17] This discourse does not touch upon justice; rather, it 'is linked with the notion of distribution, exchange, quantity', agitating for one's rights having 'something of a commercial character, essentially evocative of legal claims and arguments'.[18] It reduces the resolution of social conflict to 'a shrill nagging of claims and counter-claims' – jealous and spiteful disputes without the possibility of genuine charity or reconciliation.[19]

Justice, by contrast, deals with an expectation – namely, the 'profound and childlike and unchanging expectation of good in the heart' – that has no counterpart in the discourse of rights.[20] It deals, in short, with the *sacred*. As Weil describes it,

> at the bottom of the heart of every human being, from earliest infancy until the tomb, there is something that goes on indomitably expecting, in the teeth of all experience of crimes committed, suffered, and witnessed, that good and not evil will be done to him. It is this above all that is sacred in every human being.

Real injustice, which we must distinguish from a mere infringement of rights, evokes a heartfelt cry of protest – a cry born of surprise or incomprehension at the reason for one's suffering. And such a cry of sorrowful surprise, an appeal to the sacred within oneself, is almost inevitably inarticulate or even mute. Finding words to express this violation is difficult, if not impossible. Sometimes, in those who have suffered too much (e.g. slaves), the capacity to elicit such a cry has been permanently deadened, sinking into 'a state of dumb and ceaseless lamentation'.[21] In others, this capacity remains, but scarcely expresses its cries in coherent language. And in any case, those who are most likely to endure such suffering are often the least likely to be 'trained in the art of speech', giving them little hope of finding redress within a judicial system privileging recitation of witty retorts and trite formulas.[22] Even those who represent them, as articulate as they might be, typically cannot translate the affliction into suitable words, because either 'they are far removed from it by the circumstances of their life' or 'they put it at a distance at the first possible moment'.[23]

The capacity for expression is monopolized by the privileged, and for this reason, Weil thinks commonplace appeals to freedom of speech or expression fundamentally miss the point:

> Apart from intelligence, the only human faculty truly interested in public freedom of expression is that part of the heart which cries out against evil. But as it cannot express itself, freedom is of little use to it. What is first needed is a system of public education capable of providing it, so far as possible, with means of expression; and next, a regime in which the public expression of opinions is characterized not so much by freedom as by an atmosphere of attentive silence in which this faint and faltering cry can make itself heard; and finally, a system of institutions is needed which will, so far as possible, put power into the hands of men who are able and willing to hear and understand it.[24]

Rather than construing these anguished cries as muddled, incoherent ramblings – mere noise – as politicians and judges usually do, we need to foster an environment in which those afflicted by evil are able to articulate the truth of their pain (or able to find others, endowed with great genius, who can hypotypotically articulate it for them), and those in power are willing to listen to these cries, as muffled as they might be. Crucial in this passage is the qualifier 'so far as possible': Weil's enjoinment in no way entails the possibility that such remonstrances will ever be fully articulable in the way rights claims might be. Her equation between justice and the sacred ensures that the former always will, in some fashion, transcend expression.

Just as pivotal is Weil's claim that true justice is never personal, but *impersonal*. The inconsolable cry in question is not personal, it does not spring from injury to the person (that chimerical proper noun to which rights apply), but from an injustice touching upon the depths of the soul. 'It is always, in the last of men as in Christ himself, an impersonal protest.'[25] The sacred is impersonal, and the impersonal sacred. The sacred elements of truth in science, beauty in art and justice in law – elements of perfection, devoid of sin and error – all dwell in this impersonal and anonymous realm. In a decidedly mystical register, Weil strives to reach a truth beyond both the individual person and the aggregates within which they come to be grouped: 'the whole effort of the mystic has always been to become such that there is no part left in his soul to say "I". But the part of the soul which says "We" is infinitely more dangerous still.'[26]

Indeed, much like Kierkegaard, Weil is suspicious of collectivity, which she views – invoking Plato's image of the 'Great Beast' – as a dangerous abstraction, a fiction, furnishing only a false simulacrum of the sacred (hence her misgivings regarding Personalism, since it depends upon a collective *human person* or *personality*).[27] The attribution of sacrality to the collective, she avers, is nothing other than idolatry. Whereas the human person is always understood to be subordinate to the collective, and liable to be sacrificed to the latter, Weil values a solitude incompatible with social attachment. 'Impersonality', she explains, 'is only reached by the practice of a form of *attention* which is rare in itself and impossible except in solitude; and not only physical but mental solitude'.[28] She deploys the concept of attention, 'the creative faculty in man', frequently in her writings, designating a religious mode of comportment (the best-known example being prayer) whereby one turns away from the 'I' in order to reorient oneself towards an inconceivable truth – namely, the good.[29] To comport oneself in this manner requires a sedulous commitment in the face of intense intellectual resistance, the reward for which is the possibility of reaching those higher, pure values – truth, beauty and justice – belonging to the realm of the impersonal alone. To raise oneself above the personal, to install oneself in this realm of impersonal goodness, is to find within one's soul that which can 'bring to bear without any outside help, against any collectivity, a small but real force'.[30]

The impersonal, as much as it emerges from conditions of solitude, has nothing to do with individualism – it is not at all about cutting oneself irrevocably off from others. Everyone who comes in contact with the realm of impersonality 'is charged with a responsibility towards all human beings; to safeguard, not their persons, but whatever frail potentialities are hidden within them for passing over to the impersonal'.[31] Those who have grasped this responsibility, who have discovered that attention which permits them to transcend the personal, are in turn those most capable of understanding appeals to 'respect the sacredness of the human being' (as opposed to the human person), and it is to them that such appeals must be addressed.[32] 'This intense, pure, disinterested, gratuitous, generous attention is love.'[33] Hence the need to foster opportunities for attention within the collective, encouraging the maturation of that impersonal element harboured within the soul:

> this means, on the one hand, that for every person there should be enough room, enough freedom to plan the use of one's time, the opportunity to reach ever higher levels of attention, some solitude, some silence. At the same time

the person needs warmth, lest it be driven by distress to submerge itself in the collective.[34]

Affliction cannot be spoken of directly, in such a manner that everyone, regardless of their circumstances, is going to comprehend its implications. 'The thought of affliction', as Blanchot writes, 'is precisely the thought of that which cannot let itself be thought. Affliction is an "enigma". It is of the same nature as physical suffering, from which it is inseparable'.[35] It cannot be transmitted integrally: even though there are certainly ways of improving its articulation, better phrasing will never be a substitute for genuine understanding. Thus, in order to speak truly of justice – or more precisely, to speak in a manner that might do justice to others who are suffering – we must instead cultivate an environment in which the afflicted can voice their grievances, however muted or incoherent they might seem, and others can listen to and recognize these cries, with all the reciprocal responsibility this implies.

Higher ideas

Like all the other philosophers covered so far in this book, Weil identifies a higher principle – in her case, the good, manifesting as beauty, justice and truth depending on the circumstances at hand – that one cannot speak of and understand straightforwardly, as one might speak of democracy, rights or the human person. A principle which demands a specific manner of both speaking and listening. What stands out about Weil's take on this theme, however, in spite of the obvious Platonic resonances of such an approach (and her attendant fear of demagoguery), is that her goal is not so much to help raise her audience above the pandaemonium of everyday speech but to clear away the ossified layers of bureaucratic and legalistic discourse that have enveloped the human being in order to hear the almost imperceptible voice of the other.

'There is a natural alliance between truth and affliction', Weil explains, 'because both of them are mute suppliants, eternally condemned to stand speechless in our presence'.[36] Truth sits outside language, the latter concerning itself only with opinions. Language offers varying degrees of value: when vague or imprecise, as we already know, it is at best useless, and at worst actively detrimental to the lives of those it influences; when used with clarity, precision and rigour, however, and addressed to those capable of apprehending it adequately, it can be quite rich in significative content. Yet 'this relative wealth is abject poverty compared with the perfection which alone is desirable'.[37] Language is a prison that entraps the mind, enclosing the latter within a sphere of mere opinion, shrouding from it all those thoughts, however clear and rigorous they might be, that one cannot formulate in words.[38] In order to orient ourselves towards the truth, we must escape this prison, learning to grasp the inexpressible. And we can only do this via a fundamental transformation of our situation. 'The only way into truth is through one's own annihilation; through dwelling a long time in a state of extreme and total humiliation.'[39]

Attention demands a radical humility, an experience of one's non-being, an endurance of the void – a negation of the self by which one passes over into truth. An openness to the possibility, not just that one might also face profound suffering and affliction but that one might at any moment, due to circumstances outside of one's control, lose *everything*.[40] The wholeness or integrity of the human being is confirmed by the possibility of this total loss, this deprivation of one's own being. Human thought recoils from the reality of affliction, again and again proving itself incapable of acknowledging the truth of human suffering, and instead merely pitying those afflicted, observing their condition at a distance. The almost implacable tendency is to intellectualize suffering, and thus to rationalize it, explaining the inexplicable. To listen to those whose souls are overwhelmed and undermined by affliction, one must put oneself in their place, which is effectively to 'annihilate oneself'.[41] Hence why cries of the afflicted are so seldom heard. The comportment needed to break through this intellectual resistance, to reach a state of attention, involves a certain kind of ascesis, but it bears little resemblance to the spiritual exercises of prior philosophers, even those detailed by Plato. Attention is not *work*. It is not a product of the will and certainly not of dogged activity, however well-meaning it might be; rather, it comes from the 'supernatural working of grace'.[42] The only movement of the soul not governed by natural laws, grace enters the void that it itself hollows out.

Accordingly, to speak in a manner that does justice to affliction, we need more than just an environment in which such injuries can be articulated and made audible (as important as this is); we also need a language that gestures away from the baseness of the collective and towards higher principles – towards the supernatural. One way to do this is through beauty, which, as we already know, is a direct correlate of justice. In great works of genius (Weil points towards ancient poets and playwrights such as Homer, Aeschylus and Sophocles, modern writers like Shakespeare, Molière, Racine and Villon, and above all the four Evangelists' passion narratives), beauty's radiance 'illumines affliction with the light of the spirit of justice and love', a light through which it offers human thought some meagre opportunity to report the truth of affliction.⁴³ Via the medium of beauty, it becomes possible to evoke something language itself could never capture:

> it sometimes happens that a fragment of inexpressible truth is reflected in words which, although they cannot hold the truth that inspired them, have nevertheless so perfect a formal correspondence with it that every mind seeking that truth finds support in them.⁴⁴

Thanks to the formal parity between beauty, justice and truth, the attention beautiful poetry or prose can engender, pointing the reader or listener towards the inexpressible inspirations of these works, can also help direct their attention towards these other higher principles without travestying them through the use of crude descriptors.⁴⁵ Such a use of beauty holds out the possibility of a universal communicability, albeit still in purely formal terms. For we all possess something of the sacred within ourselves, we all long deep within our hearts for absolute goodness, and we all have the ability (however dormant) to direct our attention beyond our own worldly being. As a consequence, it is always the case that certain words, in certain contexts, when deployed by great writers, can transcend the shared acceptations of the collective (which offer nothing more than the objectified dregs of actual thought) and illuminate aspects of the good in ways that remain valid for all of us, and yet will never be contained within these words themselves.

A different way of speaking

Recourse to beauty in the service of truth and justice, however, is still likely inaccessible to those who suffer the most from said affliction. For them, Weil encourages a different application of language, one that speaks of nothing other than the good. 'If one wishes to efficaciously arm the afflicted', she propounds, 'one must put into their mouths [*mettre dans leur bouche*] only those words whose rightful abode is in heaven, beyond heaven, in the other world.'⁴⁶ Abandoning the hazy imprecision of political language, the afflicted must confine themselves to 'those words and phrases which always, everywhere, in all circumstances express only the good'.⁴⁷ Such a language of goodness – impersonal in character – is, in some sense, impossible.⁴⁸ The absolute good has no language. And yet, Weil suggests, by focusing attention upon this impossibility, one can in fact point in the direction of the good, however inexpressible it might be. Weil's explication of this suggestion is, unsurprisingly, anything but clear-cut and frustratingly cursory. But it does hint at an antidote to her habitual pessimism regarding the power of words.

Weil discerns a potency within certain words that has nothing whatsoever to do with their significative value, for they point towards objects inaccessible not just to speech but to thought as well:

> thanks to a providential arrangement, there are certain words which possess, in themselves, when properly used, a virtue which illumines and lifts up towards the good. These are the words which refer to an absolute perfection which we cannot conceive. Since the proper use of these words involves not trying to make them fit any conception, it is in the words themselves, as words, that the power to enlighten and draw upward resides. What they express is beyond our conception.[49]

The words to which she alludes here are those pointing towards higher, impersonal, even supernatural principles: words such as 'God', 'truth', 'justice', 'love' and 'good'. This is an overtly spiritual, mystical usage of language, far removed from the comforting but vacuous words that fill the institutionalized discourses of the political and legal spheres:

> it is dangerous to use words of this kind. They are like an ordeal. To use them legitimately one must avoid referring them to anything humanly conceivable and at the same time one must associate with them ideas and actions which are derived solely and directly from the light which they shed.[50]

These words, when deployed in such a manner that they symbolize nothing but pure goodness, can help orient their audience in the direction of the impersonal, divine order of the world. But they can only do so when used by those who have already grasped some sense of their higher purpose – which is precisely what affliction disposes the soul towards. It is the obligation, Weil argues, of those in positions of power, those who have the ability to sway the public's opinion, and everyone who possesses some wisp of spiritual authority 'never to hold up for human aspiration anything but the real good in its perfect purity'.[51] And in doing so, the chance might finally arrive for the afflicted to speak of their pain, in a manner that might afford them justice.

It goes without saying (appositely) that Weil is something of an enigma, and these oracular reflections on the power of words are no exception. In regard to her theory of communication, however embryonic it might be, we might well consider her one of the few authentic Platonists in the mould of the *Phaedrus*: she values discourse less for its ability to help us acquire knowledge of superlative ideas as such, and more for its capacity, via the identification of formal correspondences and privileged terms, to orient perceptive speakers and listeners in the direction of these ideas – and ultimately, to direct them towards the good.[52] Such perception must be fostered, and it is as relevant to the domains of law and politics as it is to philosophy proper. But where Plato situates philosophizing as a social activity, located within the midst of disputation, Weil conversely regards it as a solitary pursuit. As she would have it, attention is predicated upon one's decided detachment from sociality.

This necessary detachment, though, as an ongoing process of purification, does not preclude one from maintaining a social existence; in fact, 'to contemplate the social is as good a way of detachment as to retire from the world', hence her own vigorous political engagements.[53] Most pertinently, in spite of her frequent attacks on the idolatry of the collective, Weil evinces – in her life as much as her work – an indefatigable empathy for others. She cares about the suffering of her fellow human beings and wants to construct a philosophy that cares for them likewise. And notwithstanding her anxieties in regard to demagoguery, her aim is not to ring-fence philosophy, distancing it from the needs of 'ordinary' people. But as we witness in the essay in question, there is still a tacit hierarchization and exclusion operating in her work. Scholars often make reference to her occasionally vicious (albeit also somewhat equivocal) attacks on Judaism (what she refers to as 'Israel'), which she views as pursuing and perpetrating the great error of a collective, tribal or national religion, deprived of supernatural transcendence.[54] Less obvious, but more significant for our purposes, however, is the notion that affliction and justice (as two sides of the same coin) – while ineffable, even for those directly in contact with them – can be gestured towards via specific forms of communication: on the one hand, affliction can be vicariously described by those in possession of a rare and inimitable genius; on the other hand, those afflicted can shield themselves through recourse to a language of pure good.

Of course, we cannot separate Weil's description here from her polemical condemnation of Personalism and its appeal to the abstract figure of the human person: she is trying to defend the sanctity and singularity of human life, of those beings susceptible to the most brutal affliction, against a liberal discourse of rights which alienates and silences the victims of this affliction. It is admirable that she wishes to identify the underlying political and cultural conditions of this incommunicability: inequitable social relations, the failures of partisan politics, and a judicial system concerned only with legal persons and not human beings in their wholeness, all of which end up treating the ardent cries that arise from genuine injustice as little more than noise or interference. Yet at the same time, she underwrites this account with a more fundamental and deep-seated appeal to the sacred and an according dismissal of everyday speech, ensuring that true justice, as a manifestation of the good, will in every instance transcend expression.

It is difficult to ignore the fact that Weil seeks to empower the afflicted, to supply them with a mode of expression that might finally allow them to break through their silence, by expressly putting words in their mouths, prescribing a very particular means of speaking. A reasonable critique of insipid liberal platitudes and abstractions projected onto the human population as a whole slips rather effortlessly into a forceful imposition of its own. Is there not a risk that Weil's resolve in trying to give a voice to those who have been silenced actually works to further delegitimize subaltern speech? Weil presumes the afflicted, the favoured object of analysis in many of her essays, to be either mute or incapable of coherent speech – but what if this is at least partly a result of her own failure to listen? She presumes herself capable of offering a solution to this deep-rooted problem – but what if this is just another faulty translation of the cries of pain and suffering into an acceptable discursive frame? Weil positions herself as a privileged conduit for the speech of the afflicted, dispensing the means by which we might communicate the incommunicable. And while she hardly belongs to the philosophical enterprise in any conventional sense (even if she has been gradually incorporated into the margins of its canon), she still utilizes the notion of a proper way of speaking to grant herself, and those who follow her lead, a particular status vis-à-vis a discourse supposedly foreclosed to integral transmission. In short, Weil speaks *for* the afflicted, even when she aspires to give them their own voice.

8

Writing at the limits of history
Michel Foucault and unreason

In his preface to the original 1961 edition of the *History of Madness* (excised from the 1972 edition, and preserved only as a truncated fragment within the initial abridged English translation), Michel Foucault announces his desire to free madness from the objectifying analysis of medical and psychopathological positivism – discourses that, since the nineteenth century, have spoken for madness without ever entering into dialogue with it.[1] Appealing to a formalistic style of historico-philosophical writing which attempts to suspend all moralizing judgements and teleologies, he proposes that it might finally be possible to allow madness to speak on its own terms. The object of his study, as he describes it, 'is not at all a history of knowledge, but of the rudimentary movements of an experience. A history not of psychiatry, but of madness itself, in all its vivacity, before it is captured by knowledge'.[2]

This invocation of an *experience* of 'madness itself' does not hint at any kind of internal subjective or existential state, let alone a mental illness waiting to be diagnosed by a psychiatrist. It certainly does not insinuate that one can identify a static or transhistorical essence of madness, presuming that 'madness pre-exists the practices that designate and concern it'.[3] The experience to which Foucault alludes is not an individual experience and by no means an experience of what it is like to be mad; rather, it is an experience, at a historical and structural level, of the various mechanisms that constitute madness as an object of knowledge and discourse, and the variegated ways in which this constitution takes place across diverse historical periods.[4] Foucault wishes to produce a history of the experience of madness itself – which is to say, a history of the experience of *division*. An experience formed through lines of demarcation, drawing of boundaries and social practices of exclusion, separation and internment. For it is through such structural, spatial and geometrical manoeuvres that madness is constituted and the experience of madness located. We discover there is no madness other than the history of madness, no essence of madness preceding history's divisions. But also (and this reflects the impressive intricacy of Foucault's project), there is in fact no history other than the history of madness. For in the experience of division, history as it is typically presented – a continuously unfolding process of dialectical self-revelation – takes shape. Foucault equates the conditions of possibility of the historical experience of madness with the conditions of possibility of history itself.

On the face of it, Foucault structures the *History of Madness* around three distinct epochs – the Renaissance, the classical age (his principal focus), and the modern age – a tripartite periodization to which he would return in *The Order of Things* (1966). In practice though, the book traces a (dare I say it) maddeningly elaborate historical meshwork, the complexity of which I can do no justice in such a short chapter. Foucault's chief concern is to map the imbricated epistemic shifts and structural partitions that have variously characterized madness over the past six centuries, and in doing so, to gesture towards something underpinning these historical movements:

> the consciousness of madness, in European culture at least, has never formed an obvious and monolithic fact, undergoing metamorphosis as a homogeneous ensemble. For the Western consciousness, madness has always welled up simultaneously at multiple points, forming a constellation that slowly shifts from one form to another, its face perhaps hiding an enigmatic truth.[5]

This truth is Unreason, a shadowy figure – 'like a wordless institution, a gesture without commentary, an immediate knowledge' – haunting the history of Western thought, an immemorial trace of Western reason's constitutive separation from itself.[6] The guiding thread of Foucault's history is the doublet of madness and unreason, terms that sometimes overlap, but which are not inherently synonymous (even if they have been treated as such at certain points in history). If madness is, for Foucault, defined and periodized through the historical experience of division, unreason is, more nebulously, that excess which lies at the origin of and remains unsusceptible to clear and distinct definition. Unreason designates everything outside the realm of rationality, language, history, morality, common sense and good taste. It is not a concept, a discourse or a historical narrative; rather, its expurgation makes all these instruments of thought possible.[7] It is always there, always sitting on the other side of reason's divisions, and by this very fact always implicated in that from which it is separated.

In the original preface of the *History of Madness*, Frédéric Gros remarks, 'Foucault gives his book the precise dimension of a metaphysical drama', proffering an entire 'conceptual horizon' that would be abandoned when this preface came to be excised.⁸ We see this metaphysical motif first and foremost in said appeal to unreason, whereby he seeks to recapture an elusive truth which preexists the constitutive caesura between madness and reason – in his own words, the 'degree zero of the history of madness, when it was undifferentiated experience, the not-yet-divided experience of division itself'.⁹ This is the limit-experience of history itself: both the genesis of history and the point at which its continuity breaks down. He wishes to disrupt the ways of speaking that have bolstered this history, the discourses that have occluded this fundamental rupture, and to make the experience of madness (as division, disavowal, segregation, etc.) heard. In the work of reason, in the processes of demarcation and exclusion that form its *œuvre*, we uncover evidence of the former's fragility.¹⁰ Bringing the residua reason separates from itself out into the open, Foucault believes we can offer a voice to those domains of experience tarred by the label of madness, without speaking for them or distorting their words via the discursive norms of 'rational' language (in particular, those of positivist psychopathology). To do this though, he argues, we need a specific way of writing history, a particular usage of language.

The search for unreason

The original title of this book, *Folie et déraison: Histoire de la folie à l'âge classique*, highlights Foucault's foremost concerns: he conceives of his history as one of madness and unreason in the classical age (i.e. the 'age of reason'), a time when these two terms were treated as synonymous. A history taken from the perspective of his age, in which madness has been medicalized as mental illness and thus submitted to the objectifying discourse of psychopathology. Under the latter conditions, there is no possibility of dialogue between the putatively reasonable man and the madman:

> there is no common language: or rather, it no longer exists; the constitution of madness as mental illness, at the end of the eighteenth century, bears witness to the fact of a broken dialogue, treats this separation as already a given, and pushes into oblivion all those imperfect words, without fixed syntax, somewhat stammered, in which the exchange between madness and reason took place. The

language of psychiatry, which is a monologue by reason *about* madness, could only have been established upon such a silence.[11]

Foucault does not want to produce a history of said language of psychiatry but to 'draw up the archaeology of that silence', to grasp the conditions of this rupture in dialogue.[12] In this way, as we shall see, he hopes to offer a rejoinder to this monologue of reason, and to allow madness to speak on its own terms once again, uncovering that figure omitted from history proper. We should not interpret this as the hope of enabling those who have been designated 'mad' to speak; rather, Foucault is striving to give voice, counterintuitively, to the experience of madness itself insofar as it is effected via the gesture of division.

This gesture is not unique, taking place at a single point in history; its recurrence is instead the very basis of history's continuity. Foucault pinpoints several 'fundamental experiences', belonging to specific historical periods, by which such division is implemented.[13] Above all else, he privileges one particular instance of division: namely, the classical age's strict demarcation of reason and madness, locating the latter firmly and unambiguously on the side of reason's obverse. In the classical age, unreason comes to designate a negativity strictly devoid of reason. Through this division, madness comes to be silenced. The period lasting from the Middle Ages to the Renaissance, in Foucault's estimation, exhibited a certain reciprocity between reason and madness, such that the latter was not entirely excluded from the domain of the former. Madness circulated throughout society, situated within the field of everyday experience, and madmen, seldom confined (although sometimes banished), tended to live an itinerant existence, roaming the countryside or drifting along rivers (exemplified by the literary and artistic figuration of the Ship of Fools). In the works of artists such as Bosch, Brueghel, Bouts and Dürer, madness possesses 'a primitive, prophetic force, revealing that the dream-like is real and that a thin surface of illusion opens onto bottomless depths', unveiling '*the tragic madness of the world*'; and in writers such as Brant, Erasmus and the humanist tradition as a whole, we find '*a critical consciousness of man*', which confines madness to the world of discourse, treating it in an ironic manner, as 'a mere object', or even worse, 'an object of ridicule'.[14]

Over time, the conflict between these two conceptions of madness subsides, with the latter predominating. This triumph of the critical consciousness over its tragic counterpart presages the wholesale appropriation of madness by reason at the dawn of the classical age. In the seventeenth century, great houses of confinement (above all, the Hôpital Général in Paris) were established across

Europe in order to separate physically those – including the insane – who had come to be regarded as existing outside the sphere of reason. These institutions, which had an ethical rather than medical mission, did not distinguish between madness and other forms of perceived degeneracy, leading to an 'enforced fraternisation between the poor, the unemployed, the criminal and the insane'.[15] Treated as a moral failing, an error of one's own choosing, madness was viewed as just one among many ways in which an individual could stray from the path of truth and reason. Houses of confinement, as moral establishments, were tasked with enforcing virtue, administering in the same fashion as one might commerce or economics: 'sinners were locked up in these cities of pure morality, where the law that should govern the human heart was applied without mercy and without compromise, as a rigorous form of physical constraint.'[16]

This new event of large-scale confinement would, in Foucault's view, come to not only typify but determine the consciousness of madness – that is, 'how madness was perceived, and lived' – in the classical age.[17] The 'act of drawing a line around a space of confinement, of giving it a special power of segregation and assigning madness a new land', was anything but a simple procedure, encompassing new attitudes to poverty and indigence, unemployment and idleness (perceiving them as forces of disorder, in need of wholesale elimination), a new work ethic (considering idleness to be the greatest of all vices), and the aforesaid fusion of moral obligations and civic duties, all held together in a complex unity by 'authoritarian forms of constraint'.[18] Most significantly, this delineation, in which madness was lumped together with many other social ills also condemned to confinement, banished madness to the realm of silence. Many philosophers and physicians continued to write about madness, but they treated it not as a positive object but as a mere negation of all reason stood for, a non-being counterposed against truth. Madness was afforded no opportunity to speak for itself: 'there was no autonomous language for madness, and no possibility that it might express itself in a language that spoke its truth.'[19] It was excluded from the discourse that spoke of it, 'enveloped in a discourse to which it remained a stranger'.[20]

This Great Confinement produced a new experience of madness, its 'practices and regulations constituting a domain of experience that had unity, coherence and function'.[21] And accompanying these practices was a new recognition of madness as unreason. Whereas during the Renaissance, forms of 'unreasonable Reason, or reasoned Unreason' were seen to be commonplace, by the seventeenth century, unreason had been wholly severed from reason, and madness subsumed under the former.[22] This segregation, 'wrenching unreason away from its own truth and confining it in the space of the social world', facilitated the experience of madness *qua* alienation, whereby unreason was no longer treated as an experience internal to or accompanying the travails of human reason, but was instead circumvented, separated and enclosed.[23] Unreason was placed at a distance, and this distance manifested itself not only symbolically but physically, thanks to the houses of confinement. An intensification of the ostracism lepers suffered in the mediaeval age, 'unreason was made into an object and thrown into an exile where it was to remain mute for centuries'.[24]

Yet the mode of division peculiar to the classical age's experience of madness pertains not just to physical and symbolic segregation but to the partition separating the critical and practical consciousness of madness conducive to such practices of confinement, in which those deemed mad are interpellated as either legal subjects or social beings, segregating them and hiding them away from society, from the enunciative and analytical consciousness, by which the madman is immediately recognized as such and is assimilated as an object of knowledge.[25] These two domains of consciousness – the 'many specific ways', as Gros describes them, 'that reason concretely apprehends madness whilst guarding against it' – are, in a manner characteristic of the classical age (with its rigid subject/object dualism), left separated and distinct, not to mention divided within themselves.[26] This purported age of reason turns out to be an '*age of the understanding*' when it comes to the experience of madness, bringing about contradiction and alienation without reconciliation or sublation.[27]

'For a century and a half', Foucault maintains, 'madness had a rigorously divided existence', offering 'no possibility of dialogue, no confrontation between a practice that mastered all that went against nature and reduced it to silence, and a form of knowledge that tried to decipher the truths of nature'.[28] On one side, there was the suppression and expulsion of all those deemed aberrant, a violent denial of their existence within the realm of reason; on the other, the objectification of those deemed as requiring analysis, revealing the truth of madness as the negation of reason, expressed through signs devoid of content. In both cases though, 'madness was never *made manifest* on its own terms, in its own particular language'.[29] Madness was not allowed to speak for itself, for the distance between these domains and their privileged concepts granted them a certain appearance of self-evidence, neither bringing the other into dispute: the injustice of confinement, even if acknowledged, did not seem to bear upon the self-circumscription of reason itself, and doubts regarding the concept of madness and its boundaries were seen as irrelevant in the face of more concrete, practical considerations.

Despite this separation and the silence it precipitated, however, careful examination of these domains reveals a number of structural analogies between them. Foucault proposes that it is possible to describe a single experience which grounds both sides of this division:

> it is this single experience, appearing here and there, supporting, explaining, and justifying the practice of internment and the cycle of knowledge, which constitutes the classical experience of madness; and this is the experience that we can describe with the term 'unreason'. Its secret coherence stretches out beneath the great scission that we have just evoked; for unreason is both the reason for the severance and the reason for the unity that is to be found on both sides of the severance. Unreason is the explanation for the presence of the same forms of experience on *both sides* of the divide, but also for the fact that they are only ever found on one side *and* on the other. The unreason of the classical age is that unity and that division all at once.[30]

In either case, madness is utterly segregated from reason; it is nothing other than unreason. Yet in the classical age, the critical and practical consciousness of madness on the one hand and knowledge and recognition of the madman on the other are never reconciled or sublated. Two experiences of division, each possessing their own unique truth. United in the identification of madness with unreason but divergent in the ways in which they draw these lines. Thus, for Foucault, identifying this single underlying experience allows us to grasp the limits of the experience of madness in the classical age, limits that this divided state itself obscures.

Reason's separation from itself

The classical situation, Foucault suggests, in which there is no discourse capable of traversing the chasm between reason and madness, stands in stark contrast to that of the Renaissance, wherein one does in fact witness a certain dialogue between these two domains, the latter revealing the dark truths of the former. The Renaissance had, in its later years, effectively 'liberated the voice of Madness', albeit in a tamed, domesticated form, lacking the eschatological violence characterizing its fifteenth-century figuration.[31] Whereas 'the age of reason, in a strange takeover, was then to reduce it to silence'.[32] Yet this silence, Foucault propounds, would eventually come to be challenged. Beginning with Diderot, the nineteenth century is a period in which reason and unreason once again tentatively come into contact: 'men of our age, after Nietzsche and Freud, find deep within themselves the point of contestation of all truth, being capable of reading in that which they now know of themselves the hints of fragility by which unreason poses a threat.'[33]

Freud reintroduced the question of language – and in particular, a dialogue with unreason – into medical thought, as a substitution for the silent gaze of the asylum, but did so while preserving the alienating figure of the doctor, who maintains a non-reciprocal relationship with their patients. As such, 'psychoanalysis cannot and will never be able to hear the voices of unreason nor decipher on their own terms the signs of the insane', remaining 'a perpetual stranger to the sovereign work of unreason'.[34] Conversely, Nietzsche, like many other authors and artists of his time (e.g. Artaud, Hölderlin, Nerval, Roussel, Sade and Van Gogh) exemplifies the resurgence of a tragic consciousness that has always lurked behind the practices and institutions of the critical consciousness of madness masking it. At a time when madness is being detached from the other categories of unreason, observed and classified within the conceptual strictures of positivism, it is only in the work of such figures that 'the imminence of an immemorial truth', of an unreason resistant to all positivist objectification, shines forth.[35]

At the same time though, all of these figures' eventual fall into something identifiable, within the strictures of modern science and psychiatry, as madness (exhibiting, in most instances, some form of 'mental breakdown') opens up a question directly impelling Foucault's history of madness in its entirety: Why and how has unreason, in the modern era, been so deprived of language that any attempt to confront it would seem to condemn one to madness? Foucault seeks not only to restore the dialogue between reason and madness lost since the Renaissance but to gesture towards the indistinct, almost unspeakable presence throughout the history of Western thought, irreducible to the shackles of *logos*. For this bygone dialogue between reason and madness was itself facilitated by a degree of overlap between reason and unreason that came to be gradually effaced by the critical consciousness of madness. In essence, Foucault wishes to recover a cosmic, *tragic* consciousness of unreason obscured (though not obliterated) during the classical age. Following Nietzsche's lamentation for tragedy as the affirmation of 'all that is fearsome, wicked, mysterious, annihilating and fateful at the very foundations of existence', the death of which he blames on 'the dialectics, moderation, and cheerfulness of theoretical man' (as typified by Socrates and Euripides), Foucault maintains that the classical age is founded upon a blinkered retreat from the mystery, terror and anguish of existence.[36] In its recovery, he hopes, a space might be excavated in which the limits of reason and unreason are more nebulous, the latter no longer condemned to ostracism and silence.

Hence Foucault's stated aim of writing 'a history of *limits* – of those obscure gestures, necessarily forgotten as soon as they take place, whereby a culture rejects something that will be, for it, the Exterior'.[37] This is not just a history of limits though but one that takes place at the limits of history, interrogating the rifts through which a culture solidifies its values, its very positivity and thus the continuity of historical or dialectical time. 'To interrogate a culture about its limit-experiences', he argues, 'is to question it at the confines of history about a tear that is something like the very birth of its history'.[38] The limit-experience in this case is reason's separation of and from itself, this experience of division constituting not just a historical event but *the* historical event, on the basis of which history becomes legible as such. A fissure that can only be described as the origin of history, but which can also be nothing other than a non-origin, its constitutive status placing it outside the linear continuity of history as it is usually understood.[39]

The persistence of the figure of madness within Western history, Foucault maintains, is linked to the very possibility of history itself. The expulsion of madness from the realm of reason typifies the necessary exclusions upon which history's continuity (and the intelligibility of culture more generally) is constructed – the elimination of all that might destabilize its narratives. As Gros notes:

> this reason/madness division is all the more constitutive of a history in that it itself separates history from an absence of history; the œuvre from an absence of œuvre; articulate language from empty speech (madness thus being identified as a delirious repetition of the insignificant). The division by which the West separates fruitless repetition from progress, productiveness from uselessness, or meaning from nonsense, opens the very possibility of a regulated succession of cultural content. [. . .] The meaning of history finds its conditions of possibility less in a self-revealing structure of the forms of reason than in a constitutive refusal of the nonsense of madness.[40]

Writing a history of limits is about confronting this refusal, bringing this decision into question, and revealing its constitutive exteriority. Hence the repeated invocation of unreason as that which sits outside history's signification and reason's œuvre, and the yearning for a tragic consciousness that might apprehend something of it. Foucault's study of madness, as he describes it, is the first in a 'long line of enquiry which, beneath the sun of the great Nietzschean quest, would confront the dialectics of history with the immobile structures of the tragic'.[41] The 'horizontal becoming' of reason, its linear, uniform, dialectical progression, is juxtaposed against a 'constant verticality, which, throughout Western culture, confronts it with what it is not, measuring it against its own extravagance'.[42]

While adopting the outward appearance of a straightforward history of ideas, the *History of Madness* is traversed by a concern for the incommunicable, and in particular, for those experiences of suffering and indignity that cannot be transmitted integrally within the language of reason. Rather than trying to fit into words what will always remain incommensurable, Foucault gestures towards these experiences one might otherwise disregard as irredeemably senseless:

> we need to strain our ears, and bend down towards this muttering [*marmonnement*] of the world, and try to perceive so many images that have never been poetry, so many fantasies that have never attained the colours of day. But it is, no doubt, a doubly impossible task, as it would require us to reconstitute the dust of this concrete pain, and those insane [*insensées*] words that nothing anchors in time; and above all because that pain and those words only exist, and are only apparent to themselves and to others in the act of division that already denounces and masters them. It is only in the act of separation, and from it, that we can think of them as dust that has not yet been separated. Any perception that aims to apprehend them in their wild state necessarily belongs to a world that has captured them already. The liberty of madness can only be heard from the heights of the fortress in which it is imprisoned.[43]

Beneath the structures of exclusion and segregation, outside the continuity of history and unanchored in time, lie the intractable residua of those forced to endure their repression. But only through an encounter with the limit-experience of division can we hear this muttering.

As we have already seen, to furnish a history of madness *itself* is not to speak of madness as some kind of ahistorical essence or characteristic inferred through the instruments of the positivist human sciences, but to grasp it as a phenomenon constituted by a decision to which such sciences (as well as conventional historical narratives) remain oblivious:

> to write the history of madness will therefore mean making a structural study of the historical ensemble – notions, institutions, judicial and police measures, scientific concepts – which holds captive a madness whose wild state can never be reconstituted; but in the absence of that inaccessible primitive purity, the structural study must go back to that decision that both bound and separated

reason and madness; it must tend to discover the perpetual exchange, the obscure common root, the originary confrontation that gives meaning to the unity and the opposition of sense and senselessness. That will allow that fulgurant decision to appear once more, heterogeneous with the time of history, but ungraspable outside it, which separates the murmur of dark insects from the language of reason and the promises of time.[44]

This dazzling, blinding decision which separates reason from unreason – and which, in its most pronounced form, marks the transition to the classical experience of madness, and then to our own, pathologized and medicalized experience of the same – does not manifest within the continuity of history; rather, it appears as 'the point at which history freezes, in the tragic mode that both founds it and calls it into question'.[45] Foucault does not seek merely to recount history but to disrupt it.

This history of limits, which in itself amounts to a certain kind of limit-experience, a confrontation with reason's separation from itself, demands a particular language, and a particular manner of writing history. Not rejecting the language of reason per se but pushing the latter to its limit, to where all its judgements and moralisms fall away – and with them, the imperious gesture of speaking for all, even for those who reason has declared foreign to itself. After all, Foucault argues, history is built upon the exclusion of madness, the 'decisive action that extracts a significative language from the background noise and its continuous monotony', filtering out all that is unintelligible to the language of reason.[46] But this noise persists. Paradoxically, it persists in its silence. For the conceptualization of reason first established in the classical age, and still resonating today, is founded upon the bedrock of this silence: a plenitude of reason cleanly divided from the utter vacuity of its inverse. And the same goes for historical chronology, the plenitude and continuity of which relies upon this imposition of silence:

> the plenitude of history is only possible in the space, both empty and populated at the same time, of all those words without language that make, to anyone who lends an ear, a muffled sound from beneath history, the obstinate murmur of a language talking *to itself* – without any speaking subject and without an interlocutor, wrapped up in itself, with a lump in its throat, collapsing before it ever reaches any formulation and returning without a fuss to the silence from which it has never been freed. The charred root of meaning.[47]

Foucault does not wish to write a history that further contributes to the imperious designs of reason. And he does not want to write a history in the language that has worked to exclude madness.

A language without support

But in what way, one might ask, is a philosopher or a historian – even one as unorthodox as Foucault – able to bypass the stranglehold of the language of reason over history? In attempting to amplify the pathos of exclusion, how does one avoid assuming a certain mastery over this neglected discourse, or a certain capacity to translate it into the language of reason? Is his venture not predicated upon the covert presumption of a kind of *characteristica universalis*, reproducing the universalist aspirations of the classical philosophy of which Foucault is so castigatory? Can one truly compose an archaeology of silence without betraying unreason's alterity?

Foucault's preemptive rejoinder to such concerns lies in his curious, cursorily explained appeal to 'a language without support [*langage sans appui*]', a self-correcting language of pure relativity, the aim of which is 'to safeguard the *relative* at all costs, and to be *absolutely* understood'.[48] As he explains:

> in this simple problem of elocution, the greatest difficulty that faced the enterprise hid and expressed itself: it was necessary to bring to the surface of the language of reason a division and a debate that must necessarily remain below it, since this language only has meaning well beyond them. What was required was therefore a language that was neutral enough (fairly free from scientific terminology, and social or moral options) in order that it could approach these initially tangled words as closely as possible, and so that the distance by which modern man shores himself up against madness might be abolished; but a language that remained sufficiently open for the decisive words through which the truth of madness and of reason are constituted for us to be registered without misrepresentation.[49]

A neutral language (or as close to neutral as one can get) – which is to say, not the misleading objectivity of psychopathology but a formal, geometric language, stripped as much as possible of any medicalizing or moralizing accoutrements.[50] A language which speaks, in the images it employs and texts it analyses, of division. A language devoid of any intimations of a transcendental subjectivity external to the movements of history. A language that does not attempt to speak of unreason in the terms of reason (the move by which the former was first objectified, in the critical consciousness of madness), and indeed, does not claim to speak for unreason at all but which speaks a language able to account for the experience of unreason *qua* disavowal, separation and expulsion. Hence Michel Serres' description of Foucault as a geometer, writing in 'the language of an abstract theory of pure exclusion'.[51]

In writing his history, Foucault makes no recourse to an enumeration of existential states, and instead foregrounds, as we have already seen, the 'experience' of spatial divisions, separations, boundaries, limits and enclosures. As the murky, inaccessible nether world to which madness once seemed to offer an imaginary passage comes to be replaced by the designation of a pure negativity, and then again by the symptomatology of a psychological condition, the circulation and close contact symbolized in the figure of the Ship of Fools is supplanted by the outright separation of the Hôpitaux Généraux, which is in turn supposedly superseded by the objectifying gaze of psychiatric asylums and clinics and the immediate encounter between doctors and patients therein. The insistent formalism by which reason draws its borders becomes, in the hands of the philosopher-historian, the instrument by which these exclusions can be laid bare. Only through the transparency of this language without support, Foucault suggests, can one reveal the decisions undergirding the language of reason, bypassing the accumulated layers of discursive debitage concealing them. Prescribing neither content nor meaning in advance, this spatial language remains open to the discourses heretofore filtered out by the rigid mesh of Western rationality. The goal is not to render these residua explicable, conforming to the norms of reason; it is to reveal both its opacity *and* propinquity to these norms. In this way, Foucault believes, he can allow 'these words and texts, which came from beneath language [. . .] to speak for themselves', freed from the psychopathological gaze monopolizing their interpretation in the modern age.'[52]

Such neutrality also involves the extrication of all insinuations of 'progress' from historical narrativization, revealing 'in the history of an experience, a movement in its own right, uncluttered by a teleology of knowledge or the orthogenesis of learning'.[53] A history, he claims, without perspectival interpretation and value judgements. A history of those recurrent gestures whereby reason separates itself from unreason, but one which refuses to take reason's claims to its own unity and self-sufficiency at face value, focusing instead on the occluded rupture upon which these are constructed and in the face of which their tenuousness is exposed. In place of such assertions of plenitude, Foucault proffers a formal structure: a history of division, and a glimpse into a world prior to this division. For even though it still can only offer an outside perspective, Foucault suggests, it is in such a history that we find a way of 'approaching the experience of madness in its positive reality, an experience which stripped the madman of the precise individuality and status that the Renaissance had given him'.[54] This is the crux of Foucault's project here: not to describe the experience of 'being mad', which could only mark a reversion into the medicalized or positivistic discourses of psychopathology, but to unearth the experience of madness *qua* exclusion.

Writing a history of limits, tracing a complex network of divisions and dualities, in Foucault's view, affords him the opportunity to communicate the truth of madness and the truth of reason, which are, in the end, one and the same. Such a formalism, which pushes the instruments of reason towards a purity at which point all of its judgements, jargons, moralisms and teleologies reveal themselves to be *un*reasonable, might – for the first time since the Renaissance – offer a voice to madness and unreason, letting them not only speak in their own words but speak in dialogue with those domains which have excluded them for so long:

> then, and only then, can that domain appear where the man of madness and the man of reason, whilst parting from one another, are not yet separate, and who, in a language very deep-rooted, very crude, and much more matutinal than that of science, enter into the dialogue of their rupture, momentarily indicating that they are still on speaking terms. There, madness and non-madness, reason and unreason are hazily implicated in each other, inseparable since they do not yet exist, and existing for each other, in relation to each other, in the exchange that separates them.[55]

Foucault wants to both utilize and interfere with the language of reason, making its blind spots visible, disclosing its necessary but occluded counterpart. He hopes that by highlighting other modes of discourse that have been forced into silence (to the extent that they are likely unrecognizable *as* discourse), and in particular by calling attention to the means by which this silence has been imposed and their inherent fragility, it might be possible to once again destabilize the sharp divisions governing the conceptualization of madness from the classical age onward, viewing reason and unreason as two sides of the same coin. He does not promise the dissolution of such divisions, nor does he anticipate their sublation, but he hopes to bring the mutual dependence (and consequent potential for interchange) between both sides into relief. He sees an opportunity to reveal the inveterate insularity of reason, its tendency to confine itself to well-defined, secure borders, at the cost of a violent expulsion of everything that troubles its certitude. And to explain how madness is created through this expulsion.

Despite the already discussed rhetorical allusion to the man of reason and the man of madness, Foucault remains consistent in his goal of allowing madness itself (rather than those deemed 'mad') to speak. But we must take care to not misconstrue Foucault's book as attempting to grant speech to the empirical victims of the various structural exclusions it describes. To give voice in such a fashion would do little more than lending those silenced the transitory usage of a discourse that serves to exclude them. Such a discourse will never allow one to speak of madness itself, on its own terms and its own terrain. Madness will always remain for it a foreign language, translated in a crude and garbled fashion. Although his critique angered Foucault, Derrida describes this aspect of his former friend's project well:

> Foucault wanted madness to be the subject of his book in every sense of the word: its theme and its first-person narrator, its author, madness speaking about itself. Foucault wanted to write a history of madness *itself*, that is madness speaking on the basis of its own experience and under its own authority, and not a history of madness described from within the language of reason, the language of psychiatry *on* madness.[56]

Hence why Foucault reaches for a neutral language, a language that tries not to *lean upon* reason's discursive resources but to speak of those divisions (and more fundamentally, the act of division as such) reason must efface. As Derrida goes on to ask, however, who or what supports this language without support? 'Who wrote and who is to understand this history of madness?'.[57] Or more simply, who is actually speaking here?

A new role for the philosopher

The pathos pervading Foucault's book – the desire to maintain an openness to those domains of experience whose speech has been refused – no doubt represents, as it did for Weil in the preceding chapter, a genuine hope for a more empathetic, understanding mode of philosophy, freed of its imperious pretensions. Foucault, like many thinkers who came after him, signals a reversal of the classical mechanism of philosophical exclusion via reason: he does not wish to implement further exclusion, but to recognize and reverse it. Instead of providing access to a privileged discourse of identity or similitude, the incommunicable is located for Foucault in the realm of the other. His rejection of any integral transmission of the discourse of madness does not stem from a wish to protect it from the ignorant ears of the masses but to safeguard it from the domineering, distorting discourse of psychopathology that has spoken on behalf of the mad since the nineteenth century. He uses philosophical esotericism against itself, as a mechanism of inclusion.

What does it mean to listen to and speak of the experience of madness itself though? In the absence of an identifiable speaking subject, to whom are we listening? Can we still distinguish between the silent words of madness itself and those of the philosopher (or philosopher-historian) who makes use of this professedly neutral language to bring these words to the surface? If so, this latter language is surely just another example of the kinds of philosophical comportment we have examined throughout this book – an œuvre regarding the absence of œuvre, shoring up the philosophical enterprise it purports to condemn. Indeed, Foucault's sketchy, allusive presentation of this language should immediately signal to us that he intends it less as a substantive methodology for historical writing, and more as a way of marking off his own project from the positivist human sciences and safeguarding the truths it articulates from their grasp.

Foucault's relationship to and identification with philosophy is, without doubt, thorny and ambivalent. 'The breakdown of philosophical subjectivity and its dispersion in a language that dispossesses it while multiplying it within the space created by its absence', he declares, in an article published two years after the *History of Madness*, 'is probably one of the fundamental structures of contemporary thought'.[58] Yet this is not 'the end of philosophy', he clarifies, 'but rather, the end of the philosopher as the sovereign and primary form of philosophical language'.[59] Foucault's history of madness, taken at face value, abets this diminution of philosophical language, throwing discursive reason's monopoly over discourse into disarray. But he still posits the philosopher-historian as the privileged figure in possession of a tragic consciousness, peculiarly capable of allowing a subaltern discourse to speak on its own terms. This philosopher-historian is able to hear the murmurings of unreason without finding themselves condemned to the status of madness, as so many artists and writers over the past two centuries have.

Like Kant before him, Foucault perceives his role here as circumscribing the boundaries beyond which reason has no right to speak; bringing the critical powers of reason to bear upon the latter itself, in order to make room for another kind of experience. In doing so, he is able to reinvigorate the philosophical enterprise at a time of its perceived crisis, endowing the philosopher with a new role just as the sciences threaten to render it obsolete. Extending the aegis of philosophy (and history) to the unspeakable, he identifies a utility for this discipline quite distinct from the positivism of modern medicine and psychology. Which is to say, his aim of allowing madness itself to speak is, in practice, a means for allowing the philosopher-historian to continue to speak. In the absence of a discernible speaking subject, they take on this mantle.

It is telling that Foucault places so much emphasis, especially in the preface that he would soon excise, upon the need to use the fact of exclusion to gesture towards a foundational truth of Western thought: namely, the stubborn continuance of the turbulent realm of unreason, the 'obscure presence to which Western Reason owes something of its depth'.[60] Even while pining for a time when both sides of this relation were still in dialogue, Foucault also romanticizes the very fact of this decision. Thanks to the persistence of reason's separation from itself, he can allude to the possibility of fleetingly glimpsing at an originary, undifferentiated experience where reason and unreason are still indissociable.[61] It provides him with the assurance that there is always something outside of reasonable language and outside the continuity of history: a tragic consciousness through which the putative plenitude of reason and the foundational tragedy of its division can be brought into question. And it enables us, unexpectedly perhaps, to situate this early project within what Foucault would describe later that decade, in *The Order of Things* (1966), as the 'metaphysics of that never objectifiable depth from which objects rise up towards our superficial knowledge', contrasted against and yet reciprocally determined by the positivist sciences.[62]

Foucault identifies the historical experience of madness' conditions of possibility with those of history itself – which is to say, he identifies them with the separation between the reasonable and unreasonable, rational and irrational. In tracing the volatile movements and displacements by which these terms find their meaning, he locates 'the division which gives a culture the face of its positivity', the margins at which this positivity's solidity is constructed and its fragility ensured.[63] To write a history of madness, in his conception, is to write a history of this precarious constitution, to map out, in something as close as possible to a neutral language, the unreason that the positivist sciences disavow. Recounted in such a fashion, he believes, without the support of judgement, jargon, morality or teleology, the historical variances in the experience of madness will draw one towards the unobjectifiable unreason forming their condition. This figure of unreason, therefore, far from being just a simple, albeit enigmatic counterpart to reason proper (the impression one might get in the book's later editions), supplies Foucault's project, at this early stage of his career, with its *raison d'être*, positing a foundation the positivistic sciences can never apprehend and allowing for a manner of historical writing they can never appropriate. His study is still wedded to what he later describes, again in *The Order of Things*, as

> the endless controversy between philosophy, which objects to the naïveté with which the human sciences try to provide their own foundation, and those same

human sciences which claim as their rightful object what would formerly have constituted the domain of philosophy.[64]

The history of madness, in its search for the transcendental condition of history itself, grants the philosopher a renewed purpose in the face of a burgeoning positivism. And the neutral language, the language without support, in which he claims to write this history becomes the mechanism by which he can distinguish this history from those of the established human sciences, holding out the possibility that the tangled words of madness itself might at last be heard.

9

Talking with borrowed words
Strategic mimesis in Luce Irigaray

My brief explorations into the work of Weil and Foucault only scratch the surface when it comes to twentieth-century continental philosophy's condemnation of the totalizing impulses of philosophical language (which is often given the moniker 'metaphysics'). Henri Bergson's view of language as failing to capture the dynamism and continuity of lived experience; Ludwig Wittgenstein's attempt to extricate philosophy from its ensnarement within meaningless, misleading questions; Martin Heidegger's complaints regarding the transformation of philosophy into an inventory of formalized, technical apparatuses divorced from any originary relationship to language as such; the Frankfurt School's denunciation of the instrumentalized language established by logical positivism – despite their considerable differences in approach and outlook, these currents of thought all represent a growing sentiment that philosophical discourse can easily coagulate into cliché or doxa. In the second half of this century, French (post)structuralism, in its turn towards semiology as a formal model for human knowledge, also gestured insistently in the direction of all that could not be subsumed under the semiological schema (i.e. the unrepresentable, the ineffable, the differential, the outside, etc.), situating the latter not as unwanted residua, but as the occluded conditions of this schema's intelligibility.

Indeed, a number of poststructuralist and deconstructionist thinkers plausibly deserve coverage within this book. Jacques Lacan's psychoanalysis, for instance, is in large part premised upon a peculiar type of speech act – that which takes place in analytic dialogue – which begins with and yet seeks to overcome the presumption that there is a truth already contained within us, a reality beyond the confines of language. Likewise, one could see parallels in the privilege that Roland Barthes gives to the 'writerly' text; Jacques Derrida's critique of the logocentrism of Western metaphysics and the particular mode of deconstructive reading this critique demands, as well as Gayatri Chakravorty

Spivak's accordant decrial of the purportedly transparent language of Western intellectual practice; Michel Serres' concern with mathematical formalism and its empirical remainder; or Gilles Deleuze's refusal of communication in the name of conceptual heterogenesis.

In my estimation, however, it is in the psychoanalytic feminism of Luce Irigaray – and in particular, her two key early books: *Speculum of the Other Woman* (1974) and *This Sex Which Is Not One* (1977), the latter acting partly as a more accessible explication of the former – that we find the most forthright articulation, within the poststructuralist tradition, of the manoeuvre I have sought to identify throughout this book. Denouncing hegemonic discourse as phallogocentric, locked into the metaphysical postulate of sexual difference *qua* similitude, upholding the position of the phallus as a privileged signifier and thus only capable of representing woman as the defective inverse of man, Irigaray posits a different kind of speech, a strategic mimicry that does not make any attempt to speak *of* woman but instead strives to show the extent to which masculine discursivity builds its coherence and systematicity upon a ground it finds itself forced to occlude. To speak *as* a woman, implicated within this discourse and yet always exceeding its limits, able to converse on its terms but never exhausted by them, is not to posit oneself as a subject, a feminine counterpart to the masculine subject of philosophy, still determined by the latter's laws, values and schemata, but to use woman's position as the 'not-all in the sayable [*dicible*] of discourse' in order to challenge the very specular economy that has used the concept of the 'subject' to subjugate and exploit women.[1]

As Spivak observes, Irigaray's work deals with many themes common to poststructuralism, most notably 'the deconstructive *themes* of indeterminacy, critique of identity, and the absence of a totalizable analytic foothold', albeit taken from a feminist standpoint.[2] And of course it fits neatly into the *écriture féminine* described by Hélène Cixous, an undefinable practice of writing that will 'always surpass the discourse that regulates the phallocentric system', taking place 'in areas other than those subordinated to philosophico-theoretical domination'.[3] What interests me about Irigaray, though, is the emphasis she places upon mode of address, and her claim that philosophy and psychoanalysis (the latter indebted to the former) have historically used a specific way of speaking – the discourse of truth – as an instrument of exclusion and oppression.

'We must be attentive to the unsaid that dwells in the holes in discourse', suggests Lacan, so long as the unsaid is not 'understood like knocking coming from the other side of the wall'.[4] Irigaray, in effect, takes up this suggestion, but she identifies the unsaid specifically with the figure of woman. Across the two books in question, she points to a number of discourses and registers – logic, metaphysics, sexual difference, desire, pleasure, identity, nature, political economy and the mathematical sciences, among others – troubled by that state which 'has been struck mute, but is eloquent in its silence: the *real*'.[5] The deployment of these diverse registers – in a fashion that confounds traditional disciplinary boundaries – enables Irigaray to highlight the grip philosophy holds over other discourses, and to gesture towards the margins of this asserted master discourse and its prescriptions. By pointing out this discourse's limits, and most importantly, its inability to incorporate sexual difference as such into its workings, Irigaray believes one can reveal the bipartite function woman fulfils within this discourse: 'as the mute outside that sustains all systematicity; as a maternal and still silent ground that nourishes all foundations'.[6] Woman – who, in the eyes of philosophy, psychoanalysis and masculinist thought more generally, does not exist – becomes the synecdoche for a more general refusal of such thought to reckon with its own conditions: the rejected waste or residua – the 'not-all [*pas-toute*]' – on the basis of which it realizes its totalizing ambitions.[7] The taciturn material from which it draws the coherence of its voluble discourse.

The metaphysical logic of difference

A thoroughgoing critique of Freudian psychoanalysis forms the mainspring of Irigaray's approach in these two early books. This discipline, in her estimation, comprises a monologue *about* women addressed to men, systematically failing to include women within its discourse and offering no opportunities for their self-expression. 'The enigma that *is* woman' constitutes 'the *target*, the *object*, the *stake*, of a masculine discourse, of a debate among men, which would not consult her, would not concern her'.[8] In particular, Irigaray views psychoanalysis as neglecting the question of women's sexuality, desire and pleasure – and thus as unable to account for sexual difference. Freud 'insists that the so-called masculine sexual pleasure [*jouissance*] is the paradigm for all sexual pleasure, to which all representations of pleasure can but refer, standardize, and submit', with the result that his conceptualization of feminine sexuality remains obstinately shackled to the same old masculine parameters as those who preceded him.[9]

Freud strikes two crucial blows, suggests Irigaray, against the logic of representation. One of these is direct, against the metaphysics of presence, 'when he stresses secondary revision, overdetermination, repetition compulsion, the death drive, etc., or when he indicates, in his practice, the impact of so-called unconscious mechanisms on the discourse of the "subject", all of which undermines the notion of a self-present consciousness, locating a realm of thought impervious to discursive assimilation. The other is indirect, when 'he defines sexual difference in accordance with the a priori of the same', negating any such difference by rendering it in conformity with a homogeneous masculine desire, producing a sexual *indifference*.[10] Freud's recourse to similitude – and ultimately, to the signifier of the phallus – thus undercuts his representation of difference. He 'is still party to a certain logos and therefore to a certain economy of "presence", a certain representation of "presence" [. . .] able to picture the little girl becoming a woman only in terms of *lack, absence, defect,* etc.'[11] Freud's entire account of psychosexual development is dominated by 'a specular process which favours the *flat mirror* as most suitable for controlling the image, the representation, the self-representation' – a process which 'excludes the little girl from any discovery of the economy of her relationships with her mother, and with maternity'.[12] Freud thus unwittingly reveals the incapacity of his own theory to represent sexual difference as such.

This image of the *flat mirror* is central to Irigaray's argument in these two early books, symbolizing the masculine economy of similitude, a 'specular duplication, reflecting back to man "his" own image and repeating it as the "same"'.[13] It is woman who props up this planar duplication, who provides the surface upon which this mirror image appears. Woman is denied her own representation. She is treated as nothing more than an inverted image, with no prospect of genuine self-representation – the paradoxical confirmation of sexual difference as both symmetrical and asymmetrical. She 'does not have access to language, except through recourse to "masculine" systems of representation which estrange her from her relation to herself and to other women'.[14] Any utterance not conforming to such systems is denounced as abnormal, irrational or unintelligible – even pathological. The feminine is, in all instances, defined in terms of and for the benefit of the masculine, and never vice versa. All desire is indexed to the phallus.

Such a situation is not unique to psychoanalysis, which is a symptom rather than a cause. A symptom of masculinist discourse's predominance, of course, and the material relations serving as its base. But also, in a more narrow sense, a symptom of the codification of this discourse at the hands of metaphysics, with its laws of identity, non-contradiction and the excluded middle, together furnishing an impoverished conceptualization of difference *qua* indifference.[15] What stands out about psychoanalysis for Irigaray, though, is that Freud's blatant declaration of this specular depiction of difference in his account of psychosexual development finally offers up this metaphysics of *in*difference as an object of analysis:

> in devising a theory of sexuality, Freud brought to light something that had been at work all along though it remained implicit, hidden, and unrecognized: *the sexual indifference that underlies the truth of any science, the logic of every discourse*. This is readily apparent in the way Freud defines woman's sexuality. In fact, this sexuality is never defined with respect to any sex but the male. Freud does not see *two sexes* whose differences are articulated in the act of intercourse, and, more generally speaking, in the imaginary and symbolic processes that regulate the workings of a society and a culture. The 'feminine' is always described in terms of deficiency or atrophy, as the other side of the sex that alone holds a monopoly on value: the male sex.[16]

The psychoanalytic failure to account for sexual difference betrays its continued reliance upon a metaphysical logic. Freud is, in Irigaray's estimation, an 'active stakeholder in an "ideology" that he never questions', a 'prisoner of a certain economy of the logos, of a certain logic, notably of "desire", whose link to classical philosophy he fails to see', persistently deploying the same old devices – 'analogy, comparison, symmetry, dichotomic oppositions, etc.' – that have always formed part of the philosophical armature, and which never fail to reduce difference to a mere subspecies of the same.[17] But what differentiates psychoanalysis from philosophy proper is that in the former, the question of sexualization is at stake. At the same time psychoanalysis repeats the metaphysical representation of difference, it also opens it up to interpretation. Freud inadvertently brings into relief a 'crisis point in metaphysics', in which the instruments of domination propping up metaphysical coherence and systematicity are exposed, and the philosophical unconscious, its conditions of possibility, becomes apparent.[18]

We must understand Irigaray's deconstruction of psychoanalysis as just one part of a broader undertaking: an interrogation of the philosophical *logos* and the phallogocentrism underpinning it. 'It is indeed precisely philosophical discourse that we have to challenge, and *disrupt*,' she declares, 'inasmuch as this discourse sets forth the law for all others, inasmuch as it constitutes the discourse of discourses.'[19] The hegemonic power of the philosophical *logos*, suggests Irigaray, in its closure, cohesion, apparent universality and imperious pretensions to mastery 'stems in large part from its power to *reduce any other in the economy of the Same*', and most broadly, 'from its power to *eradicate the difference between the sexes* in systems that are self-representative of a "masculine subject"'.[20] And hence 'the necessity of "reopening" the figures of philosophical discourse [. . .]

in order to pry out of them what they have borrowed that is feminine, from the feminine, to make them "give back" [*rendre*] what they owe to the feminine'.²¹ Psychoanalysis, for all its drawbacks, supplies critical resources that can be brought to bear upon philosophy. Provided that it recognizes its own repetition of long-standing metaphysical tropes regarding sexual difference, of course.²²

A feminist practice's task, in Irigaray's conception, is not to speak within the confines of the dominant discourse (which would only work to uphold its specular universality) but to expose the boundedness of this discourse, to reveal its limits. And accordingly, to pave the way for other forms of discourse, other manners of speaking that put paid to this specularization. To make room for the feminine, in other words. If philosophy is the domain 'where one never gets away from the search for sameness', a house of flat mirrors, infinitely reflecting an idealized image of man (with woman representable only in terms of absence, deficiency or imitation, a defective duplicate of the male identity), Irigaray instead sets out to discover a genuine *difference* irreducible to such similitude, a *heterogeneity* of discourse, desire and materiality the upswell of which imperils the authority of the self-present, self-representing significative economy hitherto prevailing over philosophical language, securing all meaning via the master signifier of the phallus.²³

Such a task demands 'going back through the processes of specula(riza)tion that underlie our social and cultural organization', grasping the extent to which the flat mirror has shaped speculation.²⁴ It requires us 'to interpret the mirror's intervention, to discover what it may have kept suspended in an unreflected dazzle of its brilliance, what it may have clotted in its decisive cut, what it may have frozen of the "other's" flowing'.²⁵ To critique a discourse speaking interminably of and for women without ever letting them speak for themselves in their own terms. A discourse that quietens women, or dismisses their words as gossip, idle chatter, irremediably doxastic. A discourse permitting women to speak of nothing other than that of which the male subject expects her to speak, leaving her to fulfil the function of a silenced exteriority whose exclusion permits the maintenance of discursive coherence and systematicity.

Philosophy's material conditions

'If only your ears were not so informed', laments Irigaray, 'so clogged with meaning, closed off to anything that does not in any way echo that which they have previously heard'.²⁶ Philosophical discourse standardizes woman by making 'her' into a noun, a concept, stipulating 'her' meaning in advance. In spite of its frequent appeals to a pure, rarefied ideality, we find the economy of said discourse firmly embedded within the material conditions of particular relations of production. It is just one instance of an economic system which renders woman a commodity, an object of exchange, placing her on the market. A commodity used and exchanged (i.e. exploited) by men, with no rights of her own. A commodity whose value is determined in line with phallocentric general equivalence. Excluded from the laws of exchange regulating their circulation as commodities, it is thanks to this systematic oppression that women are capable of mounting not only a critique of political economy but a critique of the discourse (and its metaphysical presuppositions) through which its exploitation is carried out:

> the (male) subject gathers and reconstitutes the plurality of female merchandise – scattered in their silence, in(con)sistent chatter, or madness – as coins that have an established value in the marketplace. Thus, in order that 'she' is to begin to speak, and above all to be heard, it is crucial to first suspend and overhaul all systems of credit. In every sense. The credit, the credibility, that sustains all the current forms of monopoly, needs to be questioned.[27]

And bringing this system of credit into question means grasping that which remains unrepresentable within it – that which eludes this phallic hegemony, this masculinist symbolic order which speaks only of 'truth', fixing meaning in place once and for all.

For women, as Irigaray makes clear, will never be able to liberate themselves while still working within this masculinist order, speaking the language of men. It is fruitless to posit a 'female' subject along the same lines and within the same parameters as the male 'subject' hitherto posited as the universal subject of language and history. Such an assertion of symmetry, as appealing as it might be to those versed in the rhetoric of gender equality, can only reinforce the age-old metaphysical (and phallocratic) system of identarian representation, which has long served as a condition of possibility for mastery of the other via non-recognition. A discourse grounded in sexual indifference cannot tell us anything about the 'feminine'.

Nor does Irigaray see utility in any attempt to appropriate the flat mirror by which the male subject reproduces this indifference. Instead, she argues, even as the male subject catches a glimpse of his own reflection, he 'already has to deal with another specularization' – curved or twisted – fundamentally incapable of reflecting his representation onto the other.[28] After all, 'if an *other* image, an *other* mirror were to intervene' in his specular duplication, it 'inevitably would entail the risk of mortal crisis', calling into question the universality upon which this process grounds its legitimacy.[29] Against the flat mirror of speculation, which divides the male subject from himself in order that he might identify with his own image, Irigaray counterposes a *concave mirror*, a speculum, which proffers no reflection. In the face of this 'concave speculum, pirouetting upon itself', he encounters only 'impossible reflected images, maddening reflections, parodic transformations', disrupting his self-identification, and with it his domineering systems of representation.[30]

Central to Irigaray's account is the premise that behind the figure of 'woman' remains something unrepresentable by and uncontainable within this concept. Something which withdraws from the 'theoretical tools (geometrical, mathematical, discursive, dialogic)' man uses in his attempts to appropriate being.[31] At the same time that she functions as a muted, constitutive exteriority, she also acts as a maternal ground for all of man's supposedly solid foundations – albeit a dissimulated and derided ground, travestied by philosophical discourse and irreducible to its restricted model of knowledge.

Taking up the Aristotelian concept of *prime matter*, a pure potentiality, Irigaray identifies this 'unknowable entity' with the body of the mother, who is 'both radically lacking in all power of logos and offers, unawares, an all-powerful soil in which the logos can grow'.[32] Philosophers may speak of materiality, but they either forget or deny that the potency residing behind this concept is always already distorted by their own speculative proclivities. 'Every utterance, every assertion, is thus developed and affirmed by covering up the fact that being's unseverable relation to mother-matter has been buried.'[33] This mother-matter provides the ground and the sustenance for the philosopher's ongoing speculation, even as he tenaciously disclaims it, submitting its dynamism to his rigid categories and prefabricated teleologies. Indeed, Irigaray suggests, the figure of God *qua* creator stands as nothing more than a sublimation of this mother-matter, a conceptual purification of and an abstraction from the labour of birth.

This identification of mother-matter as the dynamic, generative and yet occluded basis for philosophical discourse reverses the usual hierarchy between form and matter, *eidos* and *hylē*, using Aristotle's suggestion of an affinity between menstrual blood and prime matter to reveal the disavowal by which man's self-identity is affirmed. It is to this identity – the absence of contradiction (the foundation of Aristotelian logic) – that such matter cannot conform. The forms philosophers impose upon woman can never exhaust her – she is always in excess of them, always morphologically incomplete. And the same goes for her desire, her *jouissance*. 'Woman is not to be related to any simple designatable being, subject, or entity. [...] One woman + one woman + one woman will never add up to some generic entity: woman.'³⁴ The common noun 'woman' is not a signifier to which one can attach a fixed meaning; it designates precisely that which eludes the strictures of self-identity. It 'refers to what cannot be defined, enumerated, formulated or *formalized*', resisting all definition.³⁵ Masculinist systems of representation locate meaning in self-identity, in a spatial discreteness and distinctness – a discursive rigidity – which cannot account for the blank spaces bestrewn across the surface of language: they cannot read between the lines. Woman inhabits these interstices. She remains elusive.

Which is not to say that 'woman' is unable to be arrogated by phallogocentric discourse (i.e. grasped as a female 'subject'). But she will never fully recognize herself in this signification. She will never have the self-knowledge, self-possession and self-resemblance characterizing such subjectivity. Representations of woman, as the expression of men's fantasies, may conceal her potency, but they cannot contain it. In fact, the former make use of these resources, which 'remain the basis of (re)production – particularly of discourse – in all its forms'.³⁶ One cannot localize woman. She is scattered, fragmented, torn apart, distributed among manifold places that one cannot definitively locate or consolidate, let alone identify with a singular 'self'. She 'is never here and now because it is she who sets up that eternal elsewhere from which the "subject" continues to draw his reserves, his re-sources, though without being able to recognize them/her' – the unacknowledged wellspring for all speculation, nourishing the male subject's attempts to break free from 'the specular matrix, the enveloping discursivity, the body of the text wherein he has become a prisoner'.³⁷ Man's speculation, and his ensuing self-identity, thus remains duplicitous: he knows himself only through his denial of the other.

The not-all

Even while she decries the dominating tendencies of metaphysics, there is something strikingly familiar in Irigaray's notion of a foundational aspect of reality – a materiality, sensibility or alterity – both preceding and exceeding the matrix of expressibility furnished by rational thought. But the incommunicability of the real is, for her, not a transcendental certitude but a historical contingency, born of chauvinism, domination and exclusion. What metaphysicians have long relegated to the position of an irretrievable outside or a stubbornly resistant and refractory remainder is not, by necessity, silent; rather, it has been *silenced* through such mechanisms of exclusion and mastery. Hence why Irigaray is hesitant to perpetuate the division between 'a language that is always subject to the postulates of ideality and an empirics that has forfeited all symbolization'.[38] She instead founds her project upon the possibility that 'something of the feminine *as limit of the philosophical* might finally be heard', and as a consequence, that the imperious coherence and systematicity of the discursive mechanism might be thwarted.[39]

The 'woman' Irigaray gestures towards, as we know, is not a concept, nor is she an object waiting to be subsumed under a concept; she is everything resistant to such subsumption. 'Woman' designates a dynamism, a potency, impervious to all imposition of form. She possesses a 'fluid' character, 'which has deprived her of all possibility of identity with herself'.[40] A fluidity not just lying outside expressibility (at least within the confines of the phallogocentric *logos*) but, in its instability, resisting formalization or representation. It provokes turbulence. In this respect, Irigaray posits, there is a homology between woman's diffuseness and the physical reality of fluids, which she claims have been routinely overlooked by the mathematical sciences. A certain precedence, she suggests, has been granted to solidity over fluidity, the latter having been dealt with in a partial, idealizing or geometrizing manner that enabled the technical and mathematical analysis of fluids, but did so while 'losing a certain relationship to the *reality of bodies in the process*'.[41] A remainder is left behind, a residue of the real that one cannot capture in any formalizing language:

> if we examine the properties of fluids, we note that this 'real' may well include, and in large measure, *a physical reality* that continues to resist adequate symbolization and/or that signifies the powerlessness of logic to capture in its writing all the characteristic features of nature. And it has often been found necessary to reduce certain of these features of nature, to envisage them, and it, only in light of an ideal status, so as to keep it/them from jamming the works of the theoretical machinery.[42]

Such an excess, therefore, does not just elude the fixed, discrete schemata of formal symbolization; it actually poses a threat to the latter. In the same way women are denied the prospect of expressing their own pleasure, on their own terms – for 'female pleasure has to remain inarticulate in language, in its own language, if it is not to threaten the underpinnings of logical operations' – fluid mechanics has been systematically neglected within physics, for fear the stochastic indeterminacy of the former's object of study might undermine the surety of the latter's congealed categories.[43]

Woman, because she experiences herself in this way, 'only fragmentarily, in the little-structured margins of a dominant ideology, as waste, or excess, what is left of a mirror invested by the (masculine) "subject" to reflect himself, to copy himself', possesses the instruments to challenge the *a priori* valorization of similitude.[44] Such an endeavour, as we already know, cannot involve the articulation of a feminine discourse corresponding to its masculine counterpart, positing woman as a subject equal to her male equivalent – an approach that can only reinforce the intelligibility of sexual difference through *in*difference alone. Likewise, it cannot posit another concept of femininity or the female subject, for this would be to assert a merely more accurate self-representation, remaining within the system of masculine representation. 'The feminine cannot signify itself in any proper meaning, proper name, or concept, not even that of woman.'[45] The question, then, is what transformations might allow for the possibility of a women's politics within a discursive order imposed by men (i.e. a phallocratic order)? How might women speak of their own exploitation and voice their own demands? How might they address their position of alterity without reinscribing it within the generalized repetition of the economy of similitude? Simply put, how might they discover or recover a language that is truly their own? To finally express themselves *as* women.

The answer, Irigaray proposes, is that instead of trying to speak as a male or gender-neutral subject, woman must 'assume the feminine role deliberately', and in doing so, 'convert a form of subordination into an affirmation'.[46] Irigaray wishes to embrace the aporia faced by woman: namely, that she can either speak in words borrowed from masculinist discourse, remaining a hollow imitation or simulacrum of the men for whom this is their natural language, or she can speak in words that the master discourse will deem unintelligible, and thus spurn as irrational or pathological, even while this discourse uses her as a mirror upon which it projects and reflects its own images:

> she can only be knowable, recognizable, under disguises that denature her; she borrows forms that will never belong to her and that she must nevertheless mimic if she is to enter even a little way into knowledge. And when she does this, she will no doubt be stigmatized, after the fact, for owing her power of seduction to *deceptive* appearances. She will be blamed for claiming to compete in this way with the real attributes of the types in her modes of being, and in the relationships she has with other beings. Whereas the logos, in order to preserve the purity of its conception, veils her in the truth of its word to the extent that it is no longer clear what she holds in reserve, and all the desires and delirium of power denied by the measuredness of Reason can be projected onto her. She is thus manifest and exalted, even as she is masked and lost, in discursive displays

that set her outside herself; offered in an ideal form to the oratorical disputes between men. *As for the rest*, it lies buried under the earth, deep down in dark caves where all is shadow and oblivion.[47]

Woman's exclusion from the dominant discourse does not preclude her from parodying it. She can use her capacity for mimicking the 'reasonable' words of her oppressors in order to demonstrate that what they regard as abnormal or incomprehensible is in fact foundational, and thus showing up the fragility of their proclaimed mastery. Her alterity, her position outside of this discourse, means her 'self' remains unscathed by this discourse even as it interrogates it. She is always elsewhere; she always holds something in reserve.

Crucially, this strategic mimesis – in line with all the thinkers discussed throughout this book – does not so much concern itself with specific propositions or concepts (even though it might point towards these as exemplars); rather, through a playful repetition, it takes aim at discourse as a whole. For in order to transform culture, we must first transform language. More precisely, it targets that discourse – the *logos* – which positions itself as *the* discourse, the sole legitimate and rational medium of communication. Irigaray describes this at various times as a masculine discourse, a phallogocentric discourse, a phallocratic discourse, even just a metaphysical or philosophical discourse, but ultimately it is what she calls a *discourse of truth*.[48] A language into which woman's pleasure, desire and sexual difference tout court remain untranslatable – and thus a perpetual threat. This discourse of truth, at the same time it claims to speak for all subjects and all beings, draws the boundaries of what is and is not expressible, and in doing so, also determines who can and cannot speak on their own terms. Irigaray's hopes lie in the prospect of 'jamming the theoretical machinery itself, of suspending its pretension to the production of a truth and of a meaning that are excessively univocal', and thus making room for another kind of utterance, another mode of speaking or writing.[49] She tries to bring into relief a properly feminist mode of address, not aligned with nor trying to replicate the discourse of truth (as one would expect from a philosopher) but set in opposition to it.

Speaking as a woman

'For Irigaray', writes Judith Butler, 'the possibility of another language or signifying economy is the only chance at escaping the "mark" of gender'.[50] Masculine language, argues Irigaray, 'gives privileged status to "self-representing", excluding all it might regard as threatening or troublesome to its ideality, covering over all those irregularities, dissymmetries and blank spaces that might interrupt the smooth operation of the *logos*.[51] But it never fully accomplishes this dissimulation. Within 'those *blank spaces* in discourse that remind us of the places of her exclusion, spacings which, by their *silent plasticity*, ensure the cohesion, articulation, and consistent spread of established forms', Irigaray sights a means of this disruption.[52] Women must insistently bring attention to the impotence of 'reasonable' words – which they access thanks to their capacity for mimicry – in the face of their disruptive excess, reinscribing these troublesome gaps within the texts themselves. They must '*shatter syntax* by suspending its always-teleological order by snipping wires, cutting off power, breaking circuits, reversing couplings, and changing continuity, alternation, frequency, and intensity' generating an endless dispersion, diffraction and deflection of energy incapable of being traced back to a single origin.[53] Women speak, superficially, in the language of reason, yet do so in a manner that will seem contradictory, unreasonable, mad and even imperceptible to the latter. Diffuse rather than linear, never settled or established, always left unfinished, they use words in such a fashion that their meaning can never congeal – a discursive practice devoid of all claims to identity, in excess of all common sense, good taste and formal coherence.

To speak as a woman then, as Irigaray would have it, is to prioritize fluidity over precision. It is to speak in a manner that does not wholly escape the dominant discourse but surreptitiously slips out of its rigid structures and prefabricated codes, making it impossible 'to trap women in the exact definition of what they mean, to make them repeat (themselves) so that it will be clear'.[54] To never speak of the same thing, in the same way, twice. To speak in a fashion that confounds linear reading, with all its teleological implications. To speak in accordance with a 'style' (although said discourse will never recognize it as such) that 'resists and explodes every firmly established form, figure, idea or concept', making no claim to closure or totality, and unable to be captured as the object of an argument or position.[55] This speech also requires a different kind of listening, one that can hear all those utterances that do not fit into readymade schemata, one that does not filter out all those sounds that do not conform to its discursive mechanisms.

Woman's status as simultaneously internal to and yet excluded from the dominant discourse – capable of mimicking it even as she remains irrecuperable by it – enables her to disrupt, and perhaps eventually even destroy this discourse and its mechanisms, by making manifest that which it must repress:

what is important is to disconcert the staging of representation according to *exclusively* 'masculine' parameters, that is, according to a phallocratic order. It is not a matter of toppling that order so as to replace it – that amounts to the same thing in the end – but of disrupting and modifying it, starting from an 'outside' that is exempt, in part, from phallocratic law.[56]

An indirect challenge, but one striking at the heart of discursive coherence in a way no claim to the dignity of subjecthood will ever manage. Through strategic mimesis, woman playfully and disingenuously adopts the language censoring, censuring and exploiting her – with all its binary oppositions and essentialist presuppositions – intervening as an outsider in order to reveal that she was always there, always underpinning the system spurning her.[57] Identified with the vertiginous manifold of the 'sensible', counterposed against the stable certitude of 'intelligible' discourse, she unveils herself as inextricably present within the latter, sustaining its very systematicity; likewise, identified with the passive receptivity of 'matter', counterposed against the active potency of 'form', she discloses herself as the condition of possibility for all reproduction, and thus for discourse as such. She renders herself visible at the same time she continues to evade the shackles of representation: she is always there, at the foundation, and yet always already elsewhere.

Accompanying this endeavour to speak (and listen) as a woman is an act of (re)reading and interpretation of phallogocentrism – a critique of the symbolic order, the masculine imaginary and their circumscription of the boundaries of possible expression. A psychoanalytic rereading of philosophical discourse:

> we need to pay attention to the way the unconscious works in each philosophy, and perhaps in philosophy in general. We need to listen (psycho)analytically to its procedures of repression, to the structuration of language that shores up its representations, separating the true from the false, the meaningful from the meaningless, and so forth. [. . .] For each philosopher, beginning with those whose names define some age in the history of philosophy, we have to point out how the break with material contiguity is made, how the system is put together, how the specular economy works.[58]

The aim of this undertaking is 'to cast phallocentrism, phallocratism, loose from its moorings in order to return the masculine to its own language, leaving open the possibility of a different language', denying it the right to define itself as a totality, to assign the values and determine the properties of things, and thus to 'leave space for the feminine'.[59]

Irigaray wishes to ensure a space for woman within sexual difference – without hierarchy or subordination, without being reduced to a mere inversion of man and without representing her alterity through the flat mirror of similitude. As was the case for Foucault, we can understand Irigaray's work, counterintuitively, as an unexpected inheritor of the Kantian critical project: she attempts to show that in its boundless ambition to speak for all, the discourse of reason actually fetters the possibility of other ways of speaking. Space for the latter can only be carved out 'if the feminine is granted its own "specificity" in its relation to language', unburdened by the demand for discursive coherence and systematicity.[60] For Irigaray then, the critique of philosophical discursivity and its inability to account for difference as such is inseparable from discursive practice:

> for woman it is not a matter of installing herself within this lack, this negative, even by denouncing it, nor of reversing the economy of sameness by turning the feminine into *the standard for 'sexual difference'*; it is rather a matter of trying to practice that difference.[61]

Discourse is thus both the terrain upon which this practice takes place and the object of its critique: it is brought to bear upon itself, highlighting its own shortcomings and occlusions, in the hopes that 'what has been serving as a condition of possibility of philosophical discourse, of rationality in general, can make itself heard'.[62]

The power of philosophical discourse

Irigaray's psychoanalytic feminism, in its subversion of philosophical *doxa*, perfectly illustrates the basic concern underlying this entire book: namely, that one can use the question of communication to gesture towards a truth residing beyond the bounds of communicability – or more specifically, beyond those of discursive reason. For Irigaray, there is something that one cannot obtain via philosophical discursion: specifically, sexual difference as such, which she contrasts with the specular representation of woman as the inverted image of man. This exclusion of anything not aligning with masculine codes of intelligibility forms the basis of discursive systematicity and coherence. But, she contends, there *is* a way of speaking (and listening) that allows one to speak in accordance with such difference, though this very fact means one can never speak of 'woman' as a concept, let alone transmit something of 'her' essence.

Hoping to ensure it can never become just another discourse of truth, Irigaray vacillates between treating this feminine mode of address, on the one hand, as a substantive and historically repressed language in its own right, capable of speaking of aspects of the real that fall through the gaps of the dominant discourse, and on the other hand, as just a parodic mimesis revealing that which will never be discursively assimilable. Whatever the case, this manner of speaking is, thanks to its continual becoming-other, incapable of integral transmission: one speaks in accordance with sexual difference, one does not speak *of* it as such. At the same time though, it is difficult to discount the fact there is a *truth* posited here, albeit an elusive one. The 'truth' that traverses Irigaray's account is the excess of the sexual relation, the excess of desire, *jouissance*, the excess of everything assigned to 'woman', 'matter', 'the sensible', 'the fluid', 'the maternal' and so on. For although she intends her parodic approach to destabilize any conventional truth claim, this mimesis supervenes upon the certainty she invests in an *a priori* condition that cannot itself be a mere parody: namely, that there are certain aspects of the real the dominant discourse can never adequately represent.

In designating the dominant, masculine mode of address a 'discourse of truth', Irigaray underscores that the philosophical mobilization of 'truth' does not need to occur via propositional truth claims alone; on the contrary, for many philosophers 'truth' must be gestured towards through the cultivation of a particular mode of comportment or manner of speaking. This ring-fencing of the sphere of properly philosophical speech enables a circumscription of who can be deemed to speak philosophically rather than doxastically. For Irigaray, this is what philosophical discourse has always done: it has demanded a fixed, inflexible manner of speaking, rooted in self-identity and incapable of conceiving of difference in its own right. And yet, as I have shown, many philosophers – spanning the history of Western philosophy – have in fact appealed to comportment in order to gesture towards the incommunicable, a truth exceeding integral transmission and bounded signification. Is Irigaray's own manoeuvre really so distinct from this, even if it reverses the basic terms? Does Irigaray not ring-fence the sphere of the properly philosophical (i.e. the masculine) to then point towards an exteriority that exceeds this sphere and a mode of address that can speak in accordance with it?

Irigaray illustrates the fundamental ambivalence of this approach. In detailing the specular, occlusive mechanisms with which phallogocentric discourse operates, she is able to depict, rather vividly and unconventionally, the ease with which the assertion of a peculiarly philosophical manner of speaking – intended to provide a critical outlook vis-à-vis the received truths saturating ordinary speech – can itself become doxastic and exclusionary, dismissing other forms of speech and modes of address. Indeed, one aspect of the strategic mimesis at work in Irigaray's texts is the parodic accentuation of philosophical inaccessibility: declaring that woman 'does not have to conform to the codes theory has set up for itself', she writes in a manner intended to confound ingrained habits of reading, hoping to generate discomfort in those still caught in the grip of the masculine imaginary and joy in those who can read between the lines, whose ears are open to other ways of communicating.[63] Her work, even as it draws upon recognizable tropes and figures from philosophy (though without the citational practices that grant them their authority), drops all pretence of universality: it is a discourse of the other, addressed to an audience for whom the identity foisted by philosophy proper has never seemed quite adequate.[64]

Of course, when considering the context of Irigaray's work, it would be hard to contest her justification for this performative exclusion, redressing a vast historical repression by turning masculine discourse's oppressive techniques back upon itself. But there is a risk that her exaggerated presentation of this discourse and its circumscription of intelligibility reinforces the metaphysical logic she wishes to undermine. Irigaray's argument presupposes the identification not just of a systematic discrimination or prejudice against women within philosophy (the historical evidence for which is incontrovertible) but of an utter exclusion of woman as such from the bounds of acceptable discourse. Woman, according to this account, cannot speak on her own terms as long as she is restricted to the laws of discursive coherence and systematicity, for she will always exceed its codified laws and values. 'For Irigaray', writes Michelle Boulous Walker, 'woman's exclusion from the project of philosophy is complete. The equation of rationality with masculinity is totalised in her account, and she argues that this equation allows no voice for the feminine Other'.[65] Irigaray's project requires this stark division, this wholesale exclusion of feminine speech from the *logos*, this incapacity of sexual difference to be incorporated into the dominant discourse, in order for her strategic mimesis to remain feasible. Woman's unambiguous position of exteriority vis-à-vis this discourse means its logic cannot contaminate her, even as she adopts its tropes and mannerisms. Ironically, for all that she claims to reject coherence, her parodic approach needs this well-ordered opposition between discourses to avoid the accusation that it is simply reproducing that which it denounces.[66]

It is questionable – even when taking into account the patently exclusionary nature of philosophy from antiquity through to the present day – whether this partition has ever been as clear-cut as Irigaray depicts it. As other feminist philosophers such as Kofman and Le Dœuff have observed, women's exclusion from both philosophy and psychoanalysis (let alone discourse as a whole) has never been absolute and is very much historically variable.⁶⁷ Irigaray overstates the power of this discourse in its capacity to draw its own boundaries, define its own terms, set its own values, fix its own significations and totalize the sayable. She creates a monolithic image of philosophical discourse in its ideal, mythical (and more than anything else, Platonic) form, attributing powers that it has never possessed, in order that she can then not only point towards everything exceeding it but guarantee that this excess will remain forever inaccessible to and unrepresentable by this discourse. She ignores the messiness, porosity and plurality of philosophy – the failure of its practice to live up to its idealities. And as such, even if she intends to mimic philosophers' own claims, even if she posits this ideality in order to subvert it, ultimately Irigaray does exactly what every figure discussed in this book attempts to do: she reifies the boundaries of properly philosophical manner of speaking in the name of a truth that can never be transmitted integrally.⁶⁸

'A discourse can poison, surround, close off, and imprison,' Irigaray reminds us, 'or it can liberate, cure, nourish and fecundate. It is rarely neutral'.⁶⁹ These two possibilities are not, however, mutually exclusive. A discourse, as we have seen over the course of this book, can illuminate and obscure simultaneously; it can open doors to new ways of thinking, gaining knowledge and forming bonds with others but at the same time also close doors, forbidding access or dismissing those who do not conform to its strictures. As Isabelle Stengers comments, 'the contemporary scene is literally saturated with the "modern" heirs of Plato. Each of these heirs denounces his "other", just as the philosopher denounced the sophists, accused them of exploiting that which he himself had triumphed over'.⁷⁰ On the face of it, of course, it would be ungenerous to portray Irigaray as performing just another repetition of this gesture. She is trying to throw a spanner in the works of the philosophical machine, strategically indicating both the impossibility and absurdity of its constitutive exclusions. She has no interest whatsoever in propping up philosophy's traditional prejudices and delimitations.

And yet, Irigaray's project still rests upon the articulation of a peculiar manner of speaking – one that cannot be taken as simply playful or ironic, lest it undermine its own political and ethical aspirations, but which cannot be taken wholly seriously either, lest it become indistinguishable from the essentialist metaphysics it aims to subvert. Irigaray's deconstruction of philosophical discourse consistently equates the latter with the Platonic *logos*, 'the neat, clear-cut, immutable, unambiguous categories that characterize, divide up, classify, and order everything', collocated against 'the phantasmagorias of *doxa*'.⁷¹ To speak as a woman, in her estimation, is to speak on the latter side of this *khorismos*, and in doing so, to unsettle this entire abiding dualism. Except that this never really occurs: she inverts its terms, but the form remains intact. For all her success in highlighting the exclusionary nature of metaphysical discursion, Irigaray's strategy of mimicry or mimesis is, ultimately, more or less indistinguishable from the broader strategy of *speaking philosophically* surveyed throughout this book. Which is not necessarily a fundamental shortcoming but it does suggest that the boundaries of the philosophical *logos* may not be as impermeable as she is wont to claim.

Notes

Introduction

1 Plato, *The Laws*, trans. Trevor J. Saunders (London: Penguin, 1970), 968c. Citations for Plato's works throughout this book refer to the standard Stephanus numbering system.
2 See Plato, *Protagoras and Meno*, trans. Adam Beresford (London: Penguin, 2005), 85b–86c; cf. *Phaedo*, 73a. For further examination of *anamnēsis* in the *Meno*, see Gail Fine, 'Inquiry in the Meno', in *Plato on Knowledge and Forms: Selected Essays* (Oxford: Clarendon Press, 2003), 44–65.
3 Samuel Taylor Coleridge, *The Collected Works of Samuel Taylor Coleridge, Volume 4 (Part I): The Friend*, ed. Barbara E. Rooke (London: Routledge & Kegan Paul, 1969), 42–3.
4 Plato, *The Republic*, trans. Robin Waterfield (Oxford: Oxford University Press, 1993), 499a.
5 Arthur Schopenhauer, *The World as Will and Representation, Vol. 1*, trans. Judith Norman, Alistair Welchman, and Christopher Janaway (Cambridge: Cambridge University Press, 2019), 507.
6 Aristotle, *Posterior Analytics*, trans. Jonathan Barnes (Oxford: Clarendon Press, 1993), 71a.
7 Ibid.
8 Max Deutscher, *Towards Continental Philosophy: Reason and Imagination in the Thought of Max Deutscher* (Lanham: Rowman & Littlefield, 2021), 94.
9 Aristotle, *Prior Analytics, Book I*, trans. Gisela Striker (Oxford: Clarendon Press, 2009), 24a. Heidegger describes the propositional form as follows: 'a statement is true if what it means and says is in accordance with the matter about which the statement is made' (*Pathmarks*, ed. William McNeill (Cambridge: Cambridge University Press, 1998), 138); cf. Peter Yates, 'Nietzsche, Aristotle, and Propositional Discourse', in *Nietzsche and Antiquity: His Reaction and Response to the Classical Tradition*, ed. Paul Bishop (Cambridge: Cambridge University Press, 2004).
10 A surface-level similarity might be picked up here between my argument and Heidegger's narrative of the 'forgetting of Being', insofar as Heidegger claims that 'it is precisely in Plato and Aristotle that the decline of the determination of *logos* sets in', a decline that would eventually render the *logos* unintelligible (*Introduction to Metaphysics*, trans. Gregory Fried and Richard Polt (New Haven: Yale University

Press, 2000), 182). I, however, reject this notion that Plato and Aristotle instigated a profound rupture in the history of philosophy.
11 Michèle Le Dœuff, *The Philosophical Imaginary*, trans. Colin Gordon (London and New York: Continuum, 1989), 114, translation altered.
12 Plato, *Republic*, 376a.
13 Ibid.
14 Ibid., 376b.
15 Ibid.
16 Sara Ahmed, *Strange Encounters: Embodied Others in Post-Coloniality* (London and New York: Routledge, 2000), 56.
17 Plato does his utmost, in Stephen Gaukroger's words, 'to carve out and shape a particular kind of discourse for its own purposes, providing it with a genealogy and characterising it in a way that marginalises its competitors' ('The Persona of the Natural Philosopher', in *The Philosopher in Early Modern Europe: The Nature of a Contested Identity*, ed. Conal Condren, Stephen Gaukroger, and Ian Hunter (Cambridge: Cambridge University Press, 2006), 17–18.
18 For a defence of ordinary language philosophy (in the sense established by Wittgenstein) vis-à-vis the stylistic norms of the continental tradition, see Sandra Laugier, *Why We Need Ordinary Language Philosophy*, trans. Daniela Ginsburg (Chicago: The University of Chicago Press, 2013). Conversely, a quintessential example of the defence of these norms, and the perceived difficulty of much continental philosophical writing, can be found in Judith Butler, 'Values of Difficulty', in *Just Being Difficult? Academic Writing in the Public Arena*, ed. Jonathan Culler and Kevin Lamb (Stanford: Stanford University Press, 2003).
19 See Sybille Krämer, *Medium, Messenger, Transmission: An Approach to Media Philosophy*, trans. Anthony Enns (Amsterdam: Amsterdam University Press, 2015), 21–2.
20 Régis Debray, *Media Manifestos: On the Technological Transmission of Cultural Forms*, trans. Eric Rauth (London and New York: Verso, 1996), 44.
21 Saint Augustine, *On Christian Teaching*, trans. R. P. H. Green (Oxford: Oxford University Press, 1997), 30.
22 On Locke's pivotal role in defining the English term *communication*, see John Guillory, 'Genesis of the Media Concept', *Critical Inquiry* 36, no. 2 (2010): 331–5.
23 John Locke, *An Essay Concerning Human Understanding* (London: Penguin, 2004), 425.
24 Ibid.
25 As Paul de Man observes, 'at times it seems as if Locke would have liked nothing better than to be allowed to forget about language altogether' ('The Epistemology of Metaphor', *Critical Inquiry* 5, no. 1 (1978): 14.
26 Régis Debray, *Transmitting Culture*, trans. Eric Rauth (New York: Columbia University Press, 2000), 6. Debray relies upon a terminological distinction between

communication (linear and synchronic transferral of knowledge) and *transmission* (diffuse and diachronic establishment of tradition) that, for clarity's sake, I have not replicated here.
27 Ibid.
28 Ibid.
29 'All communities larger than primordial villages of face-to-face contact (and perhaps even these)', argues Benedict Anderson, 'are imagined' (*Imagined Communities: Reflections on the Origin and Spread of Nationalism* (London and New York: Verso, 2006), 6).
30 See Bertrand Russell, *Mysticism and Logic* (London: George Allen & Unwin, 1917), 209–32.
31 Jean-Luc Nancy, *The Gravity of Thought*, trans. François Raffoul and Gregory Recco (Atlantic Highlands: Humanities Press, 1997), 52.
32 Pierre Hadot, *Philosophy as a Way of Life: Spiritual Exercises from Socrates to Foucault*, trans. Michael Chase (Oxford and Cambridge: Blackwell, 1995), 59.
33 There are a few modern thinkers who Hadot mentions as echoing these ancient spiritual exercises: e.g. Goethe, Schopenhauer, Nietzsche, Kierkegaard, Bergson, Wittgenstein and Foucault. But with the exception of the latter two, they are rarely his primary object of study.
34 Ian Hunter, *Rival Enlightenments: Civil and Metaphysical Philosophy in Early Modern Germany* (Cambridge: Cambridge University Press, 2003), 23. University metaphysics, in Hunter's conception, is defined principally by a fascination with the relationship between worldly finitude and infinite, pure intellection, inculcating its followers into an exercise of ascetic self-transformation reaching towards the latter.
35 Hadot, *Philosophy as a Way of Life*, 76.
36 'The widespread sense that communication means the unproblematic transmission of meaning,' remarks John Durham Peters, 'makes it seem to some people like a funny topic for an academic field' ('Doctors of Philosophy', in *Philosophical Profiles in the Theory of Communication*, ed. Jason Hannan (New York: Peter Lang, 2012), 500).
37 Gilles Deleuze and Félix Guattari, *What Is Philosophy?*, trans. Hugh Tomlinson and Graham Burchell (New York: Columbia University Press, 1994), 6.
38 Ibid., 28.
39 Ibid., 22.
40 Jacques Derrida, *Margins of Philosophy*, trans. Alan Bass (Chicago: The University of Chicago Press, 1982), 322, translation altered.
41 Debray, *Transmitting Culture*, 15.
42 Jean-François Lyotard, *The Inhuman: Reflections on Time*, trans. Geoffrey Bennington and Rachel Bowlby (Stanford: Stanford University Press, 1991), 62.
43 Nancy, *Gravity of Thought*, 38.

Chapter 1

1. Chiara Bottici, *A Philosophy of Political Myth* (Cambridge: Cambridge University Press, 2007), 26.
2. Friedrich Nietzsche, *Philosophy in the Tragic Age of the Greeks*, trans. Marianne Cowan (Washington, DC: Regnery Publishing, 1962), 35–6.
3. Aristotle, *Metaphysics*, trans. C. D. C. Reeve (Indianapolis: Hackett, 2016), 683b; cf. Harold Cherniss, *Aristotle's Criticism of Presocratic Philosophy* (Baltimore: The Johns Hopkins University Press, 1935).
4. Ibid., 984a.
5. Heraclitus B30. All translations of the Presocratics in this chapter are taken from Patricia Curd (ed.), *A Presocratics Reader: Selected Fragments and Testimonia* (Indianapolis: Hackett, 2011). Citations refer to the standard Diels–Kranz numbering system.
6. Heraclitus' claim that 'all things are an exchange for fire and fire for all things, as goods for gold and gold for goods' makes this synonymy between fire and harmonic opposition apparent (B90). As Charles Kahn argues, 'the doctrines of fire, cosmic order, and elemental transformations serve as more than illustrations; but they are significant only insofar as they reveal a general truth about the unity of opposites' (*The Art and Thought of Heraclitus* (Cambridge: Cambridge University Press, 1979), 21); cf. Patricia Curd, 'Knowledge and Unity in Heraclitus', *The Monist* 74, no. 4 (1991): 531–49.
7. An exhaustive study of the law in Heraclitus can be found in Thanos Zartaloudis, *The Birth of Nomos* (Edinburgh: Edinburgh University Press, 2019), 188–211.
8. Heraclitus propounds that one should be 'listening not to [him], but to the *logos*' (B50).
9. Heraclitus, B2.
10. Heraclitus, B114. As Kahn argues, for Heraclitus 'the *logos* is "common" because it is (or expresses) a structure that characterizes all things, and is therefore a public possession in principle available to all men, since it is "given" in the immanent structure of their shared experience', allowing for a communication that truly expresses this commonness, rather than remaining ensnared within individual worlds of subjective experience (*Art and Thought*, 101–2).
11. The divine law of the *logos* is 'the sufficient reason of laws *qua* laws, whatever the variation in content' (Marcel Conche, *Héraclite: Fragments* (Paris: Presses Universitaires de France, 1986), 218–19, my translation).
12. Heraclitus, B1.
13. Ibid., B78.
14. Since this book is concerned precisely with the exclusionary affordances of philosophical language, this chapter, as in most of the chapters of this book, I have preserved the authors' use of male pronouns when discussing the figure

of the philosopher, since it is readily apparent they imagined this figure to be a man; conversely, I have actively avoided such usage in later chapters, where such a segregation is clearly not intended. For more on this approach, see Pauline Kleingeld, 'The Problematic Status of Gender-Neutral Language in the History of Philosophy', *The Philosophical Forum* 25, no. 2 (1993): 134–50.
15 Conche, *Héraclite*, 82.
16 Heraclitus, B107.
17 Kahn, *Art and Thought*, 107.
18 Heraclitus, notes Kathryn Morgan, 'attacks men for failing to use the kind of language he thinks they should, and this criticism is extended to their mode of consciousness' (*Myth & Philosophy from the Presocratics to Plato* (Cambridge: Cambridge University Press, 2004), 28)
19 Conche, *Héraclite*, 151.
20 'A message embodied in all messages, a truth behind all truths', as Daniel Graham puts it (*Explaining the Cosmos: The Ionian Tradition of Scientific Philosophy* (Princeton: Princeton University Press, 2006), 144).
21 Heraclitus, B34.
22 Ibid., B1.
23 Ibid., B113.
24 'Those who speak with understanding (*noos*) must rely firmly on what is common to all as a city must rely on its law, and much more firmly. For all human laws are nourished by one law, the divine law; for it has as much power as it wishes and is sufficient for all and is still left over' (Ibid., B114).
25 For a rejoinder to this standard characterization of Heraclitus as a misanthropic aristocrat, refer to Kōjin Karatani, *Isonomia and the Origins of Philosophy*, trans. Joseph A. Murphy (Durham: Duke University Press, 2012), 80–3.
26 Conche, *Héraclite*, 24.
27 Heraclitus, B104 'By the very gesture of defining and demarcating what poets could hope to know or communicate', writes Glenn Most, 'the philosophers seem to be suggesting that they themselves are exempt from such limitations [. . .] carving out for themselves a discursive space that would be autonomous and privileged over other forms of social communication' ('The Poetics of Early Greek Philosophy', in *The Cambridge Companion to Early Greek Philosophy*, ed. A. A. Long (Cambridge: Cambridge University Press, 1999), 334).
28 Heraclitus, B123. On the ambiguity of Heraclitus' phrasing here, see Pierre Hadot, *The Veil of Isis: An Essay on the History of the Idea of Nature*, trans. Michael Chase (Cambridge: The Belknap Press of Harvard University Press, 2006).
29 See Conche, *Héraclite*, 253–5.
30 Heraclitus, B93.
31 Maurice Blanchot, *The Infinite Conversation*, trans. Susan Hanson (Minneapolis: University of Minnesota Press, 1993), 86, translation altered.

32 Ibid., translation altered.
33 'Heraclitian harmony', writes Jean Beaufret, 'speaks of the pressured junction of opposing forces. It is at work only in the adjoining of adverse tensions [...] Here language philosophizes by itself, and it is a play of words that precedes thought, for it is in this play that the unity of contraries is directly articulated' (*Dialogue with Heidegger*, trans. Mark Sinclair (Bloomington and Indianapolis: Indiana University Press, 2006), 22).
34 Heraclitus, B50.
35 Conche, *Héraclite*, 36.
36 On the Heraclitean usage of paradox, see in particular Mary Margaret Mackenzie, 'Heraclitus and the Art of Paradox', in *Oxford Studies in Ancient Philosophy, Vol. VI*, ed. Julia Annas (Oxford: Clarendon Press, 1988); cf. Joanne Waugh, 'Heraclitus: The Postmodern Presocratic?', *The Monist* 74, no. 4 (1991): 605–23 and Erin O'Connell, *Heraclitus and Derrida: Presocratic Deconstruction* (New York: Peter Lang, 2006).
37 See Plato, *Theaetetus*, trans. Robin Waterfield (London: Penguin, 2004), 152e, in which he pointedly singles out Parmenides as not beholden to the privileging of becoming over being.
38 Parmenides, B7.
39 Parmenides' duality between *alētheia* and *doxa* is discussed in Patricia Curd, *Eleatic Monism and Later Presocratic Thought* (Princeton: Princeton University Press, 1998), 98–126.
40 Marcel Conche, *Parménide: Le Poème: Fragments* (Presses Universitaires de France, 1996), 66. 'Ancient Greek philosophers, like ancient Greek oral poets', argues Lisa Atwood Wilkinson, 'do not claim *for themselves* an experience of the real or divine', for even while their works may have been composed in a written form, they were still likely intended to be read aloud in front of an audience, keeping in mind the comparative scarcity of written texts in the ancient world, and the labour involved in reproducing them (*Parmenides and To Eon: Reconsidering Muthos and Logos* (London and New York: Continuum, 2009), 75).
41 Hadot lumps Heraclitus and Parmenides, as well as Empedocles, together as 'aristocrats of knowledge [...] who opposed their theories to the ignorance of the mob' (*What Is Ancient Philosophy?*, trans. Michael Chase (Cambridge: The Belknap Press of Harvard University Press, 2002), 26).
42 Heraclitus, B104, B108.
43 Ibid., B51.
44 Mario Perniola, *Enigmas: The Egyptian Moment in Society and Art*, trans. Christopher Woodall (London and New York: Verso), 19; cf. Andrew Benjamin, *Place, Commonality, and Judgement: Continental Philosophy and the Ancient Greeks* (London and New York: Continuum, 2010), 29–53.
45 Conche, *Héraclite*, 49.
46 Ibid., 37.

47 Ibid., 218.
48 Ibid., 36.
49 On the complex relationship between commonality and separation (and Heraclitus' use of language more generally), see T. H. Lesher, 'Heraclitus' Epistemological Vocabulary', *Hermes* 111, no. 2 (1983): 155–70.
50 Conche, *Héraclite*, 58.
51 Ibid., 137.
52 Harold Cherniss, *Selected Papers*, ed. Leonardo Tarán (Leiden: Brill, 1977), 17. It is 'intriguing', remarks Rosalind Thomas, 'that one of the earliest known prose works, that of Heraclitus, was said to have been deposited by him in a temple – like a set of laws or an inscription of public importance' (*Oral Tradition and Written Record in Classical Athens* (Cambridge: Cambridge University Press, 1989), 31).

Chapter 2

1 Iris Murdoch, *The Fire and the Sun: Why Plato Banished the Artists* (Oxford: Clarendon Press, 1977), 21.
2 Philippe Lacoue-Labarthe, *The Subject of Philosophy*, trans. Thomas Tresize, Hugh J. Silverman, Gary M. Cole, Timothy D. Bent, Karen McPherson, and Claudette Satiliot (Minneapolis: University of Minnesota Press, 1993), 1.
3 Hadot, *Philosophy as a Way of Life*, 163.
4 Plato, *Symposium*, trans. Christopher Gill (London: Penguin, 1999), 175e.
5 See Dmitri Nikulin, *Dialectic and Dialogue* (Stanford: Stanford University Press, 2010), 1–22; cf. Christopher Rowe, *Plato and the Art of Philosophical Writing* (Cambridge: Cambridge University Press, 2007). On Socrates's role as narrator in the Platonic dialogues, and the interplay between reason and the emotions that this narration dramatizes, see Anne-Marie Schultz, *Plato's Socrates as Narrator: A Philosophical Muse* (Lanham: Lexington Books, 2013).
6 Complicated even further in later dialogues by the diminished role (and sometimes disappearance) of Socrates. On Plato's incorporation of real individuals, both historical and contemporary, into his fictionalized disputations, see Debra Nails, *The People of Plato: A Prosopography of Plato and Other Socratics* (Indianapolis: Hackett, 2002).
7 Sarah Kofman, *Socrates: Fictions of a Philosopher*, trans. Catherine Porter (London: The Athlone Press, 1998), 4–5. On the literary character of Plato's dialogues, and his use of dramatis personae, see Ruby Blondell, *The Play of Character in Plato's Dialogues* (Cambridge: Cambridge University Press, 2004) and Rebecca Bensen Cain, *The Socratic Method: Plato's Use of Philosophical Drama* (London and New York: Continuum, 2007); on the broader dramatology of Plato's dialogues, see

Catherine H. Zuckert, *Plato's Philosophers: The Coherence of the Dialogues* (Chicago: The University of Chicago Press, 2009).
8. See Mary Margaret Mackenzie, 'Paradox in Plato's "Phaedrus"', *Proceedings of the Cambridge Philological Society* 28 (1982): 64–76.
9. 'Notice', in Platon, *Phèdre*, trans. Léon Robin (Paris: Société d'Édition, 1933), liv, my translation.
10. Plato, *Phaedrus*, trans. Christopher Rowe (London: Penguin, 2005), 274d–279b. The seminal essay on this aspect of the *Phaedrus* is, of course, Jacques Derrida's *Dissemination*, trans. Barbara Johnson (London and New York: Continuum, 1981), 67–186.
11. John Durham Peters, *Speaking into the Air: A History of the Idea of Communication* (Chicago: University of Chicago Press, 1999), 37. On the role that a nascent literacy plays in Plato's philosophy, see Jack Goody and Ian Watt, 'The Consequences of Literacy', *Comparative Studies in Society and History* 5, no. 3 (1963): 304–45.
12. Plato, *Phaedrus*, 275a.
13. Robin, 'Notice', li.
14. Plato, *Phaedrus.*, 275e; cf. *Protagoras,* 329a.
15. Plato, *Phaedrus*, 278c.
16. Ibid., 278d.
17. The sophists, remarks Robin, 'taught literary or oratorial procedures by means of books and notes, typical compositions in which they had, once and for all, put these procedures into practice' (*Platon* (Paris: Presses Universitaires de France, 1935), 9, my translation).
18. Plato, *Phaedrus*, 276a.
19. Plato, *Phaedrus*, 277e.
20. Ibid., 278d.
21. 'Plato furnished the word "philosophy"', argues Hans-Georg Gadamer, 'with a somewhat artificial and decidedly unconventional emphasis; for him, philosophy was the sheer striving after wisdom or truth. For Plato, philosophy was not the possession of knowledge but only the striving for knowledge' (*The Beginning of Philosophy*, trans. Rod Coltman (London and New York: Continuum, 1998), 15).
22. See Francis Grabowski, who positions Plato as an unusual kind of empiricist, conceiving of knowledge as arising not through discursion, but through an awareness of the ideas (*Plato, Metaphysics, and the Forms* (London and New York: Continuum, 2008)).
23. Plato, *Republic*, 596e.
24. Plato, *Phaedrus*, 275d.
25. Ibid., 275e.
26. Plato, *Protagoras and Meno*, 336b.

27 Plato, *The Last Days of Socrates*, trans. Hugh Tredennick and Harold Tarrant (London: Penguin, 2003), 99e.
28 For a comprehensive survey of the role of *logos* in Plato's philosophy, see John Sallis, *Being and Logos: Reading the Platonic Dialogues* (Bloomington and Indianapolis: Indiana University Press, 1996).
29 Even though philosophy eventually moved beyond the 'drastic pre-Platonic doctrine that went so far as to proclaim unthinkable the concepts of the multiple and the changing', argues Adriana Cavarero, 'the dualistic framework founded on Parmenides' teaching still persists', preserving 'the distinction between *episteme* and *doxa*, mind and body, the world of ideas and the world of life' (*In Spite of Plato: A Feminist Reworking of Ancient Philosophy*, trans. Serena Anderlini-D'Onofrio and Áine O'Healy (New York: Routledge, 1995), 48).
30 Plato, *Republic*, 534b; cf. *Phaedo*, 76b.
31 Ibid., 454b.
32 Ibid., 534b.
33 Ibid.
34 Ibid., 517c.
35 Ibid., 508e.
36 Ibid., 518d.
37 Plato, *Republic*, 532b. See for instance, Plato's contention in the *Phaedo* that one's body invariably inhibits one's soul's grasp of the truth (65a–d).
38 Plato, *Republic*, 475b.
39 Ibid., 533b.
40 Dialogue, Plato advises in the *Statesman*, is designed 'for the sake of our becoming better dialecticians in relation to all subjects' (*Statesman*, trans. Christopher Rowe (Indianapolis: Hackett, 1995), 285d).
41 Plato, *Republic*, 534c.
42 In many cases, notes Hadot, the 'task of dialogue' for Plato 'consists essentially in pointing out the limits of language, and its inability to communicate moral and existential experience' (*Philosophy as a Way of Life*, 163).
43 Aporetic conclusions are not wholly absent from his subsequent writings, most notably the *Theaetetus*, which concludes in a deadlock regarding the definition of knowledge.
44 'What we call thought is speech that occurs without the voice, inside the soul in conversation with itself' (Plato, *Sophist*, trans. Nicholas P. White (Indianapolis: Hackett, 1993), 263e).
45 Ibid., 260a.
46 'Being the limited creatures that we are', explains Jill Gordon, 'we cannot be turned by logos alone. Plato must therefore choose to enter into another kind of relationship with us – one that grips our souls more powerfully' (*Turning Toward Philosophy: Literary Device and Dramatic Structure in Plato's Dialogues* (University Park: The Pennsylvania State University Press, 1999), 171).

47 See Plato, 'Apology', in *The Last Days of Socrates*, trans. Hugh Tredennick and Harold Tarrant (London: Penguin, 2003), 21d.
48 On beauty as highest ideal, see Plato, *Symposium*, 210a–211c.
49 Plato, *Phaedrus*, 250a.
50 Ibid., 246a. On the role of myth in guiding souls, see María Angélica Fierro, 'The Myth of the Winged Chariot in the *Phaedrus*: A Vehicle for Philosophical Thinking', in *Plato's Styles and Characters: Between Literature and Philosophy*, ed. Gabriele Cornelli (Berlin: De Gruter, 2016).
51 Plato, *Phaedrus*, 277b.
52 Plato, *Republic*, 453d; cf. *Statesman*, in which he writes of the 'boundless sea of unlikeness' (273e). For Plato, comments Kofman, 'discourses are forces which are no less disturbing and no less dangerous than the sea and its depths: like the sea and like Tartarus, the aporia of discourse are endless' ('Beyond Aporia?', in *Post-Structuralist Classics*, ed. Andrew Benjamin (London and New York: Routledge, 1988), 11)).
53 Plato, *Phaedrus*, 278a.
54 Robin, *Platon*, 9.
55 Plato, *Parmenides*, trans. Mary Louise Gill and Paul Ryan (Indianapolis: Hackett, 1996), 136d–e.
56 Plato, *Theaetetus*, 173c, translation altered.
57 'The model of the good life within classical Greek philosophy', observes Ahmed, 'was based on an exclusive concept of life: only some had the life that enabled one to achieve a good life, a life that involved self-ownership, material security, and leisure time [. . .] The classical concept of the good life relied on a political economy: some people have to work to give others the time to pursue the good life, the time, as it were, to flourish' (*The Promise of Happiness* (Durham: Duke University Press, 2010), 12–13).
58 See Plato, *Republic*, 484a–487a, 535b–541b.
59 Ibid., 433d, translation altered.
60 Ibid., 484d.
61 'Please don't think that what I've been saying', Plato notes, 'doesn't apply equally to any women in the community with the required natural abilities' (Ibid., 540c). On the role of women in *The Republic*, see Julia Annas, 'Plato's Republican Feminism', and Susan B. Levin, 'Women's Nature and Role in the Ideal Polis: Republic V Revisited', both in *Feminism and Ancient Philosophy*, ed. Julie K. Ward (London and New York: Routledge, 1996).
62 Hence why the Socratic method is sometimes referred to as maieutics, i.e. midwifery (*maieutikos*). Plato's employment of metaphors of pregnancy, childbirth and reproduction is examined in Cynthia D. Coe, 'Plato, Maternity, and Power: Can We Get a Different Midwife?', in *Coming to Life: Philosophies of Pregnancy, Childbirth, and Mothering*, ed. Sarah LaChance Adams and Caroline R. Lundquist (New York: Fordham University Press, 2013).

63 Plato, *Theaetetus*, 150b.
64 Plato, *Symposium*, 209c. In this passage, contends Page duBois, Socrates 'reinscribes the act of generation, of reproduction, and transfers it to the philosopher, whose experience in labor and birth is idealized and made to transcend that of women', such that the female is depicted as 'a defective male, defined by lack' (*Sowing the Body: Psychoanalysis and Ancient Representations of Women* (Chicago: University of Chicago Press, 1988), 181, 183).
65 'For Plato', writes Vigdis Songe-Møller, 'ideal love is the attraction between elements that are masculine, good and unifying. Like is attracted to like, where "like" is synonymous with "good"' (*Philosophy without Women: The Birth of Sexism in Western Thought*, trans. Peter Cripps (London and New York: Continuum, 2002), 96).
66 Peters, *Speaking into the Air*, 45.
67 Plato, *Republic*, 537c.

Chapter 3

1 Immanuel Kant, 'Universal Natural History and Theory of the Heavens', in *Natural Science*, ed. Eric Watkins (Cambridge: Cambridge University Press, 2012), 1:367. All citations of Kant's work follow the pagination of the standard *Kant's Gesammelte Schriften*.
2 See Peter Fenves, *Raising the Tone of Philosophy: Late Essays by Immanuel Kant, Transformative Critique by Jacques Derrida* (Baltimore: The Johns Hopkins University Press, 1993), 6–7.
3 Immanuel Kant, 'Critique of Practical Reason', in *Practical Philosophy*, ed. Mary J. Gregor (Cambridge: Cambridge University Press, 1996), 5:161.
4 Immanuel Kant, *Correspondence*, ed. Arnulf Zweig (Cambridge: Cambridge University Press, 1999), 10:351.
5 Immanuel Kant, *Critique of Pure Reason*, trans. Paul Guyer and Allen W. Wood (Cambridge: Cambridge University Press, 1998), Bxxxviii. Keep in mind that Kant is convinced that 'human nature is by nature architectonic, i.e., it considers all cognitions as belonging to a possible system, and hence it permits only such principles as at least do not render an intended cognition incapable of standing together with others in some system or other' (Ibid., A474/B502).
6 Ibid., Bxliv.
7 Kant, *Correspondence*, 10:269.
8 Ibid.
9 Theodor W. Adorno, *History and Freedom: Lectures 1964–1965*, trans. Rodney Livingstone (Cambridge and Malden: Polity Press, 2006), 241.
10 Kant, *Critique of Pure Reason*, A738/B766.

11 Ibid., A710/B738.
12 Such inferences, Kant emphasizes, 'are sophistries not of human beings but of pure reason itself, and even the wisest of all human beings cannot get free of them; perhaps after much effort he may guard himself from error, but he can never be wholly rid of the illusion, which ceaselessly teases and mocks him' (Ibid., A339/B397).
13 Kant, *Critique of Pure Reason*, A711/B739.
14 Ibid., A735/B763.
15 Ibid. Wolff, complains Kant, 'built his success in philosophy at random on mathematical presuppositions, and by application of the mathematical method confused *a priori* cognitions from pure ideas with mathematical cognitions, because he believed himself able to operate with them by the construction of concepts from *a priori* intuition just as in mathematics' ('Metaphysik Vigilantius', in *Lectures on Metaphysics*, ed. Karl Ameriks and Steve Naragon (Cambridge: Cambridge University Press, 1997), 29:959,). It is worth remembering that in spite of Kant's often vituperative criticism of Wolff, he nevertheless declares that 'in the future system of metaphysics, we will have to follow the strict method of the famous Wolff, the greatest among all dogmatic philosophers, who gave us the first example [. . .] of the way in which the secure course of a science is to be taken, through the regular ascertainment of the principles, the clear determination of concepts, the attempt at strictness in the proofs, and the prevention of audacious leaps in inferences' (*Critique of Pure Reason*, Bxxxvi). Wolff's error, from Kant's perspective, was that he failed to turn his critique back onto the organ of pure reason itself, thus leading him to believe that he could attain an immediate intuition of noumena.
16 Kant, *Critique of Pure Reason*, A727/B755.
17 Kant, 'Observations on the Feeling of the Beautiful and the Sublime', in *Anthropology, History, and Education*, ed. Günter Zöller and Robert B. Louden (Cambridge: Cambridge University Press, 2007), 2:305.
18 Ibid., 2:306.
19 Ibid.
20 Ibid.
21 Kant, 'Observations', 2:307.
22 Ibid.
23 Immanuel Kant, 'Metaphysik Mrongovius', in *Lectures on Metaphysics*, ed. Karl Ameriks and Steve Naragon (Cambridge: Cambridge University Press, 1997), 29:779.
24 Kant, *Critique of Pure Reason*, A839/B867.
25 Kant, 'Observations', 2:307.
26 Kant, *Critique of Pure Reason*, A837/B865.
27 Ibid., A837/B865.

28 Ibid., A836/B864. In this context, 'reason' designates 'the entire higher faculty of cognition', contrasted against the empirical (Ibid., A835/B863).
29 Kant, 'Observations', 2:229.
30 Ibid., 2:230.
31 This passage operates, as Claudia Moscovici puts it, via an 'ambivalent gesture of respect and condescension with which the implied [male] author at once flatters and dismisses women as both too charming and too frivolous to engage in what he (reflexively) considers deep thought' (*From Sex Objects to Sexual Subjects* (London and New York: Routledge, 1996), 46).
32 Kant, 'Observations', 2: 229. Anna Dacier was a prominent classicist, best known for her greatly admired translations of Homer into French prose. Émilie du Châtelet was a natural philosopher and mathematician who produced the still-standard French translation of Isaac Newton's *Principia*. Kant's disparagement of these esteemed women scholars is particularly spineless given they had both passed away decades prior. On his line of attack here, see Robin May Schott, 'The Gender of Enlightenment', in *Feminist Interpretations of Immanuel Kant*, ed. Robin May Schott (University Park: The Pennsylvania State University Press, 1997), 324 and Jordan Pascoe, 'Patriarchy and Enlightenment in Immanuel Kant's, in *Patriarchal Moments*, ed. Cesare Cuttica and Gaby Mahlberg (London: Bloomsbury, 2016), 117–18.
33 Immanuel Kant, *Anthropology from a Pragmatic Point of View*, trans. Robert B. Louden (Cambridge: Cambridge University Press, 2006), 307.
34 Kant, *Critique of Pure Reason*, A761/B789, translation altered; cf. the lecture notes of 1784–1785, wherein Kant avers that 'there is an immaturity of sex, namely, of woman' ('Anthropology Mrongovius', in *Lectures on Anthropology*, ed. Allen W. Wood and Robert B. Louden (Cambridge: Cambridge University Press, 2012), 25:1298). On the theme of (im)maturity in Kant, see Genevieve Lloyd, *The Man of Reason* (London: Routledge, 1993), 65–71.
35 Kant, *Critique of Pure Reason*, 25:655.
36 Kant, 'Observations', 2:253. 'Throughout the whole of his observations', remarks Ashon Crawley, 'Kant's glance alone was enough to think the various peoples of the world, prejudicial though his thoughts may have been. But when it came to the negro, to the black, to the concept and ground of thinking such being, Kant deferred to others, he entered into the very conditions that Enlightenment would escape' – namely, the sociality of thinking, thinking with the aid of others (*Blackpentecostal Breath: The Aesthetics of Possibility* (New York: Fordham University Press, 2017), 121).
37 Kant, 'Observations', 2:255. As Fred Moten bluntly summarizes, Kant believes that 'black folks are so ugly that everything they say must be stupid' (*Black and Blur* (Durham: Duke University Press, 2017), 208).
38 Achille Mbembe, *Critique of Black Reason*, trans. Laurent Dubois (Durham: Duke University Press, 2017), 28. On the question of race in Kant, see also Robert

Bernasconi, 'Kant as an Unfamiliar Source of Racism', in *Philosophers on Race*, ed. Julie K. Ward and Tommy L. Lott (Oxford and Malden: Blackwell, 2002), Charles W. Mills, 'Kant's *Untermenschen*', in *Race and Racism in Modern Philosophy*, ed. Andrew Vallis (Ithaca: Cornell University Press, 2005), and Lucy Allais, 'Kant's Racism', *Philosophical Papers* 45, no. 1–2 (2016): 1–36.

39 Kant, 'Critique of Practical Reason', 5:108.
40 Kant, 'Observations', 2:229, translation altered.
41 On the collision of Kant's critical project with its empirical (and particularly political) circumstances, see Andrew Fiala, *The Philosopher's Voice: Philosophy, Politics, and Language in the Nineteenth Century* (Albany: State University of New York Press, 2002), 47–66.
42 Kant, 'Critique of Practical Reason', 5:122. Regarding Kant's emphasis upon 'active ethical cultivation', see James J. DiCenso, *Kant, Religion, and Politics* (Cambridge: Cambridge University Press, 2011), 233–43.
43 Kant, 'Critique of Practical Reason', 5:130. Sung Ho Kim remarks that he 'Kantian package of value, rationality, and freedom as the foundation of moral agency [. . .] can be construed as a philosophical counterpart to [Max] Weber's notion of the Puritan *Berufsmensch*' (*Max Weber's Politics of Civil Society* (Cambridge: Cambridge University Press, 2004), 52–3).
44 Hunter, *Rival Enlightenments*, 299–300.
45 'Why do you castrate oxen and colts when you prepare them for the yoke and the cart', Schlosser asks, 'yet wish to develop the totality of human powers in men similarly condemned to the yoke and the cart? They will jump the furrow if you give them the wrong preparation, or kick against the traces until they die' (quoted in Klaus Epstein, *The Genesis of German Conservatism* (Princeton: Princeton University Press, 1966), 79); cf. Günter Zöller, 'Plato on Revolution: Kant and the Political Conservatism of J. G. Schlosser', in *Kant and His Critics*, ed. Antonino Falduto und Heiner F. Klemme (Hildesheim: Georg Olms Verlag, 2018).
46 Immanuel Kant, 'On a Recently Prominent Tone of Superiority in Philosophy', in *Theoretical Philosophy after 1781*, ed. Henry Allison and Peter Heath (Cambridge: Cambridge University Press, 2004), 8:389.
47 When Kant speaks of 'intellectual intuition', he is referring to an intuition of non-sensible objects, which he regards as impossible for finite rational beings. As we shall see, this becomes one of the major dividing lines between his own work and the Idealists he inspires, although the latter's use of the term often bears little resemblance to that of Kant himself – see Moltke S. Gram, 'Intellectual Intuition: The Continuity Thesis', *Journal of the History of Ideas* 42, no. 2 (1981) and Yolanda Estes, 'Intellectual Intuition: Reconsidering Continuity in Kant, Fichte, and Schelling', in *Fichte, German Idealism, and Early Romanticism*, ed. Daniel Breazeale and Tom Rockmore (Amsterdam: Rodopi, 2010).

48 On this distinction between cognition and mere thought, see the following footnote to the second edition: 'To *cognize* an object, it is required that I be able to prove its possibility (whether by the testimony of experience from its actuality or *a priori* through reason). But I can *think* whatever I like, as long as I do not contradict myself, i.e., as long as my concept is a possible thought, even if I cannot give any assurance whether or not there is a corresponding object somewhere within the sum total of all possibilities' (*Critique of Pure Reason*, Bxxxvi).

49 Again, this distinction between positive and negative noumena is introduced in the second edition, although it is implicit in the first (in, for instance, the notion of a regulative use of ideas of reason): 'If by a noumenon we understand a thing *insofar as it is not an object of our sensible intuition*, because we abstract from the manner of our intuition of it, then this is a noumenon in the negative sense. But if we understand by that an *object of a non-sensible intuition*, then we assume a special kind of intuition, namely intellectual intuition, which, however, is not our own, and the possibility of which we cannot understand, and this would be the noumenon in a *positive* sense' (Ibid., B307).

50 Kant, 'Recently Prominent Tone', 8:389.

51 Ibid. Cf. *Anthropology from a Pragmatic*, 269.

52 Kant, 'Recently Prominent Tone', 8:390.

53 Ibid.

54 Ibid., 8:393.

55 Kant, *Critique of Pure Reason*, A756/B784.

56 Ibid., A744/B772.

57 Jean-Luc Nancy, *The Discourse of the Syncope: Logodaedalus*, trans. Saul Anton (Stanford: Stanford University Press, 2008), 78.

58 Kant, *Critique of Pure Reason*, A739/B767.

59 Kant, 'Recently Prominent Tone', 8:394.

60 Ibid., 8:398.

61 Kant, *Critique of Pure Reason*, A476/B504.

62 As recalled in Pölitz's lecture notes (from the 1770s), Kant remarks that 'one can speak for more of that of which one knows nothing than of that of which one knows something' (*Lectures on Metaphysics*, 28:265, p. 78).

63 Ibid., A796/B824.

64 Kant, 'Recently Prominent Tone', 8:402, my emphasis. On Kant's metaphor of the 'voice' of reason, see Sarah Kofman, 'The Economy of Respect: Kant and Respect for Women', *Social Research* 49, no. 2 (1982): 383–404.

65 After all, Kant's practical reason involves, as Ahmed describes it, 'a technology of will that requires a *willing submission*, a willingness to be under the moral law, an act of submission that is explicitly narrated (and justified) as an act of volition' (*Willful Subjects* (Durham: Duke University Press, 2014), 92–3).

66 Kant, 'Critique of Practical Reason', 5:25.

67 Mladen Dolar, *A Voice and Nothing More* (Cambridge, MA: The MIT Press, 2006), 90.
68 Kant, 'Critique of Practical Reason', 5:79.
69 Kant, 'Recently Prominent Tone', 8:402.
70 Ibid.
71 Hence why, after Kant, argues Justin Clemens, the 'question of freedom rapidly becomes a question of the subjective transgression of established limits' (*The Romanticism of Contemporary Theory: Institution, Aesthetics, Nihilism* (Aldershot: Ashgate, 2003), 16).
72 Kant, 'Recently Prominent Tone', 8:403, my emphasis.
73 Ibid., 8:403.
74 Ibid.
75 Kant, *Critique of Pure Reason*, A752/B780. Elsewhere, Kant famously defines enlightenment as the 'freedom to make *public use* of one's reason in all matters' ('An Answer to the Question: What Is Enlightenment?', in *Practical Philosophy*, ed. Mary J. Gregor (Cambridge: Cambridge University Press, 1996), 8:36).
76 Kant, *Critique of Pure Reason*, A831/B859.
77 Derrida, 'On a Newly Arisen Apocalyptic Tone', in *Raising the Tone of Philosophy: Late Essays by Immanuel Kant, Transformative Critique by Jacques Derrida*, ed. Peter Fenves (Baltimore: The Johns Hopkins University Press, 1993), 130, translation altered.

Chapter 4

1 *Kant's Early Critics*, ed. Brigitte Sassen (Cambridge: Cambridge University Press, 2000), 53.
2 Johann Gottlieb Fichte, *Early Philosophical Writings*, trans. Daniel Breazeale (Ithaca: Cornell University Press, 1988), 420. Citations throughout follow the pagination of the appurtenant English-language translations.
3 Karl Leonhard Reinhold, *Letters on the Kantian Philosophy*, trans. James Hebbeler (Cambridge: Cambridge University Press, 2005), 15–16.
4 'Standing historically between the two intellectual giants, Kant and Hegel, Fichte is often considered as a mere "mediator" in the dialogue of the two genii', observes Marina Bykova, and yet, 'Fichte's deep revision of the Kantian concept of the subject is key to the emergence of post-Kantian German Idealism' ('The Self as the World Into Itself', in *Fichte, German Idealism, and Early Romanticism*, ed. Daniel Breazeale and Tom Rockmore (Amsterdam: Rodopi, 2010), 131).
5 Karl Leonhard Reinhold, 'The Foundation of Philosophical Knowledge', in *Between Kant and Hegel: Texts in the Development of Post-Kantian Idealism*, trans. George di Giovanni and H. S. Harris (Indianapolis: Hackett, 2000), 71.

6 Fichte, *Early Philosophical Writings*, 357.
7 Fichte, *Early Philosophical Writings*, 207; cf. Violetta L. Waibel, 'Kant and Fichte on the Notion of (Transcendental) Freedom', in *Transcendental Inquiry: Its History, Methods and Critiques*, ed. Halla Kim and Steven Hoeltzel (Cham: Palgrave Macmillan, 2016).
8 Fichte, *Early Philosophical Writings*, 174.
9 For the sake of concision, this chapter will focus almost entirely upon Fichte's earliest and best-known works written during his tenure at the University of Jena (1794–9), prior to his dismissal in the aftermath of the atheism dispute in which he became embroiled. For a concise, straightforward overview of Fichte's project at this time, see Daniel Breazeale, 'Fichte's Project: The Jena *Wissenschaftslehre*', in *Kant, Fichte, and the Legacy of Transcendental Idealism*, ed. Halla Kim and Steven Hoeltzel (Lanham: Lexington Books, 2015).
10 Fichte, *Early Philosophical Writings*, 411.
11 See Angelica Nuzzo, 'Phenomenologies of Intersubjectivity: Fichte between Hegel and Husserl', in *Fichte and the Phenomenological Tradition*, ed. Violette L. Waibel, Daniel Breazeale, and Tom Rockmore (Berlin: De Gruyter, 2010), 99.
12 Alexis Philonenko, *La liberté humaine dans la philosophie de Fichte* (Paris: Librairie Philosophique J. Vrin, 1999), 21, my translation; cf. Robert R. Williams, 'The Question of the Other in Fichte's Thought', in *Fichte: Historical Contexts/Contemporary Controversies*, ed. Daniel Breazeale and Tom Rockmore (New Jersey: Humanities Press, 1994).
13 Fichte, *Early Philosophical Writings*, 171.
14 Ibid., 171.
15 Ibid., 174.
16 Ibid., 147.
17 Johann Gottlieb Fichte, *Foundations of Transcendental Philosophy (Wissenschaftslehre nova methodo 1796/99)*, trans. Daniel Breazeale (Ithaca: Cornell University Press, 1992), 105; cf. Janet Roccanova, 'First Steps: Lessons on Becoming a Philosopher from the Early Chapters of the *Wissenschaftslehre nova methodo*', in *New Essays on Fichte's Later Jena Wissenschaftslehre*, ed. Daniel Breazeale and Tom Rockmore (Evanston: Northwestern University Press, 2002).
18 On the concept of the transcendental, and the divergence between Kant and Fichte in this regard, refer to Daniel Breazeale, 'Doing Philosophy: Fichte vs. Kant on Transcendental Method', in *Fichte, German Idealism, and Early Romanticism*, ed. Daniel Breazeale and Tom Rockmore (Amsterdam: Rodopi, 2010) and Elena Ficara, '"Transcendental" in Kant and Fichte: A Conceptual Shift and Its Philosophical Meaning', in *The Enigma of Fichte's First Principles*, ed. David W. Wood (Leiden: Brill, 2021).
19 Fichte, *Foundations of Transcendental Philosophy*, 106. This approach takes its inspiration largely from J. S. Beck's 'doctrine of the standpoint' (*Standpunctslehre*).

20 Ibid., 97.
21 Fichte, *Foundations of Transcendental Philosophy*, 115.
22 Fichte, *Early Philosophical Writings*, 207–8.
23 Ibid., 156.
24 Ibid., 165.
25 Ibid., 164.
26 Ibid. 'It is by means of absolute freedom and not by means of any law of nature nor as a consequence of any such law', declares Fichte, 'that we raise ourselves to [the standpoint of] reason – not by means of any *transition*, but by means of a *leap*' (*Foundation of the Entire Wissenschaftslehre and Related Writings (1794-95)*, trans. Daniel Breazeale (Oxford: Oxford University Press, 2021), 355).
27 Fichte, *Early Philosophical Writings*, 163.
28 Ibid., 174.
29 Ibid.
30 Ibid., 171.
31 Ibid., 146.
32 Ibid., 200.
33 On Fichte's critique of Reinhold, see *Foundation of the Entire Wissenschaftslehre*, 206; *Early Philosophical Writings*, 400–1.
34 Fichte, *Foundations of Transcendental Philosophy*, 95.
35 Ibid., 114. See Esma Kayar, 'The First Principle of the *Wissenschaftslehre* and the Logical Principle of Identity', in *The Enigma of Fichte's First Principles*, ed. David W. Wood (Leiden: Brill, 2021).
36 Fichte, *Foundations of Transcendental Philosophy*, 119.
37 Most problematically, Fichte vacillates – sometimes seemingly within the span of a single passage – between intellectual intuition as the I's free and originary act of self-positing (its self-presence as a subject-object), and as a fact of consciousness that must be attained through a specifically transcendental standpoint. On the complexity of this concept, see Daniel Breazeale, *Thinking Through the Wissenschaftslehre: Themes from Fichte's Early Philosophy* (Oxford: Oxford University Press, 2013), 197–229; cf. C. Jeffery Kinlaw, 'Intellectual Intuition', in *The Bloomsbury Handbook of Fichte*, ed. Marina Bykova (London: Bloomsbury, 2020).
38 Fichte, *Foundations of Transcendental Philosophy*, 118.
39 Johann Gottlieb Fichte, *Introductions to the Wissenschaftslehre and Other Writings (1797-1800)*, trans. Daniel Breazeale (Indianapolis: Hackett, 1994), 46.
40 Fichte, *Foundations of Transcendental Philosophy*, 117.
41 Ibid., 423; cf. *Early Philosophical Writings*, 399.
42 Fichte, *Foundations of Transcendental Philosophy*, 103.
43 Ibid.
44 Ibid., 84.

45 Ibid., 184. 'As soon as we say "explain"', Fichte propounds, 'we have already entered the domain of finitude, inasmuch as all *explaining* (in contrast with grasping something all at once) is a continual process of progressing from one point to the next' (*Foundation of the Entire Wissenschaftslehre*, 343).
46 Fichte, *Foundations of Transcendental Philosophy*, 110.
47 Ibid., 110.
48 Fichte, *Early Philosophical Writings*, 398–9.
49 See Jodie Lee Heap, *The Creative Imagination: Indeterminacy and Embodiment in the Writings of Kant, Fichte, and Castoriadis* (Latham: Rowman & Littlefield, 2021), 99–156.
50 Fichte, *Early Philosophical Writings*, 205.
51 See Fichte's letter to Jacobi, 26th of April, 1796.
52 Fichte, *Early Philosophical Writings*, 103.
53 Fichte, *Foundations of Transcendental Philosophy*, 101.
54 Ibid., 102. It was, notes Breazeale, 'Fichte's deliberate and life-long policy to adopt a new philosophical vocabulary for virtually every new presentation of his system', in large part because 'he remained profoundly distrustful of the ability of mere words to convey the essence of his thought and always professed to judge the success of his written presentations only by the standard of how well or poorly a particular term or text seemed to achieve its intended effect' ('The Wissenschaftslehre of 1796-99 [*nova methodo*]', in *The Cambridge Companion to Fichte*, ed. David James and Günter Zöller (Cambridge: Cambridge University Press, 2016), 123).
55 Fichte, *Early Philosophical Writings*, 153.
56 Fichte, *Introductions to the Wissenschaftslehre and Other Writings*, 18.
57 Ibid., 20.
58 Ibid., 94.
59 Ibid.
60 Ibid.
61 Ibid., 95.
62 Ibid., 96.
63 Ibid., 95.
64 Johann Gottlieb Fichte, *New Exposition of the Science of Knowledge*, trans. A. E. Kroeger (St Louis, 1869), 61, translation altered.
65 Fichte, *Early Philosophical Writings*, 145.
66 Fichte, *Introductions to the Wissenschaftslehre and Other Writings*, 91.
67 Ibid.
68 Ibid.
69 Ibid., 92.
70 It would seem that Fichte's audience, those who were actually able to attend his lectures, did include at least some women. See the introduction to Johann Gottlieb

Fichte, *The Science of Knowing*, trans. Walter E. Wright (Albany: State University of New York Press, 2005), 3.
71 Le Dœuff, *Philosophical Imaginary*, 103.
72 Dale Snow, *Schelling and the End of Idealism* (Albany: State University of New York Press, 1996), 98.
73 Johann Gottlieb Fichte, *Foundations of Natural Right*, trans. Michael Baur (Cambridge: Cambridge University Press, 2000), 298.
74 Ibid., 299.
75 Ibid., 274. See also Isabel V. Hull, *Sexuality, State, and Civil Society in Germany, 1700–1815* (Ithaca: Cornell University Press, 1996), 319. On Fichte's equation of marriage with organic wholeness, see Stefani Engelstein, 'The Allure of Wholeness: The Eighteenth-Century Organism and the Same-Sex Marriage Debate', *Critical Inquiry* 39, no. 4 (2013): 754–76.
76 Fichte, *Introductions to the Wissenschaftslehre and Other Writings*, 45.
77 Fichte, *Foundations of Natural Right*, 303.
78 Ibid.
79 Ibid.
80 Ibid., 304.
81 Ibid.
82 Ibid.
83 Ibid.
84 Fichte implies 'savages or children' are also incapable of this, 'since to them, lost in wondering astonishment, both representation and the thing merge together, and cannot be kept apart' (*New Exposition of the Science of Knowledge*, 78).
85 Fichte, *Early Philosophical Writings*, 192.
86 Helen Watanabe-O'Kelly, *Beauty or Beast?: The Woman Warrior in the German Imagination from the Renaissance to the Present* (Oxford: Oxford University Press, 2010), 26.
87 Karen Kenkel, 'The Personal and the Philosophical in Fichte's Theory of Sexual Difference', in *Impure Reason: Dialectic of Enlightenment in Germany*, ed. W. Daniel Wilson and Robert C. Holub (Detroit: Wayne State University Press, 1993), 279.
88 Fichte, *Foundations of Natural Right*, 304.
89 Ibid., 304–5.
90 Ibid.
91 Ibid.
92 Bärbel Frischmann, 'Fichte's Theory of Gender Relations in his Foundations of Natural Right', in *Rights, Bodies, and Recognition: New Essays on Fichte's Foundations of Natural Right*, ed. Tom Rockmore and Daniel Breazeale (London and New York: Routledge, 2006), 161. For a rather more optimistic interpretation of sexual difference in Fichte, see Yolanda Estes, 'Fichte's Account of Human Sexuality:

Gender Difference as the Basis of Human Equality within a Just Society', *Social Philosophy Today* 25 (2009): 63–73.
93   Breazeale remarks upon Fichte's 'growing frustration, sometimes bordering on despair, at the apparent failure of his writings to achieve their stated goal' ('The *Wissenschaftslehre* of 1796–1799', 123).
94   Fichte, *Foundations of Transcendental Philosophy*, 102.

Chapter 5

1   Friedrich Nietzsche, 'Ecce Homo', in *The Anti-Christ, Ecce Homo, Twilight of the Idols, and Other Writings*, trans. Judith Norman (Cambridge: Cambridge University Press, 2005), Why I Am So Clever, §8. Citations to Nietzsche's work throughout refer to original chapter and section headings, with the sole exception of *Philosophy in the Tragic Age of the Greeks*, for which the page numbers of the English-language translation are used instead.
2   Gianni Vattimo, *Dialogue with Nietzsche*, trans. William McCuaig (New York: Columbia University Press, 2006), 34.
3   Friedrich Nietzsche, *Untimely Meditations*, trans. R. J. Hollingdale (Cambridge: Cambridge University Press, 1997), Schopenhauer as Educator, §3. It became clear to Nietzsche, following Schopenhauer's example, Martine Béland observes, that 'the most important philosophical attitude cannot take place within academia' ('Vocation as Therapy: Nietzsche and the Conflict between Profession and Calling in Academia', in *Nietzsche's Therapeutic Teaching: For Individuals and Culture*, ed. Horst Hutter and Eli Friedland (London: Bloomsbury, 2013), 25).
4   Nietzsche, *Untimely Meditations*, Schopenhauer as Educator, §3.
5   'If Kant ever should begin to exercise any wide influence', Nietzsche notes mockingly, 'we shall be aware of it in the form of a gnawing and disintegrating scepticism and relativism; and only in the most active and noble spirits who have never been able to exist in a state of doubt would there appear instead that undermining and despair of all truth' (Ibid.).
6   Ibid.
7   Nietzsche, *Untimely Meditations*, Schopenhauer as Educator, §5.
8   Schopenhauer, *World as Will*, 18.
9   Ibid.
10 Ibid., 25.
11 Ibid., 17.
12 Friedrich Nietzsche, *Writings from the Early Notebooks*, trans. Ladislaus Löb (Cambridge: Cambridge University Press, 2009), 19[103].
13 Ibid., 29[8].

14 Nietzsche, *Philosophy in the Tragic Age*, 44–5.
15 Nietzsche, *Early Notebooks*, 255.
16 See Thomas Hobbes, *Leviathan* (Cambridge: Cambridge University Press, 1996), 24.
17 Nietzsche, *Early Notebooks*, 255. As Sarah Kofman notes, this forgetting of the metaphorical does not occur at a particular moment in human history; rather, 'it is originary, the necessary correlate of metaphorical activity itself: man has always already forgotten that he is an "artist from the beginning", and that he remains one in all his activities' (*Nietzsche and Metaphor*, trans. Duncan Large (London: The Athlone Press, 1993), 25).
18 Nietzsche, *Early Notebooks*, 256.
19 Ibid., 257.
20 Ibid., 259.
21 Ibid., translation altered.
22 Nietzsche, *Early Notebooks*, 258.
23 Friedrich Nietzsche, *Beyond Good and Evil: Prelude to a Philosophy of the Future*, trans. Judith Norman (Cambridge: Cambridge University Press, 2002), §16.
24 Friedrich Nietzsche, *Human, All Too Human*, trans. R. J. Hollingdale (Cambridge: Cambridge University Press, 1996), I, §483.
25 Ibid., II, §190.
26 Friedrich Nietzsche, *Writings from the Late Notebooks*, trans. Kate Sturge (Cambridge: Cambridge University Press, 2003), 6[13].
27 Nietzsche, *Beyond Good and Evil*, §5. For Nietzsche, as Arthur C. Danto puts it, 'philosophy has been not so much an independent user of language as a supine accepter of the crusted categories of daily speech, flattering, rather than rectifying or purifying the entrenched erroneousness of the human mind so far' (*Nietzsche as Philosopher* (New York: Columbia University Press, 2005), 104).
28 Nietzsche, *Human, All Too Human*, I, §11.
29 Friedrich Nietzsche, *The Gay Science*, trans. Josefine Nauckhoff and Adrian Del Caro (Cambridge: Cambridge University Press, 2001), III, §189.
30 Nietzsche, *Late Notebooks*, 34[247].
31 Friedrich Nietzsche, 'Twilight of the Idols', in *The Anti-Christ, Ecce Homo, Twilight of the Idols, and Other Writings*, trans. Judith Norman (Cambridge: Cambridge University Press, 2005), §26.
32 Following the German orthographic reforms that took place in 1901, the word is nowadays spelt *mitteilen*.
33 Nietzsche, *Late Notebooks*, 9[106], 161.
34 Nietzsche, *Gay Science*, V, §354, 213.
35 A clear account of Nietzsche's perspectivism, in its various manifestations, can be found in Tsarina Doyle, *Nietzsche on Epistemology and Metaphysics: The World in View* (Edinburgh: Edinburgh University Press, 2009), 59–69.
36 Nietzsche, *Late Notebooks*, 7[60]; cf. *Gay Science*, V, §374.

37 Ibid., 14[122].
38 Helpful explication of Nietzsche's naturalistic account of truth, language and communication is provided in Vanessa Lemm, *Nietzsche's Animal Philosophy: Culture, Politics, and the Animality of the Human Being* (New York: Fordham University Press, 2009), 111–51, as well as Béatrice Han-Pile, 'Transcendental Aspects, Ontological Commitments, and Naturalistic Elements in Nietzsche's Thought', in *The Transcendental Turn*, ed. Sebastian Gardner and Matthew Grist (Oxford: Oxford University Press, 2015).
39 Nietzsche, *Beyond Good and Evil*, §3.
40 Ibid., §4.
41 Nietzsche, *Gay Science*, III, §110.
42 Ibid.
43 Nietzsche, *Beyond Good and Evil*, §36.
44 Nietzsche, *Late Notebooks*, 7[60].
45 Ibid., 43[1].
46 Ibid., 34[88].
47 Nietzsche, *Beyond Good and Evil*, §6.
48 Friedrich Nietzsche, *Daybreak: Thoughts on the Prejudices of Morality*, trans. R. J. Hollingdale (Cambridge: Cambridge University Press, 1997), §507.
49 Nietzsche, *Gay Science*, V, §355.
50 Nietzsche, *Beyond Good and Evil*, §4, translation altered.
51 Ibid., §211.
52 Ibid.
53 Ibid., §14. At other times, of course, Nietzsche is scathing of both Socrates and Plato.
54 Nietzsche, *Early Notebooks*, 262.
55 Ibid., 263.
56 Ibid.
57 Nietzsche, *Beyond Good and Evil*, §203. The eschatological tenor of Nietzsche's writings, and the way that this informs his critique of morality, is explored in Tracy B. Strong's seminal *Friedrich Nietzsche and the Politics of Transfiguration* (Berkeley and Los Angeles: University of California Press, 1988).
58 Nietzsche, *Beyond Good and Evil*, §2.
59 Ibid., §10.
60 Nietzsche, 'Ecce Homo', Preface, §3.
61 Friedrich Nietzsche, *Thus Spoke Zarathustra*, trans. Adrian Del Caro (Cambridge: Cambridge University Press, 2006), I, On the Flies of the Market Place.
62 Ibid.
63 Vattimo, *Dialogue with Nietzsche*, 67.
64 Seán Burke, *The Ethics of Writing: Authorship and Legacy in Plato and Nietzsche* (Edinburgh: Edinburgh University Press, 2008), 202.

65 Nietzsche, *Thus Spoke Zarathustra*, II, On the Blessed Isles.
66 Nietzsche, *Beyond Good and Evil*, §9.
67 Nietzsche, *Late Notebooks*, 11[157].
68 Nietzsche, *Beyond Good and Evil*, §43.
69 Nietzsche, *Daybreak*, §119.
70 Nietzsche, *Beyond Good and Evil*, §213.
71 Nietzsche, *Human, All Too Human*, I, §262.
72 Nietzsche, *Beyond Good and Evil*, §203.
73 Nietzsche, *Human, All Too Human*, I, §4. On Nietzsche's ongoing fascination with superlative individuals, see Manuel Knoll, 'The "Übermensch" as a Social and Political Task: A Study in the Continuity of Nietzsche's Political Thought', in *Nietzsche as Political Philosopher*, ed. Manuel Knoll and Barry Stocker (Berlin: De Gruyter, 2014).
74 Nietzsche, *Beyond Good and Evil*, §44.
75 Friedrich Nietzsche, *On the Genealogy of Morality*, trans. Carol Diethe (Cambridge: Cambridge University Press, 1997), II §24.
76 Nietzsche, *Gay Science*, IV, §325.
77 Daniel Conway, *Nietzsche & the Political* (London and New York: Routledge, 1997), 6–7; cf. Herman Siemens, 'Yes, No, Maybe So . . . Nietzsche's Equivocations on the Relation between Democracy and "Grosse Politik"', in *Nietzsche, Power and Politics: Rethinking Nietzsche's Legacy for Political Thought*, ed. Herman Siemens and Vasti Roodt (Berlin: De Gruyter, 2008).
78 Nietzsche, *Beyond Good and Evil*, §44. On the value of Nietzsche's anti-democratic critique for theories of democracy, see Wendy Brown, *Politics out of History* (Princeton: Princeton University Press, 2001), 121–37.
79 Ibid., §203. Nietzsche's political conclusions, Mark Warren maintains, 'stem primarily from erroneous assumptions about the nature and limits of modern institutions, assumptions that impoverished his thinking about social structures, and caused him to mistake their historical limitations for ontological ones' (*Nietzsche and Political Thought* (Cambridge, MA: The MIT Press, 1988), 3).
80 Nietzsche, *Beyond Good and Evil*, §259.
81 Sarah Kofman, 'Scorning Jews: Nietzsche, the Jews, Anti-Semitism', in *Selected Writings*, ed. Thomas Albrecht (Stanford: Stanford University Press, 2007), 148. Nietzsche's doctrine of the *Übermensch* or higher man, notes Vattimo, 'amounts to a polemic against evolutionism; it maintains that modern man, far from being the culmination of a process of evolution, is in reality a form that must be changed and overcome, not by further development but by nothing less than a mutation' (*The Adventure of Difference: Philosophy after Nietzsche and Heidegger*, trans. Cyprian Blamires (Cambridge: Polity Press, 1993), 44). On the influence of race theory upon Nietzsche's work, see Nicholas Martin, 'Breeding Greeks: Nietzsche, Gobineau, and Classical Theories of Race', in *Nietzsche and Antiquity: His Reaction*

    and Response to the Classical Tradition, ed. Paul Bishop (Cambridge: Cambridge University Press, 2004).
82 Nietzsche, *Beyond Good and Evil*, §203.
83 Ibid., §258. 'Nietzsche's conception of "great politics"', notes Nandita Biswas Mellamphy, 'is grounded in the pre-eminence of his conception of body in which the superiority of the "philosophy of the future" will lie in directly measuring and justifying the "health" and vitality of the species in terms of the "health" and vitality of the philosopher's innermost physiological and psychological workings' (*The Three Stigmata of Friedrich Nietzsche: Political Physiology in the Age of Nihilism* (Basingstoke: Palgrave Macmillan, 2011), 25).
84 Nietzsche, *Gay Science*, I, §18.
85 Ibid.
86 Life, Nietzsche exclaims, 'wants to build itself up into the heights with pillars and steps; it wants to gaze into vast distances and out upon beatific beauties – *therefore it needs height!*' (*Thus Spoke Zarathustra*, II, On the Tarantulas, translation altered).
87 Nietzsche, *Gay Science*, I, §2; '*Twilight of the Idols*', §37.
88 Nietzsche, *Beyond Good and Evil*, §257. For a more optimistic take, see Rosalyn Diprose, 'Nietzsche and the Pathos of Distance', in *Nietzsche, Feminism, and Political Theory*, ed. Paul Patton (London and New York: Routledge, 1993).
89 Nietzsche, *Late Notebooks*, 2[57].
90 Regarding Nietzsche's views on women, and his ambiguous feminist/anti-feminist leanings, see as a starting point Sarah Kofman, 'The Psychologist of the Eternal Feminine (Why I Write Such Good Books, 5)', *Yale French Studies* 87 (1995): 173–89 and Maudemarie Clark, 'Nietzsche's Misogyny', in *Feminist Interpretations of Friedrich Nietzsche*, ed. Kelly Oliver and Marilyn Pearsall (University Park: The Pennsylvania State University Press, 1998).
91 Nietzsche, *Human, All Too Human*, I, §300.
92 Nietzsche, *Late Notebooks*, 1[120].
93 As Kofman remarks, Nietzsche 'multiplies his metaphors, using them to correct or complete each other; he joins unheard-of metaphors to others of long standing, for purposes which are no longer simply didactic but strategic' (Sarah Kofman, *Camera Obscura: Of Ideology*, trans. Will Straw (Ithaca: Cornell University Press, 1998), 29). Likewise, Daniela Vallega-Neu observes that 'for Nietzsche every*thing* that enters our consciousness is mere appearance to which nothing real corresponds; it is interpreted according to categories and schemata that do not find any hold in a given fact; it is a mask without a face behind. Nietzsche's style expresses precisely this. Again and again he withdraws any ground from his readers' (*The Bodily Dimension in Thinking* (Albany: State University of New York Press, 2005), 29).
94 'To the extent that Nietzsche's political views are integral with the rest of his thought – to the extent that they are made possible by it and in some ways even

required by it', writes Bruce Detwiler, 'we stand guilty of both sanitizing and trivializing his contribution when we deliberately sweep under the rug its unsavory political implications' (*Nietzsche and the Politics of Aristocratic Radicalism* (Chicago: The University of Chicago Press, 1990), 5); cf. Ofelia Schutte, 'Nietzsche's Politics', in *Feminist Interpretations of Friedrich Nietzsche*, ed. Kelly Oliver and Marilyn Pearsall (University Park: The Pennsylvania State University Press, 1998) and Marina Cominos, 'The Question of Nietzsche's Anti-Politics and Human Transfiguration', in *Nietzsche, Power and Politics: Rethinking Nietzsche's Legacy for Political Thought*, ed. Herman Siemens and Vasti Roodt (Berlin: De Gruyter, 2008).
95 Nietzsche, *Beyond Good and Evil*, §39.
96 Nietzsche, *Genealogy of Morality*, III, §14, translation altered.
97 Nietzsche, *Beyond Good and Evil*, §30.
98 Ibid., §30.
99 Nietzsche, *Gay Science*, V, §381.
100 Joanne Faulkner, *Dead Letters to Nietzsche; or, the Necromantic Art of Reading Philosophy* (Athens: Ohio University Press, 2010), 63.

Chapter 6

1 Vattimo, *Dialogue with Nietzsche*, 34.
2 Søren Kierkegaard, *Concluding Unscientific Postscript to the Philosophical Crumbs*, trans. Alastair Hannay (Cambridge: Cambridge University Press, 2009), 5.
3 Søren Kierkegaard, *Repetition and Philosophical Crumbs*, trans. M. G. Piety (Oxford: Oxford University Press, 2009), 124. On Kierkegaard's connection to the metaphysical tradition, especially Plato and Hegel, see Michael Weston, *Kierkegaard and Modern Continental Philosophy: An Introduction* (London and New York: Routledge, 1994), 11–32; cf. Mark C. Taylor, *Journeys to Selfhood: Hegel & Kierkegaard* (New York: Fordham University Press, 2000). On Kierkegaard's debt to F. W. J. Schelling (whose lectures he attended), see Saitya Brata Das, *The Political Theology of Kierkegaard* (Edinburgh: Edinburgh University Press, 2020), 17–34.
4 'Kierkegaard's goal', writes Hadot, 'was to make the reader aware of his mistakes, not by directly refuting them but by setting them forth in such a way that their absurdity would become clearly apparent' (*Philosophy as a Way of Life*, 150–1); cf. Sophie Wennerscheid, in 'Kierkegaard's Scene Changes: Authorship as Theatrical Practice', in *Authorship and Authority in Kierkegaard's Writings*, ed. Joseph Westfall (London: Bloomsbury, 2019).
5 Kierkegaard, *Concluding Unscientific Postscript*, 170.
6 Helpful summaries and explanations of Kierkegaard's strategy of indirect communication include the highly accessible Julia Watkin, *Kierkegaard* (London

and New York: Continuum, 1997), 46–55 and Clare Carlisle, *Kierkegaard: A Guide for the Perplexed* (London and New York: Continuum, 2006), 25–32, as well as the more comprehensive Roger Poole, *Kierkegaard: The Indirect Communication* (Charlottesville: University of Virginia Press, 1993), which presents Kierkegaard as a deconstructionist *avant la lettre*.
7 A trend typified by thinkers such as Henri Bergson, Edmund Husserl and William James.
8 Kierkegaard, *Concluding Unscientific Postscript*, 16. In Kierkegaard's view, writes Sylvia Walsh, 'the awareness of being a single individual constitutes the basic consciousness of a human being inasmuch as it forms the conscience or one's eternal consciousness by which one is opened to the eternal and becomes aware of having an eternal responsibility to give an accounting of oneself as a single individual before God' (*Kierkegaard and Religion: Personality, Character, and Virtue* (Cambridge: Cambridge University Press, 2018), 3); cf. Alison Assiter, *Kierkegaard, Metaphysics and Political Theory* (London and New York: Continuum, 2009) and Patrick Stokes, *The Naked Self: Kierkegaard and Personal Identity* (Oxford: Oxford University Press, 2015).
9 Kierkegaard, *Concluding Unscientific Postscript*, 16, 33.
10 Ibid., 17.
11 Ibid., 50.
12 Ibid., 37.
13 Ibid., 33.
14 Ibid., 41.
15 'All decision, all essential decision, lies in subjectivity. At no point does an observer (and that is what objective subjectivity is) have any infinite need of a decision, and at no point sees it' (Kierkegaard, *Concluding Unscientific Postscript*, 29).
16 Søren Kierkegaard, *The Point of View*, trans. Howard V. Hong and Edna H. Hong (Princeton: Princeton University Press, 1998), 7.
17 Ibid., 117.
18 Ibid., 25; cf. Christine Battersby, 'Kierkegaard, the Phantom of the Public, and the Sexual Politics of Crowds', in *Kierkegaard and the Political*, ed. Alison Assiter and Margherita Tonon (Newcastle: Cambridge Scholars Publishing, 2012).
19 Søren Kierkegaard, *The Concept of Irony With Continual Reference to Socrates*, trans. Howard V. Hong and Edna H. Hong (Princeton: Princeton University Press, 1989), 246–7.
20 Ibid., 327.
21 Søren Kierkegaard, *Fear and Trembling*, trans. Sylvia Walsh (Cambridge: Cambridge University Press, 2006), 3, 5.
22 Kierkegaard, *Concluding Unscientific Postscript*, 137.
23 Ibid., 322.
24 Ibid., 170.

25 Ibid., 45.
26 Ibid., 37.
27 'The time of childhood (in a literal sense)', Kierkegaard protests, 'is not the true age for becoming a Christian; on the contrary, it is the more advanced age. The time for deciding whether or not a person will be one is the age of maturity. The religiousness of childhood is the universal, abstract, and yet heartfelt imaginative basis of all later religiousness, becoming a Christian is a decision that belongs to a much later age' (Ibid., 506).
28 John 5:44 (New Revised Standard Version).
29 Ibid., 179.
30 Kierkegaard, *Point of View*, 110.
31 As Kierkegaard himself puts it, 'double reflection is implicit in the very idea of conveying something, that the subject existing in the isolation of his inwardness [. . .] nevertheless wishes to convey something personal, and hence wants to have his thinking in the inwardness of his subjective existence and at the same time convey it to others' (Kierkegaard, *Concluding Unscientific Postscript*, 62).
32 Kierkegaard, *Point of View*, 9.
33 Kierkegaard, *Concluding Unscientific Postscript*, 207.
34 Ibid., 43.
35 Kierkegaard, *Point of View*, 9.
36 Ibid., 10.
37 On the question of authorial authority, see Geoffrey A. Hale, *Kierkegaard and the Ends of Language* (Minneapolis: University of Minnesota Press, 2002), 1–36.
38 Kierkegaard, *Concluding Unscientific Postscript*, 65.
39 Ibid., 67.
40 Ibid.
41 Ibid., 73.
42 Although this account of appropriation *qua* becoming is clearly indebted to German Idealism, Kierkegaard is nevertheless scathing about the Idealists' teleological proclivities: 'everything said in Hegel's philosophy about process and becoming is an illusion. That is why the system lacks an ethics, why the system knows nothing when the living generation and the living individual seriously pose the question of becoming in order to act. So, in spite of all his talk of process, Hegel understands history not from the point of view of becoming, but helped by the illusion of pastness, in terms of a finality from which all becoming is excluded' (Ibid., 257).
43 Ibid., 209; cf. Claudine Davidshofer, 'Johannes Climacus and the Dialectical Method', in *The Kierkegaardian Mind*, ed. Adam Buben, Eleanor Helms, and Patrick Stokes (London and New York: Routledge, 2019).
44 Kierkegaard, *Concluding Unscientific Postscript*, 204.
45 Ibid., 205.

46 Kierkegaard, *Point of View*, 23.
47 Ibid., 41.
48 Ibid., 20.
49 Ibid., 111.
50 Ibid., 106.
51 Ibid.
52 Ibid., 57.
53 Ibid., 111. Disputing the common notion that Kierkegaard spurns love for other humans in favour of love of the eternal being, see Sharon Krishek, 'Love for Humans: Morality as the Heart of Kierkegaard's Religious Philosophy', in *The Kierkegaardian Mind*, ed. Adam Buben, Eleanor Helms, and Patrick Stokes (London and New York: Routledge, 2019); cf. Ulrika Carlsson, *Kierkegaard and Philosophical Eros: Between Ironic Reflection and Aesthetic Meaning* (London: Bloomsbury, 2021).
54 Kierkegaard, *Point of View*, 10–11.
55 Kierkegaard, *Concluding Unscientific Postscript*, 41. It is worth keeping in mind that, as Rita Felski reminds us, these kinds of 'visions of the horror of repetition', characteristic of existentialism, 'are distinctively modern. For most of human history, activities have gained value precisely because they repeat what has gone before' (*Doing Time: Feminist Theory and Postmodernism* (New York: New York University Press, 2000), 83).
56 Kierkegaard, *Point of View*, 133.
57 Kierkegaard, *Concluding Unscientific Postscript*, 321.
58 Ibid., 494.

Chapter 7

1 See Krista E. Duttenhaver and Coy D. Jones, 'Power, Subjectivity, and Resistance in the Thought of Simone Weil and Michel Foucault', in *The Relevance of the Radical: Simone Weil 100 Years Later*, ed. A. Rebecca Rozelle-Stone and Lucian Stone (London: Bloomsbury, 2009).
2 In the writings dealt with in this chapter, Weil frequently counterposes the abstract *la personne* against the lived, flesh and blood *l'homme*. Although usage of the latter ('man') as a generic term for humans or humankind was, of course, standard at the time she was writing, I have avoided it in this chapter, to avoid unintended implications about who Weil deems worthy of speech.
3 Regarding Weil's response to the war in her final works, and the growing mysticism therein, see Alexander Irwin, *Saints of the Impossible: Bataille, Weil, and the Politics of the Sacred* (Minneapolis: University of Minnesota Press, 2002), 169–212.

4 Simone Weil, 'The Power of Words', in *Simone Weil: An Anthology*, ed. Siân Miles (London: Penguin, 2005), 241.
5 Ibid., 245.
6 Ibid., 240. On Weil's use of classical Greek literature, and Homer specifically, see Catherine Burke, 'Female Homers: A Feminist *nostos*', in *Homer's Daughters: Women's Responses to Homer in the Twentieth Century and Beyond*, ed. Fiona Cox and Elena Theodorakopoulos (Oxford: Oxford University Press, 2019); cf. Marie Cabaud Meaney, *Simone Weil's Apologetic Use of Literature: Her Christological Interpretations of Ancient Greek Texts* (Oxford: Oxford University Press, 2007).
7 Weil, 'Power of Words', 241.
8 Ibid., 243. Weil, notes Andrea Nye, 'produced no system of signs: no deduction from logical intuitions, no structures or deconstructions. She condemned words that are only "signs". Wars are fought for signs, she said, against people who have another symbol on their helmets, but labels have no concrete meaning outside the realities of human life' (*Philosophia: The Thought of Rosa Luxemborg, Simone Weil, and Hannah Arendt* (New York and London: Routledge, 1994), 58).
9 Ibid., 257.
10 For Weil, 'words and phrases', write A. Rebecca Rozelle-Stone and Lucian Stone, 'naturally become slogans or clichés because they provide the energy and satisfaction echoing the collective which speaks them, while not demanding anything of them in the way of ethical or intellectual responsibility' ('The "War" on Error? Violent Metaphor and Words with Capital Letters', in *The Relevance of the Radical: Simone Weil 100 Years Later*, ed. A. Rebecca Rozelle-Stone and Lucian Stone (London: Bloomsbury, 2009), 144, 153).
11 Weil, 'Power of Words', 242.
12 Ibid.
13 Simone Weil, 'Human Personality', in *Simone Weil: An Anthology*, ed. Siân Miles (London: Penguin, 2005), 93.
14 See Eric O. Springsted, 'Beyond the Personal: Weil's Critique of Maritain', The *Harvard Theological Review* 98, no. 2 (2005): 209–18.
15 Weil, 'Human Personality', 70.
16 Ibid., 70–1, translation altered.
17 Ibid., 71.
18 Ibid., 81, translation altered.
19 Ibid., 83.
20 Ibid., 71.
21 Ibid., 72.
22 Ibid., 73.
23 Ibid., 85.
24 Ibid., 73, translation altered.
25 Ibid., H 74.

26 Ibid., 75–6.
27 In *The Republic*, Socrates asks Adeimantus, Plato's brother, to imagine 'the keeper of a huge, strong beast' who has taken note of 'what makes it angry, what it desires, how it has to be approached and handled, the circumstances and the conditions under which it becomes particularly fierce or calm, what provokes its typical cries, and what tones of voice make it gentle or wild', and asks whether there's any difference between this keeper and 'someone who's noticed what makes the motley masses collectively angry and happy and thinks he has knowledge' (493a–d). In both cases, they are simply giving assent to the capricious whims of the beast or the rabble. Clearly enamoured with this analogy, Weil argues that 'the Great Beast is the only object of idolatry, the only *ersatz* of God, the only imitation of something which is infinitely far from me and which is I myself' (*Gravity and Grace*, trans. Emma Crawford and Mario von der Ruhr (London and New York: Routledge, 1999), 164).
28 Weil, 'Human Personality', 76, my emphasis.
29 Weil, *Gravity and Grace*, 117. With respect to this central concept of attention, see Sharon Cameron, 'The Practice of Attention: Simone Weil's Performance of Impersonality', *Critical Inquiry* 29, no. 2 (2003): 216–52 and Silvia Caprioglio Panizza, *The Ethics of Attention: Engaging the Real with Iris Murdoch and Simone Weil* (London and New York: Routledge, 2022).
30 Weil, 'Human Personality', 77.
31 Ibid., 77–8.
32 Ibid., 78.
33 Ibid., 92.
34 Ibid., 79.
35 Blanchot, *Infinite Conversation*, 120. 'The unsettling obscurity of [Weil's] thought', Elizabeth Hardwick affirms, 'is not so much in the description of the condition as in the leap beyond it to affliction as a sort of open door to reality and truth, to creation. Affliction is the kind and degree of suffering that separate one from others. It inspires repulsion and withdrawal, fear and dread. It is the "mark of slaves", the terrible isolation brought about by extremity' ('Reflections on Simone Weil', *Signs* 1, no. 1 (1975): 87).
36 Ibid., 88.
37 Ibid., 88–9.
38 On Weil's broader account of language, see J. P. Little, 'Simone Weil and the Limits of Language', in *The Beauty that Saves: Essays on Aesthetics and Language in Simone Weil*, ed. John M. Dunaway and Eric O. Springsted (Macon: Mercer University Press, 1996).
39 Ibid., 90.
40 Weil, comments Henry Leroy Finch, 'came to regard Christianity as something like a science of affliction', for it is 'the only religion that finds a use for (or meaning in) suffering instead of trying to escape from it' (*Simone Weil and the Intellect of Grace* (New York: Continuum, 1999), 15).

41 Ibid., 91.
42 Ibid. On the connections between Weil's 'attention' and Hadot's 'spiritual exercises', see Simone Kotva, *Effort and Grace: On the Spiritual Exercise of Philosophy* (London: Bloomsbury, 2020).
43 Ibid., 92. On Weil's relationship to literature, and to tragedy in particular, see Katherine T. Brueck, *The Redemption of Tragedy: The Literary Vision of Simone Weil* (Albany: State University of New York Press, 1995).
44 Ibid., 92–3.
45 'That action is good', Weil instructs, 'which we are able to accomplish while keeping our attention and intention totally directed towards pure and impossible goodness, without veiling from ourselves by any falsehood either the attraction or the impossibility of pure goodness. In this way virtue is entirely analogous to artistic inspiration. The beautiful poem is the one which is composed while the attention is kept directed towards inexpressible inspiration, in so far as it is inexpressible' (*Gravity and Grace*, 97).
46 Weil, 'Human Personality', 86, translation altered.
47 Ibid., 87.
48 For Weil, writes Lissa McCullough, 'there is no such thing as a secular morality because it is not possible for us to "do good" or "be good" except insofar as we receive that good from outside ourselves, seeking it from a transcendent source. It is never the product of our rational mind, our will, or our natural being, but always and only the fruit of that impersonal core that is sacred in us' (*The Religious Philosophy of Simone Weil: An Introduction* (London and New York: I.B. Tauris, 2014), 56).
49 Ibid., 96.
50 Ibid., 97.
51 Ibid., 96.
52 'If it is true that [Weil] is a Christian', Blanchot comments, 'she owes it to Plato, for it is first of all in Plato that she found the Good, and it is through the beauty of the Greek texts that the name of the Good revealed itself to her as the sole reality, the unique response capable of illuminating the true reality of her desire and the unreality of all the rest' (*Infinite Conversation*, 109).
53 Weil, *Gravity and Grace*, 166.
54 For a reflection upon Weil's complicated relationship to Judaism, see Palle Yourgrau, *Simone Weil* (London: Reaktion Books, 2011), 117–35.

Chapter 8

1 Until 2006, the only version of the book available in English was a severely abridged translation, *Madness and Civilization: A History of Insanity in the Age of Reason*,

trans. Richard Howard (London and New York: Routledge, 1967). The abridgement extended to the preface, which was significantly cut down, removing much of Foucault's enigmatic, but methodologically vital material describing his aims in writing this history. In subsequent printings of the French edition, this preface was entirely absent, replaced by a pointedly cursory, self-deprecating reflection on the very purpose of writing a preface, giving almost no sense whatsoever of the guiding themes and motifs sketched out in the original. The unavailability of the full text in English also substantially affected the reception of this book and the secondary literature that proceeded from it. See Colin Gordon, '*Histoire de la folie*: An Unknown Book by Michel Foucault', in *Rewriting the History of Madness*, ed. Arthur Still and Irvin Velody (London and New York: Routledge, 1992).
2 Michel Foucault, *History of Madness*, trans. Jonathan Murphy and Jean Khalfa (London and New York: Routledge, 2006), xxxii. Translations of this book have been altered throughout.
3 Ibid., 438. Regarding Foucault's relationship to phenomenology, see Johanna Oksala, *Foucault on Freedom* (Cambridge: Cambridge University Press, 2005), 40–69 and John Iliopoulos, *The History of Reason in the Age of Madness: Foucault's Enlightenment and a Radical Critique of Psychiatry* (London: Bloomsbury, 2017).
4 'An age's experience of madness', explains Gary Gutting, 'is its distinctive way of viewing madness, its manner of "constituting" madness as an object' (*Michel Foucault's Archaeology of Scientific Reason* (Cambridge: Cambridge University Press, 1989), 70).
5 Foucault, *History of Madness*, 163.
6 Ibid., xxxiv.
7 On this foundational (non-)concept of Unreason, which tends to be brushed over in the secondary literature, see especially Ian Hacking, 'Déraison', *History of the Human Sciences* 24, no. 4 (2011): 13–23 and Nancy Tuana and Charles E. Scott, *Beyond Philosophy: Nietzsche, Foucault, Anzaldúa* (Bloomington and Indianapolis: Indiana University Press, 2020), 71–107.
8 Frédéric Gros, *Foucault et la folie* (Paris: Presses Universitaires de France, 1997), 29, my translation.
9 Foucault, *History of Madness*, xxvii.
10 Throughout this chapter, I adhere to the decision of the *History of Madness*' translator to stick with the French '*œuvre*', rather than rendering it as 'work'. Whether this is more or less obfuscatory than the latter I am undecided.
11 Foucault, *History of Madness*, xxviii.
12 Ibid.
13 Ibid., 174.
14 Ibid., 26–7.
15 Ibid., 47.
16 Ibid., 74.

17 Ibid., 55.
18 Ibid., 54.
19 Ibid., 516.
20 Ibid., 517.
21 Ibid., 82.
22 Ibid., 47.
23 Ibid., 103.
24 Ibid.
25 Ibid. 164–7. Foucault's analysis of this divided experience in the classical age is painfully oblique. The best explanation of this aspect of his work (the *only* adequate explanation in English of which I am aware) can be found in Hannah Lyn Venable, *Madness in Experience and History: Merleau-Ponty's Phenomenology and Foucault's Archaeology* (London and New York: Routledge, 2022), 99–105.
26 Gros, *Foucault et la folie*, 38.
27 Foucault, *History of Madness*, 171. 'As long as the Western world was entirely devoted to the age of reason', Foucault remarks, 'madness remained subject to the division of understanding' (Ibid.). On this odd allusion Pierre Billouet writes: 'In characterizing the classical age as "an age of the understanding", Foucault uses one of Hegel's expressions aimed at the subject/object split in Kant; its pejorative value, in Hegel, is to stipulate that philosophy think the "speculative" reconciliation of the same and the other, the identical and the different. Foucault keeps the pejorative aspect but objects to the reconciliation' (*Foucault* (Paris: Les Belles Lettres, 1999), 33, my translation). In other words, for Hegel, the understanding is characterized by 'the activity of separating', producing reified, discrete concepts (*à la* the Kantian faculty of the same name); he thus sets his sights towards the speculative moment of reason, which 'consists in actualizing and spiritually animating the universal through the sublation of fixed and determinate thoughts' (*The Phenomenology of Spirit*, trans. Terry Pinkard (Cambridge: Cambridge University Press, 2018), §32–3). Accordingly, in Foucault's eyes, the classical age is an age of understanding to the extent that its experience of madness is rigidly divided. Foucault does not seek sublation of this division, however, which would reinscribe his history within the teleologies he wishes to challenge.
28 Foucault, *History of Madness*, 171.
29 Ibid.
30 Ibid., 173.
31 Ibid., 44.
32 Ibid. 'After the seventeenth century', Foucault suggests, 'unreason in its widest sense was no longer considered to teach anything much at all. The reversibility of reason, which had been such a real danger for the Renaissance, was forgotten, and its scandal disappeared' (Ibid., 152).
33 Ibid., 157.

34 Ibid., 511.
35 Ibid., 377.
36 Friedrich Nietzsche, *The Birth of Tragedy and Other Writings*, trans. Ronald Speirs (Cambridge: Cambridge University Press, 1999), §1, translation altered.
37 Foucault, *History of Madness*, xxix.
38 Ibid.
39 And in fact, as Judith Revel observes, a demonstration of the non-originarity of reason also, inasmuch as reason is constituted in its identification of that which it is not: 'it is thus not reason which is originary, but the caesura which allows it to exist; and it is from this division between reason and non-reason that Foucault seeks to make a history at a very precise moment in our culture' (*Le vocabulaire de Foucault* (Paris: Ellipses, 2002), 51, my translation).
40 Gros, *Foucault et la folie*, 32–3.
41 Foucault, *History of Madness*, xxx.
42 Ibid., xxix.
43 Ibid., xxxii.
44 Ibid., xxxiii.
45 Ibid., xxxiv.
46 Ibid., xxxii.
47 Ibid., xxxi–xxxii.
48 Ibid., xxxv.
49 Ibid.
50 On Foucault's spatialized language, see Stuart Elden, *Mapping the Present: Heidegger, Foucault and the Project of a Spatial History* (London and New York: Continuum, 2001).
51 Michel Serres, 'The Geometry of the Incommunicable: Madness', in *Foucault and His Interlocutors*, ed. Arnold I. Davidson (Chicago: The University of Chicago Press, 1997), 39. This essay originally appears in the first volume of Serres' *Hermes* pentalogy, alongside a complementary essay examining *The Order of Things*. Serres' take on Foucault is read through the lens of his own peculiar structuralism, with its emphasis upon the purity of formal abstraction as a means for drawing transversal lines across seemingly unconnected disciplines and domains.
52 Foucault, *History of Madness*, xxxiv–xxxv.
53 Ibid., 122.
54 Ibid.
55 Ibid., xxviii.
56 Jacques Derrida, *Writing and Difference*, trans. Alan Bass (London and New York: Routledge, 1978), 39. On this rather bitter debate between Foucault and his former student, see *Foucault/Derrida: Fifty Years Later*, ed. Olivia Custer, Penelope Deutscher, and Samir Haddad (New York: Columbia University Press, 2016).
57 Derrida, *Writing and Difference*, 45.

58 Michel Foucault, 'A Preface to Transgression', in *Language, Counter-Memory, Practice: Selected Essays and Interviews*, ed. Donald F. Bouchard (Ithaca: Cornell University Press, 1977), 42.
59 Ibid.
60 Foucault, *History of Madness*, xxix.
61 'The attempt to write the history of the decision, division, difference', maintains Derrida, 'runs the risk of construing the division as an event or a structure subsequent to the unity of an original presence, thereby confirming metaphysics in its fundamental operation' (*Writing and Difference*, 48). Foucault's vague but suggestive assertion that 'the Greek Logos had no opposite' (*History of Madness*, xxix) reinforces this impression.
62 Michel Foucault, *The Order of Things: An Archaeology of the Human Sciences*, trans. A. M. Sheridan Smith (London and New York: Routledge, 1970), 266.
63 Foucault, *History of Madness*, xxix.
64 OT 377. In later works, Hubert L. Dreyfus and Paul Rabinow observe, Foucault will come to repudiate this 'recourse to an ontological boundary which defines us but is necessarily inaccessible to us' (*Michel Foucault: Beyond Structuralism and Hermeneutics* (Chicago: The University of Chicago Press, 1983), 11).

Chapter 9

1 Luce Irigaray, *This Sex Which Is Not One*, trans. Catherine Porter (Ithaca: Cornell University Press, 1985), 98. Translations of Irigaray's books have been altered throughout. It is also worth noting certain almost intractable difficulties that come with translating Irigaray's work: most notably, *masculin* and *féminin* in French can mean not only 'masculine' and 'feminine' (i.e. referring to gendered behaviours or attributes) but also 'male' or 'female' (as in *le sexe masculin* or *le sexe féminin*).
2 Gayatri Chakravorty Spivak, *In Other Worlds: Essays in Cultural Politics* (London and New York: Routledge, 2006), 205.
3 Hélène Cixous, 'The Laugh of the Medusa', *Signs* 1, no. 4 (1976): 883. Within the genre of *l'écriture féminine*, writes Ann Rosalind Jones, 'symbolic discourse (language, in various contexts) is another means through which man objectifies the world, reduces it to his terms, speaks in place of everything and everyone else – including women' ('Writing the Body: Toward an Understanding of "L'Écriture Feminine"', *Feminist Studies* 7, no. 2 (1981): 248).
4 Jacques Lacan, *Écrits*, trans. Bruce Fink (New York and London: W.W. Norton & Company, 2006), 308.
5 Irigaray, *This Sex*, 111.
6 Luce Irigaray, *Speculum of the Other Woman*, trans. Gillian C. Gill (Ithaca: Cornell University Press, 1985), 365. As Mary Beth Mader remarks, the English title of this

book would be more accurately rendered *'Speculum of the Woman Other'* ('Luce Irigaray', in *The History of Continental Philosophy, Vol. 6: Poststructuralism and Critical Theory's Second Generation*, ed. Alan D. Schrift (Chicago: The University of Chicago Press, 2010), 347).

7 As with many of Irigaray's central conceits, she is implicitly drawing from the concepts of Lacan here, who declares that '*woman* does not exist, woman is *not all*' (*Book XX, Encore 1972–1973: On Feminine Sexuality, The Limits of Love and Knowledge*, trans. Bruce Fink (New York and London: W.W. Norton & Company, 1998), 7, translation altered). Specifically, what Lacan means here is that *la femme* (emphasis on the definite article) does not exist – woman cannot be universalized, she is not whole. 'French feminists,' comments Moira Gatens, 'did not embrace just any old Freud (there are several), they embraced Lacan's Freud. French feminists, unlike their Anglo-American counterparts, are much more closely aligned with philosophical than sociological theories. And Lacan's version of Freud is a highly philosophical one' (*Feminism and Philosophy: Perspectives on Difference and Equality* (Bloomington and Indianapolis: Indiana University Press, 1991), 112).
8 Irigaray, *Speculum*, 13.
9 Ibid., 28.
10 Ibid.
11 Ibid., 41–2.
12 Ibid., 77.
13 Ibid., 54. Irigaray's frequent references to the *flat mirror* are, predictably, an allusion to Lacan's mirror stage, which 'manifests the affective dynamism by which the subject primordially identifies with the visual gestalt of his own body', this gestalt being 'an ideal unity, a salutary imago' (*Écrits*, 92).
14 Irigaray, *This Sex*, 85. Woman 'can only come into being as the inverted other of the masculine subject (his *alter ego*), or as the place of emergence and veiling of the cause of his (phallic) desire, or again as lack' (Ibid., 129).
15 See Rebecca Hill, *The Interval: Relation and Becoming in Irigaray, Aristotle, and Bergson* (New York: Fordham University Press, 2012), 12–18 on the role of Aristotelian logic in Irigaray's thought.
16 Irigaray, *This Sex*, 69.
17 Irigaray, *Speculum*, 28.
18 Ibid.
19 Irigaray, *This Sex*, 74.
20 Ibid.
21 Ibid.
22 'If Freudian theory indeed contributes what is needed to upset the philosophic order of discourse,' argues Irigaray, 'the theory remains paradoxically subject to that discourse where the definition of sexual difference is concerned' (Ibid., 72).

23 Irigaray, *Speculum*, 322.
24 Irigaray, *This Sex*, 154.
25 Ibid.
26 Ibid., 113.
27 Irigaray, *Speculum*, 234; cf. *This Sex*, 85. A particularly helpful guide to the political stakes of Irigaray's project can be found in Laura Roberts, *Irigaray and Politics* (Edinburgh: Edinburgh University Press, 2019).
28 Irigaray, *Speculum*, 134.
29 Ibid., 54.
30 Ibid., 134, 144.
31 Ibid., 151.
32 Ibid., 161–2.
33 Ibid., 162.
34 Ibid., 229.
35 Ibid., 230.
36 Ibid., 227.
37 Ibid., 227–8.
38 Irigaray, *This Sex*, 107.
39 Ibid., 150, my emphasis.
40 Ibid., 109. Rachel Jones describes this aspect of Irigaray's project well: 'the morphology of the male subject is interpreted in ways that make it isomorphic with this One whose self-sameness is secured against an "Other" that plays the role of desirable object, sustaining plenitude and terrifying lack, and that is thus figured as an unruly excess capable of shifting between these conflicting positions or inhabiting them all at once. *Speculum* exposes these multiple projections of "woman" as an Other who is always, within this metaphysics, the Other of the Same' ('Thinking Otherwise with Irigaray and Maximin', in *Thought: A Philosophical History*, ed. Panayiota Vassilopoulou and Daniel Whistler (London and New York: Routledge, 2021), 237).
41 Irigaray, *This Sex*, 109.
42 Ibid., 106–7.
43 Ibid., 77.
44 Ibid., 30.
45 Ibid., 156.
46 Ibid., 76.
47 Irigaray, *Speculum*, 344.
48 'Psychoanalytic discourse on sexuality', declares Irigaray, 'is the discourse of truth. A discourse that tells the truth about the logic of truth: namely, that *the feminine occurs only within models and laws devised by male subjects*. Which implies that there are not really two sexes, but only one. A single practice and representation of the sexual' (*This Sex*, 86).

49. Ibid., 78.
50. Judith Butler, *Gender Trouble: Feminism and the Subversion of Identity* (London and New York: Routledge, 2007), 36.
51. Irigaray, *Speculum*, 232.
52. Ibid., 142.
53. Ibid.
54. Irigaray, *This Sex*, 29.
55. Ibid., 78.
56. Ibid., 68.
57. This strategic mimesis, and the delicate (or perilous, depending on how one looks at it) usage it makes of essentialist gender tropes, is examined in Diana Fuss, *Essentially Speaking: Feminism, Nature & Difference* (London and New York: Routledge, 1989), 55–72 and Tina Chanter, *Ethics of Eros: Irigaray's Rewriting of the Philosophers* (London and New York: Routledge, 1995), 21–46. On the limitations of Irigaray's ontologization of sexual difference, see Eleni Varikas, 'Who Cares about the Greeks? Uses and Misuses of Tradition in the Articulation of Difference and Plurality', in *Rewriting Difference: Luce Irigaray and 'the Greeks'*, ed. Elena Tzelepis and Athena Athanasiou (Albany: State University of New York Press, 2010).
58. Ibid., 75.
59. Ibid., 79–80.
60. Ibid., 153.
61. Ibid., 159.
62. Ibid., 168.
63. Irigaray, *Speculum*, 365. For a detailed study of similar stylistic tropes in Derrida's work, through which he repurposes the discarded residua of Hegelian systematicity, see Jessica Marian, 'Styling Against Absolute Knowledge in Derrida's *Glas*', *Parrhesia* 24 (2015): 217–38.
64. Though Irigaray's forbidding writing style (even by the already abstruse standards of continental philosophy) and said citational practices (or lack thereof) potentially introduces its own forms of exclusion. Rosi Braidotti, for example, comments on 'the undemocratic and often self-referential nature of a great deal of the feminist texts produced in France in the 1980s by the generation of high poststructuralism, starting from the holy trinity of French feminism itself: Irigaray, Cixous, and Kristeva', absent of footnotes and bibliographies ('Feminist Philosophy: Coming of Age', in *The History of Continental Philosophy, Vol. 7: After Poststructuralism*, ed. Rosi Braidotti (Chicago: The University of Chicago Press, 2010), 232).
65. Michelle Boulous Walker, *Philosophy and the Maternal Body: Reading Silence* (London and New York: Routledge, 2002), 10.
66. And this well-ordered opposition risks also effacing other consequential forms of both mimicry and exclusion. Irigaray, suggests Anne McClintock, 'elides the theatrical and strategic possibilities of male masquerade: camp, voguing, drag,

passing, transvestism and so on' (*Imperial Leather: Race, Gender, and Sexuality in the Colonial Context* (London and New York: Routledge, 1995), 62). Likewise, 'Irigaray's emphasis on the ontological and ethical priority of sexual difference,' writes Joanne Faulkner 'involuntarily risks silencing questions of Western philosophy's racism' ('Settler Colonialism's "Miscarriage": Thinking the Failure of Relationality through Irigaray's "Interval"', *Angelaki: Journal of the Theoretical Humanities* 24, no. 3 (2019): 139).

67 Kofman, despite pursuing her own feminist critique of Freudian psychoanalysis, reckons that 'nothing in the text justifies Luce Irigaray's reading (according to which Freud, like Aristotle, deprives women of the right to the logos and to the phallus alike)' (*The Enigma of Woman*, trans. Catherine Porter (Ithaca: Cornell University Press, 1985), 104). Likewise, Le Dœuff notes that 'some women [. . .] have had access to philosophical theorizing; and let us add that the philosophical was not so forbidden to them that they had to pay for their transgression by losing their female "nature" in the eyes of observers' (*Philosophical Imaginary*, 102). On the relationship between these three seminal thinkers, refer to Penelope Deutscher, *Yielding Gender: Feminism, Deconstruction and the History of Philosophy* (London and New York: Routledge, 1997), 59–88.

68 Perhaps there is a risk that, as Butler puts it, Irigaray (in her reading of Plato), 'redoubles the effect of foreclosure performed by the phallogocentric discourse itself, one which "mimes" its founding violence' (*Bodies That Matter: On the Discursive Limits of 'Sex'* (London and New York: Routledge, 2011), 21).

69 Luce Irigaray, *To Speak Is Never Neutral*, trans. Gail Schwab (London: Continuum, 2002), 4.

70 Isabelle Stengers, *Cosmopolitics I*, trans. Robert Bononno (Minneapolis: University of Minnesota Press, 2010), 29.

71 Irigaray, *Speculum*, 281.

Bibliography

Adorno, Theodor W. *History and Freedom: Lectures 1964–1965*. Translated by Rodney Livingstone. Cambridge and Malden, MA: Polity Press, 2006.
Ahmed, Sara. *Strange Encounters: Embodied Others in Post-Coloniality*. London and New York: Routledge, 2000.
Ahmed, Sara. *The Promise of Happiness*. Durham, NC: Duke University Press, 2010.
Ahmed, Sara. *Willful Subjects*. Durham, NC: Duke University Press, 2014.
Allais, Lucy. 'Kant's Racism'. *Philosophical Papers* 45, no. 1–2 (2016): 1–36.
Anderson, Benedict. *Imagined Communities: Reflections on the Origin and Spread of Nationalism*. London and New York: Verso, 2006.
Annas, Julia. 'Plato's Republican Feminism'. In *Feminism and Ancient Philosophy*, edited by Julie K. Ward, 3–12. London and New York: Routledge, 1996.
Aristotle. *Posterior Analytics*. Translated by Jonathan Barnes. Oxford: Clarendon Press, 1993.
Aristotle. *Prior Analytics, Book I*. Translated by Gisela Striker. Oxford: Clarendon Press, 2009.
Aristotle. *Metaphysics*. Translated by C. D. C. Reeve. Indianapolis, IN: Hackett, 2016.
Assiter, Alison. *Kierkegaard, Metaphysics and Political Theory*. London and New York: Continuum, 2009.
Augustine. *On Christian Teaching*. Translated by R. P. H. Green. Oxford: Oxford University Press, 1997.
Battersby, Christine. 'Kierkegaard, the Phantom of the Public, and the Sexual Politics of Crowds'. In *Kierkegaard and the Political*, edited by Alison Assiter and Margherita Tonon, 27–44. Newcastle: Cambridge Scholars Publishing, 2012.
Beaufret, Jean. *Dialogue with Heidegger*. Translated by Mark Sinclair. Bloomington and Indianapolis, IN: Indiana University Press, 2006.
Béland, Martine. 'Vocation as Therapy: Nietzsche and the Conflict between Profession and Calling in Academia'. In *Nietzsche's Therapeutic Teaching: For Individuals and Culture*, edited by Horst Hutter and Eli Friedland, 13–30. London: Bloomsbury, 2013.
Benjamin, Andrew. *Place, Commonality, and Judgement: Continental Philosophy and the Ancient Greeks*. London and New York: Continuum, 2010.
Bernasconi, Robert. 'Kant as an Unfamiliar Source of Racism'. In *Philosophers on Race*, edited by Julie K. Ward and Tommy L. Lott, 145–66. Oxford and Malden, MA: Blackwell, 2002.
Billouet, Pierre. *Foucault*. Paris: Les Belles Lettres, 1999.

Blanchot, Maurice. *The Infinite Conversation*. Translated by Susan Hanson. Minneapolis, MN: University of Minnesota Press, 1993.

Blondell, Ruby. *The Play of Character in Plato's Dialogues*. Cambridge: Cambridge University Press, 2004.

Bottici, Chiara. *A Philosophy of Political Myth*. Cambridge: Cambridge University Press, 2007.

Braidotti, Rosi. 'Feminist Philosophy: Coming of Age'. In *The History of Continental Philosophy, Vol. 7: After Poststructuralism*, edited by Rosi Braidotti, 221–46. Chicago: The University of Chicago Press, 2010.

Breazeale, Daniel. 'Doing Philosophy: Fichte vs. Kant on Transcendental Method'. In *Fichte, German Idealism, and Early Romanticism*, edited by Daniel Breazeale and Tom Rockmore, 41–62. Amsterdam: Rodopi, 2010.

Breazeale, Daniel. *Thinking Through the Wissenschaftslehre: Themes from Fichte's Early Philosophy*. Oxford: Oxford University Press, 2013.

Breazeale, Daniel. 'Fichte's Project: The Jena *Wissenschaftslehre*'. In *Kant, Fichte, and the Legacy of Transcendental Idealism*, edited by Halla Kim and Steven Hoeltzel, 101–27. Lanham, MD: Lexington Books, 2015.

Breazeale, Daniel. 'The *Wissenschaftslehre* of 1796-99 [*nova methodo*]'. In *The Cambridge Companion to Fichte*, edited by David James and Günter Zöller, 93–138. Cambridge: Cambridge University Press, 2016.

Brown, Wendy. *Politics Out of History*. Princeton, NJ: Princeton University Press, 2001.

Brueck, Katherine T. *The Redemption of Tragedy: The Literary Vision of Simone Weil*. Albany, NY: State University of New York Press, 1995.

Burke, Catherine. 'Female Homers: A Feminist *nostos*'. In *Homer's Daughters: Women's Responses to Homer in the Twentieth Century and Beyond*, edited by Fiona Cox and Elena Theodorakopoulos, 57–72. Oxford: Oxford University Press, 2019.

Burke, Seán. *The Ethics of Writing: Authorship and Legacy in Plato and Nietzsche*. Edinburgh: Edinburgh University Press, 2008.

Butler, Judith. *Gender Trouble: Feminism and the Subversion of Identity*. London and New York: Routledge, 1990.

Butler, Judith. *Bodies That Matter: On the Discursive Limits of 'Sex'*. London and New York: Routledge, 1993.

Butler, Judith. 'Values of Difficulty'. In *Just Being Difficult? Academic Writing in the Public Arena*, edited by Jonathan Culler and Kevin Lamb, 199–215. Stanford, CA: Stanford University Press, 2003.

Bykova, Marina. 'The Self as the World Into Itself'. In *Fichte, German Idealism, and Early Romanticism*, edited Daniel Breazeale and Tom Rockmore, 131–47. Amsterdam: Rodopi, 2010.

Cain, Rebecca Bensen. *The Socratic Method: Plato's Use of Philosophical Drama*. London and New York: Continuum, 2007.

Cameron, Sharon. 'The Practice of Attention: Simone Weil's Performance of Impersonality'. *Critical Inquiry* 29, no. 2 (2003): 216–52.

Carlisle, Clare. *Kierkegaard: A Guide for the Perplexed*. London and New York: Continuum, 2006.

Carlsson, Ulrika. *Kierkegaard and Philosophical Eros: Between Ironic Reflection and Aesthetic Meaning*. London: Bloomsbury, 2021.

Cavarero, Adriana. *In Spite of Plato: A Feminist Reworking of Ancient Philosophy*. Translated by Serena Anderlini-D'Onofrio and Áine O'Healy. New York: Routledge, 1995.

Chanter, Tina. *Ethics of Eros: Irigaray's Rewriting of the Philosophers*. London and New York: Routledge, 1995.

Cherniss, Harold. *Aristotle's Criticism of Presocratic Philosophy*. Baltimore, MD: The Johns Hopkins University Press, 1935.

Cherniss, Harold. *Selected Papers*. Edited by Leonardo Tarán. Leiden: Brill, 1977.

Cixous, Hélène. 'The Laugh of the Medusa'. *Signs* 1, no. 4 (1976): 875–93.

Clark, Maudemarie. 'Nietzsche's Misogyny'. In *Feminist Interpretations of Friedrich Nietzsche*, edited by Kelly Oliver and Marilyn Pearsall, 187–98. University Park, PA: The Pennsylvania State University Press, 1998.

Clemens, Justin. *The Romanticism of Contemporary Theory: Institution, Aesthetics, Nihilism*. Aldershot: Ashgate, 2003.

Coe, Cynthia D. 'Plato, Maternity, and Power: Can We Get a Different Midwife?'. In *Coming to Life: Philosophies of Pregnancy, Childbirth, and Mothering*, edited by Sarah LaChance Adams and Caroline R. Lundquist, 31–46. New York: Fordham University Press, 2013.

Coleridge, Samuel Taylor. *The Collected Works of Samuel Taylor Coleridge, Volume 4 (Part I): The Friend*. Edited by Barbara E. Rooke. London: Routledge & Kegan Paul, 1969.

Cominos, Marina. 'The Question of Nietzsche's Anti-Politics and Human Transfiguration'. In *Nietzsche, Power and Politics: Rethinking Nietzsche's Legacy for Political Thought*, edited by Herman Siemens and Vasti Roodt, 85–103. Berlin: De Gruyter, 2008.

Conche, Marcel. *Héraclite: Fragments*. Paris: Presses Universitaires de France, 1986.

Conche, Marcel. *Parménide: Le Poème: Fragments*. Paris: Presses Universitaires de France, 1996.

Conway, Daniel. *Nietzsche & the Political*. London and New York: Routledge, 1997.

Crawley, Ashon. *Blackpentecostal Breath: The Aesthetics of Possibility*. New York: Fordham University Press, 2017.

Curd, Patricia. 'Knowledge and Unity in Heraclitus'. *The Monist* 74, no. 4 (1991): 531–49.

Curd, Patricia. *Eleatic Monism and Later Presocratic Thought*. Princeton, NJ: Princeton University Press, 1998.

Curd, Patricia, ed. *A Presocratics Reader: Selected Fragments and Testimonia*. Indianapolis, IN: Hackett, 2011.

Custer, Olivia, Penelope Deutscher and Samir Haddad, eds. *Foucault/Derrida: Fifty Years Later*. New York: Columbia University Press, 2016.

Danto, Arthur C. *Nietzsche as Philosopher*. New York: Columbia University Press, 2005.

Das, Saitya Brata. *The Political Theology of Kierkegaard*. Edinburgh: Edinburgh University Press, 2020.

Davidshofer, Claudine. 'Johannes Climacus and the Dialectical Method'. In *The Kierkegaardian Mind*, edited by Adam Buben, Eleanor Helms and Patrick Stokes, 28–38. London and New York: Routledge, 2019.

Debray, Régis. *Media Manifestos: On the Technological Transmission of Cultural Forms*. Translated by Eric Rauth. London and New York: Verso, 1996.

Debray, Régis. *Transmitting Culture*. Translated by Eric Rauth. New York: Columbia University Press, 2000.

Deleuze, Gilles and Félix Guattari. *What Is Philosophy?*. Translated by Hugh Tomlinson and Graham Burchell. New York: Columbia University Press, 1994.

Derrida, Jacques. *Writing and Difference*. Translated Alan Bass. London and New York: Routledge, 1978.

Derrida, Jacques. *Dissemination*. Translated by Barbara Johnson. London and New York: Continuum, 1981.

Derrida, Jacques. *Margins of Philosophy*. Translated by Alan Bass. Chicago: The University of Chicago Press, 1982.

Detwiler, Bruce. *Nietzsche and the Politics of Aristocratic Radicalism*. Chicago: The University of Chicago Press, 1990.

Deutscher, Max. *Towards Continental Philosophy: Reason and Imagination in the Thought of Max Deutscher*. Lanham, MD: Rowman & Littlefield, 2021.

Deutscher, Penelope. *Yielding Gender: Feminism, Deconstruction and the History of Philosophy*. London and New York: Routledge, 1997.

DiCenso, James J. *Kant, Religion, and Politics*. Cambridge: Cambridge University Press, 2011.

Diprose, Rosalyn. 'Nietzsche and the Pathos of Distance'. In *Nietzsche, Feminism, and Political Theory*, edited by Paul Patton, 1–26. London and New York: Routledge, 1993.

Le Dœuff, Michèle. *The Philosophical Imaginary*. Translated by Colin Gordon. London and New York: Continuum, 1989.

Dolar, Mladen. *A Voice and Nothing More*. Cambridge, MA: The MIT Press, 2006.

Doyle, Tsarina. *Nietzsche on Epistemology and Metaphysics: The World in View*. Edinburgh: Edinburgh University Press, 2009.

Dreyfus, Hubert L. and Paul Rabinow. *Michel Foucault: Beyond Structuralism and Hermeneutics*. Chicago: The University of Chicago Press, 1983.

DuBois, Page. *Sowing the Body: Psychoanalysis and Ancient Representations of Women*. Chicago: University of Chicago Press, 1988.

Duttenhaver, Krista E. and Coy D. Jones. 'Power, Subjectivity, and Resistance in the Thought of Simone Weil and Michel Foucault'. In *The Relevance of the Radical: Simone Weil 100 Years Later*, edited by A. Rebecca Rozelle-Stone and Lucian Stone, 176–92. London: Bloomsbury, 2009.

Elden, Stuart. *Mapping the Present: Heidegger, Foucault and the Project of a Spatial History*. London and New York: Continuum, 2001.

Engelstein, Stefani. 'The Allure of Wholeness: The Eighteenth-Century Organism and the Same-Sex Marriage Debate'. *Critical Inquiry* 39, no. 4 (2013): 754–76.

Epstein, Klaus. *The Genesis of German Conservatism*. Princeton, NJ: Princeton University Press, 1966.

Estes, Yolanda. 'Fichte's Account of Human Sexuality: Gender Difference as the Basis of Human Equality within a Just Society'. *Social Philosophy Today* 25 (2009): 63–73.

Estes, Yolanda. 'Intellectual Intuition: Reconsidering Continuity in Kant, Fichte, and Schelling'. In *Fichte, German Idealism, and Early Romanticism*, edited by Daniel Breazeale and Tom Rockmore, 165–78. Amsterdam: Rodopi, 2010.

Faulkner, Joanne. *Dead Letters to Nietzsche; or, the Necromantic Art of Reading Philosophy*. Athens, OH: Ohio University Press, 2010.

Faulkner, Joanne. 'Settler Colonialism's "Miscarriage": Thinking the Failure of Relationality Through Irigaray's "Interval"'. *Angelaki: Journal of the Theoretical Humanities* 24, no. 3 (2019): 137–54.

Felski, Rita. *Doing Time: Feminist Theory and Postmodernism*. New York: New York University Press, 2000.

Fenves, Peter. *Raising the Tone of Philosophy: Late Essays by Immanuel Kant, Transformative Critique by Jacques Derrida*. Baltimore, MD: The Johns Hopkins University Press, 1993.

Fiala, Andrew. *The Philosopher's Voice: Philosophy, Politics, and Language in the Nineteenth Century*. Albany, NY: State University of New York Press, 2002.

Ficara, Elena. '"Transcendental" in Kant and Fichte: A Conceptual Shift and Its Philosophical Meaning'. In *The Enigma of Fichte's First Principles*, edited by David W. Wood, 333–52. Leiden: Brill, 2021.

Fichte, Johann Gottlieb. *New Exposition of the Science of Knowledge*. Translated by A. E. Kroeger. St Louis, MO, 1869.

Fichte, Johann Gottlieb. *Early Philosophical Writings*. Translated by Daniel Breazeale. Ithaca, NY: Cornell University Press, 1988.

Fichte, Johann Gottlieb. *Foundations of Transcendental Philosophy (Wissenschaftslehre nova methodo 1796/99)*. Translated by Daniel Breazeale. Ithaca, NY: Cornell University Press, 1992.

Fichte, Johann Gottlieb. *Introductions to the Wissenschaftslehre and Other Writings (1797–1800)*. Translated by Daniel Breazeale. Indianapolis, IN: Hackett, 1994.

Fichte, Johann Gottlieb. *Foundations of Natural Right*. Translated by Michael Baur. Cambridge: Cambridge University Press, 2000.

Fichte, Johann Gottlieb. *The Science of Knowing*. Translated by Walter E. Wright. Albany, NY: State University of New York Press, 2005.

Fichte, Johann Gottlieb. *Foundation of the Entire Wissenschaftslehre and Related Writings (1794–95)*. Translated by Daniel Breazeale. Oxford: Oxford University Press, 2021.

Fierro, María Angélica. 'The Myth of the Winged Chariot in the *Phaedrus*: A Vehicle for Philosophical Thinking'. In *Plato's Styles and Characters: Between Literature and Philosophy*, edited by Gabriele Cornelli, 47–62. Berlin: De Gruyter, 2016.

Finch, Henry Leroy. *Simone Weil and the Intellect of Grace*. New York: Continuum, 1999.

Fine, Gail. *Plato on Knowledge and Forms: Selected Essays*. Oxford: Clarendon Press, 2003.

Foucault, Michel. *Madness and Civilization: A History of Insanity in the Age of Reason*. Translated by Richard Howard. London and New York: Routledge, 1967.

Foucault, Michel. *The Order of Things: An Archaeology of the Human Sciences*, translated by A.M. Sheridan Smith. London and New York: Routledge, 1970.

Foucault, Michel. 'A Preface to Transgression'. In *Language, Counter-Memory, Practice: Selected Essays and Interviews*, edited by Donald F. Bouchard, 29–52. Ithaca, NY: Cornell University Press, 1977.

Foucault, Michel. *History of Madness*. Translated by Jonathan Murphy and Jean Khalfa. London and New York: Routledge, 2006.

Frischmann, Bärbel. 'Fichte's Theory of Gender Relations in his Foundations of Natural Right'. In *Rights, Bodies, and Recognition: New Essays on Fichte's Foundations of Natural Right*, edited by Tom Rockmore and Daniel Breazeale, 152–65. London and New York: Routledge, 2006.

Fuss, Diana. *Essentially Speaking: Feminism, Nature & Difference*. London and New York: Routledge, 1989.

Gadamer, Hans-Georg. *The Beginning of Philosophy*. Translated by Rod Coltman. London and New York: Continuum, 1998.

Gatens, Moira. *Feminism and Philosophy: Perspectives on Difference and Equality*. Bloomington and Indianapolis, IN: Indiana University Press, 1991.

Gaukroger, Stephen. 'The Persona of the Natural Philosopher'. In *The Philosopher in Early Modern Europe: The Nature of a Contested Identity*, edited by Conal Condren, Stephen Gaukroger and Ian Hunter, 17–34. Cambridge: Cambridge University Press, 2006.

Goody, Jack and Ian Watt. 'The Consequences of Literacy'. *Comparative Studies in Society and History* 5, no. 3 (1963): 304–45.

Gordon, Colin. '*Histoire de la folie*: An Unknown Book by Michel Foucault'. In *Rewriting the History of Madness*, edited by Arthur Still and Irvin Velody, 19–42. London and New York: Routledge, 1992.

Gordon, Jill. *Turning Toward Philosophy: Literary Device and Dramatic Structure in Plato's Dialogues*. University Park, PA: The Pennsylvania State University Press, 1999.

Grabowski, Francis. *Plato, Metaphysics, and the Forms*. London and New York: Continuum, 2008.

Graham, Daniel. *Explaining the Cosmos: The Ionian Tradition of Scientific Philosophy*. Princeton, NJ: Princeton University Press, 2006.

Gram, Moltke S. 'Intellectual Intuition: The Continuity Thesis'. *Journal of the History of Ideas* 42, no. 2 (1981): 287–304.
Gros, Frédéric. *Foucault et la folie*. Paris: Presses Universitaires de France, 1997.
Guillory, John. 'Genesis of the Media Concept'. *Critical Inquiry* 36, no. 2 (2010): 321–62.
Gutting, Gary. *Michel Foucault's Archaeology of Scientific Reason*. Cambridge: Cambridge University Press, 1989.
Hacking, Ian. 'Déraison'. *History of the Human Sciences* 24, no. 4 (2011): 13–23.
Hadot, Pierre. *Philosophy as a Way of Life: Spiritual Exercises from Socrates to Foucault*. Translated Michael Chase. Oxford and Cambridge: Blackwell, 1995.
Hadot, Pierre. *What Is Ancient Philosophy?*. Translated by Michael Chase. Cambridge, MA: The Belknap Press of Harvard University Press, 2002.
Hadot, Pierre. *The Veil of Isis: An Essay on the History of the Idea of Nature*. Translated by Michael Chase. Cambridge, MA: The Belknap Press of Harvard University Press, 2006.
Hale, Geoffrey A. *Kierkegaard and the Ends of Language*. Minneapolis, MN: University of Minnesota Press, 2002.
Han-Pile, Béatrice. 'Transcendental Aspects, Ontological Commitments, and Naturalistic Elements in Nietzsche's Thought'. In *The Transcendental Turn*, edited by Sebastian Gardner and Matthew Grist, 195–227. Oxford: Oxford University Press, 2015.
Hardwick, Elizabeth. 'Reflections on Simone Weil'. *Signs* 1, no. 1 (1975): 83–91.
Heap, Jodie Lee. *The Creative Imagination: Indeterminacy and Embodiment in the Writings of Kant, Fichte, and Castoriadis*. Latham, MD: Rowman & Littlefield, 2021.
Hegel, Georg Wilhelm Friedrich. *The Phenomenology of Spirit*. Translated by Terry Pinkard. Cambridge: Cambridge University Press, 2018.
Heidegger, Martin. *Pathmarks*. Edited by William McNeill. Cambridge: Cambridge University Press, 1998.
Heidegger, Martin. *Introduction to Metaphysics*. Translated by Gregory Fried and Richard Polt. New Haven, CT: Yale University Press, 2000.
Hill, Rebecca. *The Interval: Relation and Becoming in Irigaray, Aristotle, and Bergson*. New York: Fordham University Press, 2012.
Hobbes, Thomas. *Leviathan*. Cambridge: Cambridge University Press, 1996.
Hull, Isabel V. *Sexuality, State, and Civil Society in Germany, 1700–1815*. Ithaca, NY: Cornell University Press, 1996.
Hunter, Ian. *Rival Enlightenments: Civil and Metaphysical Philosophy in Early Modern Germany*. Cambridge: Cambridge University Press, 2003.
Iliopoulos, John. *The History of Reason in the Age of Madness: Foucault's Enlightenment and a Radical Critique of Psychiatry*. London: Bloomsbury, 2017.
Irigaray, Luce. *Speculum of the Other Woman*. Translated by Gillian C. Gill. Ithaca, NY: Cornell University Press, 1985.
Irigaray, Luce. *This Sex Which Is Not One*. Translated by Catherine Porter. Ithaca, NY: Cornell University Press, 1985.

Irigaray, Luce. *To Speak Is Never Neutral*. Translated by Gail Schwab. London: Continuum, 2002.

Irwin, Alexander. *Saints of the Impossible: Bataille, Weil, and the Politics of the Sacred*. Minneapolis, MN: University of Minnesota Press, 2002.

Jones, Ann Rosalind. 'Writing the Body: Toward an Understanding of "L'Écriture Feminine"'. *Feminist Studies* 7, no. 2 (1981): 247–63.

Jones, Rachel. 'Thinking Otherwise with Irigaray and Maximin'. In *Thought: A Philosophical History*, edited by Panayiota Vassilopoulou and Daniel Whistler, 236–50. London and New York: Routledge, 2021.

Kahn, Charles H. *The Art and Thought of Heraclitus*. Cambridge: Cambridge University Press, 1979.

Kant, Immanuel. *Practical Philosophy*. Edited by Mary J. Gregor. Cambridge: Cambridge University Press, 1996.

Kant, Immanuel. *Lectures on Metaphysics*. Edited by Karl Ameriks and Steve Naragon. Cambridge: Cambridge University Press, 1997.

Kant, Immanuel. *Critique of Pure Reason*. Translated by Paul Guyer and Allen W. Wood. Cambridge: Cambridge University Press, 1998.

Kant, Immanuel. *Correspondence*. Edited by Arnulf Zweig. Cambridge: Cambridge University Press, 1999.

Kant, Immanuel. *Critique of the Power of Judgment*. Translated by Paul Guyer and Eric Matthews. Cambridge: Cambridge University Press, 2000.

Kant, Immanuel. *Theoretical Philosophy after 1781*. Edited by Henry Allison and Peter Heath. Cambridge: Cambridge University Press, 2004.

Kant, Immanuel. *Anthropology from a Pragmatic Point of View*. Translated by Robert B. Louden. Cambridge: Cambridge University Press, 2006.

Kant, Immanuel. *Anthropology, History, and Education*. Edited by Günter Zöller and Robert B. Louden. Cambridge: Cambridge University Press, 2007.

Kant, Immanuel. *Lectures on Anthropology*. Edited by Allen W. Wood and Robert B. Louden. Cambridge: Cambridge University Press, 2012.

Kant, Immanuel. *Natural Science*. Edited by Eric Watkins. Cambridge: Cambridge University Press, 2012.

Karatani, Kōjin. *Isonomia and the Origins of Philosophy*. Translated by Joseph A. Murphy. Durham, NC: Duke University Press, 2012.

Kayar, Esma. 'The First Principle of the *Wissenschaftslehre* and the Logical Principle of Identity'. In *The Enigma of Fichte's First Principles*, edited by David W. Wood, 161–76. Leiden: Brill, 2021.

Kenkel, Karen. 'The Personal and the Philosophical in Fichte's Theory of Sexual Difference'. In *Impure Reason: Dialectic of Enlightenment in Germany*, edited by W. Daniel Wilson and Robert C. Holub, 278–97. Detroit, MI: Wayne State University Press, 1993.

Kierkegaard, Søren. *The Concept of Irony With Continual Reference to Socrates*. Translated by Howard V. Hong and Edna H. Hong. Princeton, NJ: Princeton University Press, 1989.

Kierkegaard, Søren. *The Point of View*. Translated by Howard V. Hong and Edna H. Hong. Princeton, NJ: Princeton University Press, 1998.

Kierkegaard, Søren. *Fear and Trembling*. Translated by Sylvia Walsh. Cambridge: Cambridge University Press, 2006.

Kierkegaard, Søren. *Concluding Unscientific Postscript to the Philosophical Crumbs*. Translated by Alastair Hannay. Cambridge: Cambridge University Press, 2009.

Kierkegaard, Søren. *Repetition and Philosophical Crumbs*. Translated by M. G. Piety. Oxford: Oxford University Press, 2009.

Kim, Sung Ho. *Max Weber's Politics of Civil Society*. Cambridge: Cambridge University Press, 2004.

Kinlaw, C. Jeffery. 'Intellectual Intuition'. In *The Bloomsbury Handbook of Fichte*, edited by Marina Bykova. London: Bloomsbury, 2020.

Kleingeld, Pauline. 'The Problematic Status of Gender-Neutral Language in the History of Philosophy'. *The Philosophical Forum* 25, no. 2 (1993): 134–50.

Knoll, Manuel. 'The "Übermensch" as a Social and Political Task: A Study in the Continuity of Nietzsche's Political Thought'. In *Nietzsche as Political Philosopher*, edited by Manuel Knoll and Barry Stocker, 239–66. Berlin: De Gruyter, 2014.

Kofman, Sarah. 'The Economy of Respect: Kant and Respect for Women'. *Social Research* 49, no. 2 (1982): 383–404.

Kofman, Sarah. *The Enigma of Woman*. Translated by Catherine Porter. Ithaca, NY: Cornell University Press, 1985.

Kofman, Sarah. 'Beyond Aporia?'. In *Post-Structuralist Classics*, edited by Andrew Benjamin, 7–44. London and New York: Routledge, 1988.

Kofman, Sarah. *Nietzsche and Metaphor*. Translated by Duncan Large. London: The Athlone Press, 1993.

Kofman, Sarah. 'The Psychologist of the Eternal Feminine (Why I Write Such Good Books, 5)'. *Yale French Studies* 87 (1995): 173–89.

Kofman, Sarah. *Camera Obscura: Of Ideology*. Translated Will Straw. Ithaca, NY: Cornell University Press, 1998.

Kofman, Sarah. *Socrates: Fictions of a Philosopher*. Translated by Catherine Porter. London: The Athlone Press, 1998.

Kofman, Sarah. 'Scorning Jews: Nietzsche, the Jews, Anti-Semitism'. In *Selected Writings*, edited by Thomas Albrecht, 123–56. Stanford, CA: Stanford University Press, 2007.

Kotva, Simone. *Effort and Grace: On the Spiritual Exercise of Philosophy*. London: Bloomsbury, 2020.

Krämer, Sybille. *Medium, Messenger, Transmission: An Approach to Media Philosophy*. Translated by Anthony Enns. Amsterdam: Amsterdam University Press, 2015.

Krishek, Sharon. 'Love for Humans: Morality as the Heart of Kierkegaard's Religious Philosophy'. In *The Kierkegaardian Mind*, edited by Adam Buben, Eleanor Helms, and Patrick Stokes, 122–32. London and New York: Routledge, 2019.

Lacan, Jacques. *Book XX, Encore 1972–1973: On Feminine Sexuality, The Limits of Love and Knowledge*. Translated by Bruce Fink. New York and London: W.W. Norton & Company, 1998.

Lacan, Jacques. *Écrits*. Translated by Bruce Fink. New York and London: W.W. Norton & Company, 2006.

Lacoue-Labarthe, Philippe. *The Subject of Philosophy*. Translated by Thomas Tresize, Hugh J. Silverman, Gary M. Cole, Timothy D. Bent, Karen McPherson and Claudette Satiliot. Minneapolis, MN: University of Minnesota Press, 1993.

Laugier, Sandra. *Why We Need Ordinary Language Philosophy*. Translated by Daniela Ginsburg. Chicago: The University of Chicago Press, 2013.

Lemm, Vanessa. *Nietzsche's Animal Philosophy: Culture, Politics, and the Animality of the Human Being*. New York: Fordham University Press, 2009.

Lesher, T. H. 'Heraclitus' Epistemological Vocabulary'. *Hermes* 111, no. 2 (1983): 155–70.

Levin, Susan B. 'Women's Nature and Role in the Ideal Polis: Republic V Revisited'. In *Feminism and Ancient Philosophy*, edited by Julie K. Ward, 13–30. London and New York: Routledge, 1996.

Little, J. P. 'Simone Weil and the Limits of Language'. In *The Beauty that Saves: Essays on Aesthetics and Language in Simone Weil*, edited by John M. Dunaway and Eric O. Springsted, 39–54. Macon, GA: Mercer University Press, 1996.

Lloyd, Genevieve. *The Man of Reason*. London: Routledge, 1993.

Locke, John. *An Essay Concerning Human Understanding*. London: Penguin, 2004.

Lyotard, Jean-François. *The Inhuman: Reflections on Time*. Translated by Geoffrey Bennington and Rachel Bowlby. Stanford: Stanford University Press, 1991.

Mackenzie, Mary Margaret. 'Paradox in Plato's "Phaedrus"'. *Proceedings of the Cambridge Philological Society* 28 (1982): 64–76.

Mackenzie, Mary Margaret. 'Heraclitus and the Art of Paradox'. In *Oxford Studies in Ancient Philosophy, Vol. VI*, edited by Julia Annas, 1–37. Oxford: Clarendon Press, 1988.

Mader, Mary Beth. 'Luce Irigaray'. In *The History of Continental Philosophy, Vol. 6: Poststructuralism and Critical Theory's Second Generation*, edited by Alan D. Schrift, 337–58. Chicago: The University of Chicago Press, 2010.

De Man, Paul. 'The Epistemology of Metaphor'. *Critical Inquiry* 5, no. 1 (1978): 13–30.

Marian, Jessica. 'Styling Against Absolute Knowledge in Derrida's Glas'. *Parrhesia* 24 (2015): 217–38.

Martin, Nicholas. 'Breeding Greeks: Nietzsche, Gobineau, and Classical Theories of Race'. In *Nietzsche and Antiquity: His Reaction and Response to the Classical Tradition*, edited by Paul Bishop, 40–53. Cambridge: Cambridge University Press, 2004.

Mbembe, Achille. *Critique of Black Reason*. Translated by Laurent Dubois. Durham, NC: Duke University Press, 2017.

McClintock, Anne. *Imperial Leather: Race, Gender, and Sexuality in the Colonial Context*. London and New York: Routledge, 1995.

McCullough, Lissa. *The Religious Philosophy of Simone Weil: An Introduction*. London and New York: I.B. Tauris, 2014.
Meaney, Marie Cabaud. *Simone Weil's Apologetic Use of Literature: Her Christological Interpretations of Ancient Greek Texts*. Oxford: Oxford University Press, 2007.
Mellamphy, Nandita Biswas. *The Three Stigmata of Friedrich Nietzsche: Political Physiology in the Age of Nihilism*. Basingstoke: Palgrave Macmillan, 2011.
Mills, Charles W. 'Kant's *Untermenschen*'. In *Race and Racism in Modern Philosophy*, edited by Andrew Vallis, 169–93. Ithaca, NY: Cornell University Press, 2005.
Morgan, Kathryn. *Myth & Philosophy from the Presocratics to Plato*. Cambridge: Cambridge University Press, 2004.
Moscovici, Claudia. *From Sex Objects to Sexual Subjects*. London and New York: Routledge, 1996.
Most, Glenn W. 'The Poetics of Early Greek Philosophy'. In *The Cambridge Companion to Early Greek Philosophy*, edited by A. A. Long, 332–62. Cambridge: Cambridge University Press, 1999.
Moten, Fred. *Black and Blur*. Durham, NC: Duke University Press, 2017.
Murdoch, Iris. *The Fire and the Sun: Why Plato Banished the Artists*. Oxford: Clarendon Press, 1977.
Nails, Debra. *The People of Plato: A Prosopography of Plato and Other Socratics*. Indianapolis, IN: Hackett, 2002.
Nancy, Jean-Luc. *The Gravity of Thought*. Translated by François Raffoul and Gregory Recco. Atlantic Highlands, NJ: Humanities Press, 1997.
Nancy, Jean-Luc. *The Discourse of the Syncope: Logodaedalus*. Translated by Saul Anton. Stanford, CA: Stanford University Press, 2008.
Nietzsche, Friedrich. *Philosophy in the Tragic Age of the Greeks*. Translated by Marianne Cowan, 35–6. Washington, DC: Regnery Publishing, 1962.
Nietzsche, Friedrich. *Human, All Too Human*. Translated by R. J. Hollingdale. Cambridge: Cambridge University Press, 1996.
Nietzsche, Friedrich. *Daybreak: Thoughts on the Prejudices of Morality*. Translated by R. J. Hollingdale. Cambridge: Cambridge University Press, 1997.
Nietzsche, Friedrich. *On the Genealogy of Morality*. Translated by Carol Diethe. Cambridge: Cambridge University Press, 1997.
Nietzsche, Friedrich. *Untimely Meditations*. Translated by R. J. Hollingdale. Cambridge: Cambridge University Press, 1997.
Nietzsche, Friedrich. *The Birth of Tragedy and Other Writings*. Translated by Ronald Speirs. Cambridge: Cambridge University Press, 1999.
Nietzsche, Friedrich. *The Gay Science*. Translated by Josefine Nauckhoff and Adrian Del Caro. Cambridge: Cambridge University Press, 2001.
Nietzsche, Friedrich. *Beyond Good and Evil: Prelude to a Philosophy of the Future*. Translated by Judith Norman. Cambridge: Cambridge University Press, 2002.
Nietzsche, Friedrich. *Writings from the Late Notebooks*. Translated by Kate Sturge. Cambridge: Cambridge University Press, 2003.

Nietzsche, Friedrich. *The Anti-Christ, Ecce Homo, Twilight of the Idols, and Other Writings*. Translated by Judith Norman. Cambridge: Cambridge University Press, 2005.

Nietzsche, Friedrich. *Thus Spoke Zarathustra*. Translated by Adrian Del Caro. Cambridge: Cambridge University Press, 2006.

Nietzsche, Friedrich. *Writings from the Early Notebooks*. Translated by Ladislaus Löb. Cambridge: Cambridge University Press, 2009.

Nikulin, Dmitri. *Dialectic and Dialogue*. Stanford, CA: Stanford University Press, 2010.

Nuzzo, Angelica. 'Phenomenologies of Intersubjectivity: Fichte between Hegel and Husserl'. In *Fichte and the Phenomenological Tradition*, edited by Violette L. Waibel, Daniel Breazeale and Tom Rockmore, 97–117. Berlin: De Gruyter, 2010.

Nye, Andrea. *Philosophia: The Thought of Rosa Luxemborg, Simone Weil, and Hannah Arendt*. New York and London: Routledge, 1994.

O'Connell, Erin. *Heraclitus and Derrida: Presocratic Deconstruction*. New York: Peter Lang, 2006.

Oksala, Johanna. *Foucault on Freedom*. Cambridge: Cambridge University Press, 2005.

Panizza, Silvia Caprioglio. *The Ethics of Attention: Engaging the Real with Iris Murdoch and Simone Weil*. London and New York: Routledge, 2022.

Pascoe, Jordan. 'Patriarchy and Enlightenment in Immanuel Kant'. In *Patriarchal Moments*, edited by Cesare Cuttica and Gaby Mahlberg, 115–22. London: Bloomsbury, 2016.

Perniola, Mario. *Enigmas: The Egyptian Moment in Society and Art*. Translated by Christopher Woodall. London and New York: Verso.

Peters, John Durham. *Speaking into the Air: A History of the Idea of Communication*. Chicago: The University of Chicago Press, 1999.

Peters, John Durham. 'Doctors of Philosophy'. In *Philosophical Profiles in the Theory of Communication*, edited by Jason Hannan, 499–509. New York: Peter Lang, 2012.

Philonenko, Alexis. *La liberté humaine dans la philosophie de Fichte*. Paris: Librairie Philosophique J. Vrin, 1999.

Plato. *The Laws*. Translated by Trevor J. Saunders. London: Penguin, 1970.

Plato. *The Republic*. Translated by Robin Waterfield. Oxford: Oxford University Press, 1993.

Plato. *Sophist*. Translated by Nicholas P. White. Indianapolis, IN: Hackett, 1993.

Plato. *Statesman*. Translated by Christopher Rowe. Indianapolis, IN: Hackett, 1995.

Plato. *Parmenides*. Translated by Mary Louise Gill and Paul Ryan. Indianapolis, IN: Hackett, 1996.

Plato. *Symposium*. Translated by Christopher Gill. London: Penguin, 1999.

Plato. *The Last Days of Socrates*. Translated by Hugh Tredennick and Harold Tarrant. London: Penguin, 2003.

Plato. *Theaetetus*. Translated by Robin Waterfield. London: Penguin, 2004.

Plato. *Phaedrus*. Translated by Christopher Rowe. London: Penguin, 2005.

Plato. *Protagoras and Meno*. Translated by Adam Beresford. London: Penguin, 2005.
Platon, *Phèdre*. Translated by Léon Robin. Paris: Société d'Édition, 1933.
Poole, Roger. *Kierkegaard: The Indirect Communication*. Charlottesville, VA: University of Virginia Press, 1993.
De Quincey, Thomas. *Letters of De Quincey, the English Opium-eater, to a Young Man Whose Education Has Been Neglected*. Philadelphia, PA: John Penington, 1843.
Reinhold, Karl Leonhard. 'The Foundation of Philosophical Knowledge'. In *Between Kant and Hegel: Texts in the Development of Post-Kantian Idealism*. Translated by George di Giovanni and H. S. Harris, 51–103. Indianapolis, IN: Hackett, 2000.
Reinhold, Karl Leonhard. *Letters on the Kantian Philosophy*. Translated by James Hebbeler. Cambridge: Cambridge University Press, 2005.
Revel, Judith. *Le vocabulaire de Foucault*. Paris: Ellipses, 2002.
Roberts, Laura. *Irigaray and Politics*. Edinburgh: Edinburgh University Press, 2019.
Robin, Léon. *Platon*. Paris: Presses Universitaires de France, 1935.
Roccanova, Janet. 'First Steps: Lessons on Becoming a Philosopher from the Early Chapters of the *Wissenschaftslehre nova methodo*'. In *New Essays on Fichte's Later Jena Wissenschaftslehre*, edited by Daniel Breazeale and Tom Rockmore, 101–19. Evanston, IL: Northwestern University Press, 2002.
Rowe, Christopher. *Plato and the Art of Philosophical Writing*. Cambridge: Cambridge University Press, 2007.
Rozelle-Stone, A. Rebecca and Lucian Stone. 'The "War" on Error? Violent Metaphor and Words with Capital Letters'. In *The Relevance of the Radical: Simone Weil 100 Years Later*, edited by A. Rebecca Rozelle-Stone and Lucian Stone, 139–58. London: Bloomsbury, 2009.
Russell, Bertrand. *Mysticism and Logic*. London: George Allen & Unwin, 1917.
Sallis, John. *Being and Logos: Reading the Platonic Dialogues*. Bloomington and Indianapolis, IN: Indiana University Press, 1996.
Sassen Brigitte, ed. *Kant's Early Critics*. Cambridge: Cambridge University Press, 2000.
Schopenhauer, Arthur. *The World as Will and Representation, Vol. 1*. Translated by Judith Norman, Alistair Welchman and Christopher Janaway. Cambridge: Cambridge University Press, 2019.
Schott, Robin May. 'The Gender of Enlightenment'. In *Feminist Interpretations of Immanuel Kant*, edited by Robin May Schott, 319–37. University Park, PA: The Pennsylvania State University Press, 1997.
Schultz, Anne-Marie. *Plato's Socrates as Narrator: A Philosophical Muse*. Lanham, MD: Lexington Books, 2013.
Schutte, Ofelia. 'Nietzsche's Politics'. In *Feminist Interpretations of Friedrich Nietzsche*, edited by Kelly Oliver and Marilyn Pearsall, 282–305. University Park, PA: The Pennsylvania State University Press, 1998.
Seneca. *Dialogues and Essays*. Translated by John Davie. Oxford: Oxford University Press, 2007.

Serres, Michel. 'The Geometry of the Incommunicable: Madness'. In *Foucault and His Interlocutors*, edited by Arnold I. Davidson, 36–56. Chicago: The University of Chicago Press, 1997.

Siemens, Herman. 'Yes, No, Maybe So . . . Nietzsche's Equivocations on the Relation between Democracy and "Grosse Politik"'. In *Nietzsche, Power and Politics: Rethinking Nietzsche's Legacy for Political Thought*, edited by Herman Siemens and Vasti Roodt, 231–68. Berlin: De Gruyter, 2008.

Snow, Dale. *Schelling and the End of Idealism*. Albany, NY: State University of New York Press, 1996.

Songe-Møller, Vigdis. *Philosophy Without Women: The Birth of Sexism in Western Thought*. Translated by Peter Cripps. London and New York: Continuum, 2002.

Spivak, Gayatri Chakravorty. *In Other Worlds: Essays In Cultural Politics*. London and New York: Routledge, 2006.

Springsted, Eric O. 'Beyond the Personal: Weil's Critique of Maritain'. *The Harvard Theological Review* 98, no. 2 (2005): 209–18.

Stengers, Isabelle. *Cosmopolitics I*. Translated by Robert Bononno. Minneapolis, MN: University of Minnesota Press, 2010.

Stokes, Patrick. *The Naked Self: Kierkegaard and Personal Identity*. Oxford: Oxford University Press, 2015.

Strong, Tracy B. *Friedrich Nietzsche and the Politics of Transfiguration*. Berkeley and Los Angeles, CA: University of California Press, 1988.

Taylor, Mark C. *Journeys to Selfhood: Hegel & Kierkegaard*. New York: Fordham University Press, 2000.

Thomas, Rosalind. *Oral Tradition and Written Record in Classical Athens*. Cambridge: Cambridge University Press, 1989.

Tuana, Nancy and Charles E. Scott. *Beyond Philosophy: Nietzsche, Foucault, Anzaldúa*. Bloomington and Indianapolis, IN: Indiana University Press, 2020.

Vallega-Neu, Daniela. *The Bodily Dimension in Thinking*. Albany, NY: State University of New York Press, 2005.

Varikas, Eleni. 'Who Cares about the Greeks? Uses and Misuses of Tradition in the Articulation of Difference and Plurality'. In *Rewriting Difference: Luce Irigaray and 'the Greeks'*, edited by Elena Tzelepis and Athena Athanasiou, 231–46. Albany, NY: State University of New York Press, 2010.

Vattimo, Gianni. *The Adventure of Difference: Philosophy after Nietzsche and Heidegger*. Translated by Cyprian Blamires. Cambridge: Polity Press, 1993.

Vattimo, Gianni. *Dialogue with Nietzsche*. Translated by William McCuaig. New York: Columbia University Press, 2006.

Venable, Hannah Lyn. *Madness in Experience and History: Merleau-Ponty's Phenomenology and Foucault's Archaeology*. London and New York: Routledge, 2022.

Waibel, Violetta L. 'Kant and Fichte on the Notion of (Transcendental) Freedom'. In *Transcendental Inquiry: Its History, Methods and Critiques*, edited by Halla Kim and Steven Hoeltzel, 35–54. Cham: Palgrave Macmillan, 2016.

Walker, Michelle Boulous. *Philosophy and the Maternal Body: Reading Silence*. London and New York: Routledge, 2002.

Walsh, Sylvia. *Kierkegaard and Religion: Personality, Character, and Virtue*. Cambridge: Cambridge University Press, 2018.

Warren, Mark. *Nietzsche and Political Thought*. Cambridge, MA: The MIT Press, 1988.

Watanabe-O'Kelly, Helen. *Beauty or Beast?: The Woman Warrior in the German Imagination from the Renaissance to the Present*. Oxford: Oxford University Press, 2010.

Watkin, Julia. *Kierkegaard*. London and New York: Continuum, 1997.

Waugh, Joanne. 'Heraclitus: The Postmodern Presocratic?'. *The Monist* 74, no. 4 (1991): 605–23.

Weil, Simone. *Gravity and Grace*. Translated by Emma Crawford and Mario von der Ruhr. London and New York: Routledge, 1999.

Weil, Simone. *Simone Weil: An Anthology*. Edited by Siân Miles. London: Penguin, 2005.

Wennerscheid, Sophie. 'Kierkegaard's Scene Changes: Authorship as Theatrical Practice'. In *Authorship and Authority in Kierkegaard's Writings*, edited by Joseph Westfall, 75–90. London: Bloomsbury, 2019.

Weston, Michael. *Kierkegaard and Modern Continental Philosophy: An Introduction*. London and New York: Routledge, 1994.

Wilkinson, Lisa Atwood. *Parmenides and To Eon: Reconsidering Muthos and Logos*. London and New York: Continuum, 2009.

Williams, Robert R. 'The Question of the Other in Fichte's Thought'. In *Fichte: Historical Contexts/Contemporary Controversies*, ed. Daniel Breazeale and Tom Rockmore, 142–57. Atlantic Highlands, NJ: Humanities Press, 1994.

Yourgrau, Palle. *Simone Weil*. London: Reaktion Books, 2011.

Zartaloudis, Thanos. *The Birth of Nomos*. Edinburgh: Edinburgh University Press, 2019.

Zöller, Günter. 'Plato on Revolution: Kant and the Political Conservatism of J. G. Schlosser'. In *Kant and His Critics*, edited by Antonino Falduto und Heiner F. Klemme, 113–26. Hildesheim: Georg Olms Verlag, 2018.

Zuckert, Catherine H. *Plato's Philosophers: The Coherence of the Dialogues*. Chicago: The University of Chicago Press, 2009.

Index

Abstraction   8, 17, 22, 51, 62, 86–92, 94, 96–7, 103, 107, 113, 119, 124–5, 128, 133–4, 146, 160, 187, 200–1, 207
adequation   1, 7, 11, 18–19, 28, 34–5, 37–9, 54, 70, 88–9, 92–3, 162, 168
Adorno, Theodor   46
Ahmed, Sara   4, 182, 187
alterity   4, 127, 146, 161, 163–4, 167
aporia   23, 30, 36–9, 163, 181–2
Aristotle   2–3, 9, 12, 17–18, 41, 160, 173–4, 209, 212
ascesis   8, 23, 55, 110, 123, 130, 133, 175
audience   2, 4, 6–8, 11, 20, 23–8, 30–5, 37–40, 42–3, 48, 54, 65, 68, 73, 75, 81–3, 103–4, 108, 113–16, 119, 121, 129, 132, 169, 178
authenticity   5, 8, 15, 30, 49, 53, 59, 61, 65, 72, 104, 110, 117, 120–1
Barthes, Roland   153
Bergson, Henri   153, 175, 199
The Bible   110, 112, 114, 130–1
Blanchot, Maurice   23, 129, 204
Butler, Judith   164, 174, 212
Cherniss, Harold   28
Christianity   12, 107–21, 200, 203–4
Cixous, Hélène   154, 211
cliché   85, 93, 97, 102, 153, 202
Coleridge, Samuel Taylor   1
commonality   6–7, 9, 19, 21, 24–7, 31, 59, 61–2, 68, 77, 85–6, 88, 93, 97–8, 102–3, 114–15, 131, 137, 176–7, 179
communicability   2–3, 7–8, 10–11, 19, 28, 34, 37–8, 45–6, 58, 60–1, 65, 70–1, 73–9, 81–3, 85, 92, 104, 108–9, 112–13, 116, 121, 130–4, 144, 146–50, 154–5, 158–71, 181
community   4, 7, 25–7, 34, 41–2, 54, 83, 101, 110, 114–15, 175, 182
comportment   4–12, 15–16, 19, 23, 28, 30, 33–7, 40–1, 43, 53, 58, 62, 65, 70, 73, 83, 85, 92, 98–101, 108–9, 113–17, 121, 128–34, 137, 145–52, 158, 163–71
Conche, Marcel   20–1, 23–4, 26–7, 176
Debray, Régis   5–6, 11, 174–5
Deleuze, Gilles   9, 154
Delphic oracle   22–3
democracy   31, 42, 61, 86, 100, 105, 129, 196, 211
Derrida, Jacques   11, 61, 149, 153, 180, 207–8, 211
difference   4, 18–20, 22–8, 35, 86, 92, 99, 101, 105
   sexual difference   41–2, 51–2, 78–81, 154–9, 163–9, 192–3, 206, 208, 211–12
discursive reason   7, 9–10, 15–16, 72, 150, 171
distance   4, 18, 22, 27, 30, 34, 86, 92, 101, 103–5, 110, 127, 130, 133, 140, 146, 197
doxa   2–3, 5, 16, 18, 23–8, 35, 98, 153, 158, 167–8, 170–1, 178, 181
dramatis personae   1, 30, 108, 117, 179–80
duty   54, 59–60, 64, 67–8, 100–1, 104, 118, 139
écriture feminine   154, 208
education   1, 4, 15, 31–2, 41, 43, 48–51, 55, 63–5, 67–8, 70, 72–5, 78–82, 99, 127
Empedocles   178
equality   31, 57–8, 61–2, 68, 78, 83–4, 86, 97–8, 100–5, 119–20, 133, 159
exclusion   4–5, 7, 10–11, 15–17, 25, 27, 40–3, 51–4, 65, 70, 73–84, 86, 97–105, 117, 120–1, 123, 127, 133–5, 137–52, 154–71, 176–7, 182, 211

feminism 154, 158, 164, 167, 169, 182, 185, 197, 201, 208–9, 211–12
Fichte, J. G. 15–16, 117
   Concerning the Difference between the Spirit and the Letter within Philosophy 72
   discursive concepts 70–1, 82
   dogmatism 64–5, 74–7, 82–3
   egoism 65
   first principle 63–4, 69–74, 78, 82–3
   Foundations of Natural Right 78–80
   intersubjectivity 65–7, 83
   role of the scholar 64–8, 70–82
   Some Lectures Concerning the Scholar's Vocation 65–6, 72
   spirit of philosophy 72–3, 76, 80, 82–3
   transcendental and ordinary standpoints 66–7, 70, 73–4, 76–80, 189–90
   Wissenschaftslehre 64, 66, 72–3, 76–8, 80, 83
finitude 54, 58, 60, 67–8, 70–1, 107, 109–13, 175, 186, 191
Foucault, Michel 123, 153, 167, 175
   archaeology 138, 146
   classical age 136–8, 140–2, 145, 148, 206
   confinement 138–40
   consciousness, critical 138, 142, 146
   consciousness, tragic 138, 142–4, 150–1
   continuity 136–8, 143–5, 151
   division 135–8, 140–9, 151, 206–8
   formalism 135, 146–8, 207
   geometrical space 135, 146, 207
   history of limits 143–5, 148
   language without support 146–9, 152
   modern age 136, 142, 146–7, 150
   œuvre 137, 143, 150, 205
   The Order of Things 136, 151–2
   positivism 135, 137, 142, 144, 148, 150–1
   psychiatry 135, 137–8, 142, 146–50
   Renaissance 136, 138–9, 141–2, 147–8, 206
   unreason 136–43, 145–8, 150–1, 205–6
Frankfurt School 153

freedom 16, 39, 57–8, 60–1, 64–5, 68–70, 74–9, 83, 117–18, 120, 128, 186, 188, 190
Freud, Sigmund 142, 155–7, 209, 212
genius 56, 70, 75, 78, 81, 100, 127, 130, 133
God 7, 107, 110, 112–13, 116–21, 123, 132, 160, 199, 203
Gros, Frédéric 137, 140, 143
Hadot, Pierre 8–9, 29, 37, 175, 177–8, 181, 198, 204
Hegel, G. W. F. 78, 109, 188, 198, 200, 206, 211
Heidegger, Martin 153, 173–4
Heraclitus 2, 110
   becoming 18, 22, 24–6, 178
   cosmic fire 18, 176
   ignorance of the general populace 18–22, 25–6
   law 19–23, 26–7, 176–7, 179
   listening 18–21, 23, 25–6, 28, 176
   the masses as barbarians 20–1, 25, 27
   nature 18–20, 22, 26–7
   unity of opposites 18–19, 22–3, 26–7, 178
history 3, 8, 10–11, 17–18, 45–50, 53, 60, 62, 81, 99, 100, 123, 135–8, 142–52, 154, 159, 161, 166–70, 174, 179, 188, 194, 196, 200–1, 205–8
Hobbes, Thomas 89
Homer 22, 124, 130, 185, 202
Hume, David 52
Hunter, Ian 8, 54, 175
idealism 65, 70, 74–5, 78, 117, 186, 188, 200
identity 12, 18, 22–3, 30, 35, 90, 92, 105, 149, 154–6, 158, 160–2, 165, 168–9
idle talk 3, 25, 47, 120–1, 158
intellectual intuition 55–6, 58, 67, 69–71, 77, 186–7, 190
Irigaray, Luce
   commodity, woman as 158–9
   desire 155–8, 161, 163–4, 168, 209–10
   discourse of truth 154, 164, 167–8, 210

flat mirror 156, 158–60, 163, 167, 209
fluidity 162, 165, 168
indifference 156–7, 159, 163
not-all 154–5
phallogocentrism 154, 157, 159, 161–2, 164, 166, 168, 212
the real 155, 161–3, 168
strategic mimesis 154, 163–6, 168–71, 211
the subject 154, 156–64, 166, 209–10
Jacobi, F. H. 55, 65, 191
Kahn, Charles 20–1, 176
Kant, Immanuel 8, 15–16, 63–4, 67, 73–4, 78, 86–7, 95, 105, 167, 188–9, 193, 206
  Anthropology from a Pragmatic Point of View 52
  Critique of Practical Reason 45, 59, 64, 83
  Critique of Pure Reason 45–6, 49–50, 57–8, 61, 63, 187
  discipline 47–8, 57
  historical *vs.* rational cognition 45–50, 53, 56–7, 60–2
  labour, philosophy as 46–7, 54–61, 186
  moral law 45, 54, 59–60
  Observations on the Feeling of the Beautiful and Sublime 51–3
  'On a Recently Prominent Tone of Superiority in Philosophy' 55–7, 61
  practical reason 54–5, 59–61, 187
  Prolegomena to Any Future Metaphysics 63
  public expression 56–8, 61, 188
  speculative reason 46–7, 51, 54–5, 57–8, 60
  tone 46, 55–62
  'Universal Natural History and Theory of the Heavens' 45
  voice of reason 59–62
Kierkegaard, Søren 123, 128, 175
  authority 107, 110, 114–16, 118, 120, 200
  becoming 107, 111, 114, 116, 119, 200
  the crowd 108, 114–15, 118–20

decision 107, 110–12, 114–15, 118, 120, 199–200
double reflection 114–17, 200
Fear and Trembling 111
happiness 109–11, 115, 120
indirect communication 108, 112–17, 121, 198–9
individuality 107–15, 118–21, 199–200
interest 108–12, 117–19, 123
On the Concept of Irony with Continual Reference to Socrates 110
the press 119
speculation 109, 112
Kofman, Sarah 30–1, 100, 169, 182, 187, 194, 197, 212
Lacan, Jacques 153–4, 209
Lacoue-Labarthe, Philippe 29
Le Dœuff, Michèle 3, 78, 169, 212
Locke, John 6, 174
logos 3, 16, 173, 208
  as divine speech 18–23, 25–8, 176
  as method of reasoning 24–5
  as reasoned account 30, 33–8, 181
  as repressive 142, 156–7, 160, 162–5, 169–71, 212
Lyotard, Jean-François 11
the masses 11, 19–22, 26–7, 31, 35, 40, 43, 85–6, 97, 101, 103–5, 108, 110, 113–15, 118–20, 132, 150, 203
Mbembe, Achille 52
mediation 20, 89, 92
metaphysics 8, 37, 47, 49, 58, 67, 74, 91, 94–6, 98, 137, 151, 153–9, 161, 164, 169–71, 175, 184, 198, 208, 210
Murdoch, Iris 29
mysticism 45, 54–7, 60, 127, 132, 201
Nancy, Jean-Luc 7, 16, 57
negative theology 7
Nietzsche, Friedrich 17, 107, 110, 142–4, 175
  Beyond Good and Evil 97, 102
  breeding higher types 97–103, 196
  custom 86, 89, 91, 94–7
  domination 86, 92, 94–7, 99–102
  herd morality 86, 89, 93, 95, 97–100
  Human, All Too Human 86

Index

invention   85–7, 89–92, 94–9, 103, 105
language   86, 88–93, 95–6, 103
metaphor   88–90, 92, 96, 194, 197
naturalism   93–4, 195
On the Genealogy of Morality   102
'On Truth and Lie in an Extra-Moral Sense'   89–90, 96
pathos of distance   86, 101, 103–5
perfectionism   100
perspectivism   90–4, 96–7, 102–3, 107, 194
ressentiment   99
Thus Spoke Zarathustra   97, 197
tragic   87, 142–4
will to power   85, 94, 97–8, 100, 102–3
noise   5, 26–7, 97, 127, 133, 145
objectivity   49–50, 53, 56–7, 61, 91–3, 107–9, 111–17, 119–21, 124, 146, 199
the other   10, 76, 129, 149, 159, 161, 169, 189, 209–10
paradox   18–19, 23–5, 27, 102, 107, 113, 121, 145, 156, 178, 180, 209
Parmenides   2, 20, 24–5, 35, 178, 181
Perniola, Mario   25
Peters, John Durham   32, 42, 175
Plato   1–4, 17, 55, 78, 96, 108, 110, 128–30, 132–3, 170, 173–4, 178, 195, 198, 203–4, 212
   academy   31, 40–2
   beauty   38–9, 42, 182
   dialectic   1–2, 29–31, 34–6, 38, 40, 43, 181
   the Good   30, 35–6, 38–9, 132–3, 182, 204
   ideas   1, 29–30, 33–4, 38–9, 42, 132–3, 180–1
   The Laws   1
   love   1, 4, 33, 38, 41–2, 183
   Meno   1, 173
   midwifery   41–2, 182–3
   Parmenides   40
   Phaedo   34, 39, 181
   Phaedrus   30–1, 34, 38–9, 42, 132–3
   presence   29–30, 32–4, 36–8, 40, 42
   Protagoras   34
   recollection   1, 4, 31, 38, 96, 173

The Republic   1–2, 4, 30–1, 33, 35–6, 39, 41, 78, 182, 203
Sophist   37, 181
speechmaking   31, 33–4, 39–40
Statesman   181–2
The Symposium   30, 38, 41–2, 182
Theaetetus   40–1, 178, 181
poetry   5, 22, 24, 32, 56, 89–90, 110, 130–1, 144, 177–8, 204
propositions   1–3, 5–7, 9–10, 15–16, 18, 23, 30, 33, 40, 42, 46, 48–9, 52–3, 57–8, 61–2, 64, 71–3, 75, 85, 109, 111, 114, 164, 168, 173
race   52, 62, 100, 102, 185–6, 192, 196–7, 212
reasoning   2–3, 24–5, 79, 86, 88–9, 92–3, 107, 113
Reinhold, K. L.   63–4, 68–9, 71, 190
religion   19, 27, 54, 86, 108–21, 123–4, 128, 133, 200, 203
representation   2, 5, 10–11, 22, 25–6, 28, 33, 35, 37, 64, 67–71, 82, 87–8, 108–9, 153–64, 166–8, 170, 192, 210
rhetoric   2–4, 40, 58, 61, 90, 115
Robin, Léon   31–2, 40, 180
Schlosser, J. G.   55–6, 186
Schopenhauer, Arthur   2, 86–90, 175, 193
science   47–9, 51–2, 55, 59, 64, 68, 73, 75, 81–2, 87–8, 109, 113, 124, 127, 142, 144, 146, 148, 150–2, 155, 157, 162, 184, 203
semiology   153
Serres, Michel   146, 154, 207
slavery   40–1, 52, 88, 99, 101, 126, 182, 203
social contract   89, 96
Socrates   30, 34, 38, 41–2, 108, 110, 142, 179, 182–3, 195, 203
solitude   27, 29, 68, 97, 99, 107, 110–11, 115, 120, 128, 133
sophistry   33–4, 39–40, 47, 58, 82, 170, 180, 184
Spivak, Gayatri Chakravorty   153–4
St. Augustine   6
style   1–2, 4–5, 23–4, 46, 63, 73, 85–6, 102, 108, 116–17, 135, 146, 165, 174, 191, 197, 211

systematicity 2, 4, 8, 71, 73, 77, 83, 85, 109, 117, 154–5, 157–9, 162, 166–7, 169, 211
Temple of Artemis 27, 179
Thales 18, 88
theology 7, 12, 16, 80, 85, 107–10, 113, 117
thing in itself 35, 74, 85, 88–9, 91, 93
transmission 1, 3, 5–7, 9–11, 16, 17, 19–20, 22–3, 28, 30–3, 35, 37–8, 40–1, 46, 48–53, 61, 68, 71–2, 77, 82–3, 86, 100, 103, 108, 112–13, 121, 123, 129, 134, 144, 149, 167–8, 170, 175
universality 2–3, 19, 21, 26–7, 40–1, 45–6, 51–2, 54, 58–9, 61–2, 75–8, 80–2, 85, 87–9, 99–100, 116, 131, 146, 157–60, 169, 200, 206, 209
Vattimo, Gianni 86, 98, 107, 196
Weber, Max 185
Weil, Simone 149, 153
    affliction 123, 126–7, 129–34, 203
    attention 123, 128, 130–1, 133, 203–4
    beauty 124–5, 127–31, 204
    collectivity 124, 127–31, 133, 202–3
    freedom of speech 127
    the Good 126, 128–9, 131–4, 204
    grace 130
    the impersonal 123, 127–8, 131–2, 203–4
    justice 125–34
    Personalism 125–6, 128–9, 133
    the sacred 124–8, 131, 134, 201, 204
    war 124–5
Wittgenstein, Ludwig 153, 174–5
Wolff, Christian 47, 49–50, 184
women 41–2, 51–4, 62, 65, 70, 78–84, 99, 102, 153–71, 182–3, 185, 191–3, 197, 202, 208, 212
writing 1–3, 12, 17–18, 28–34, 37, 39–42, 66, 72, 81–2, 85, 102–4, 108, 117, 135, 137, 143, 145–8, 150–1, 154, 162, 164, 174, 178, 180, 191, 211

www.ingramcontent.com/pod-product-compliance
Lightning Source LLC
Chambersburg PA
CBHW062214300426
44115CB00012BA/2060